IMAGES
of America

Loudoun County Fair

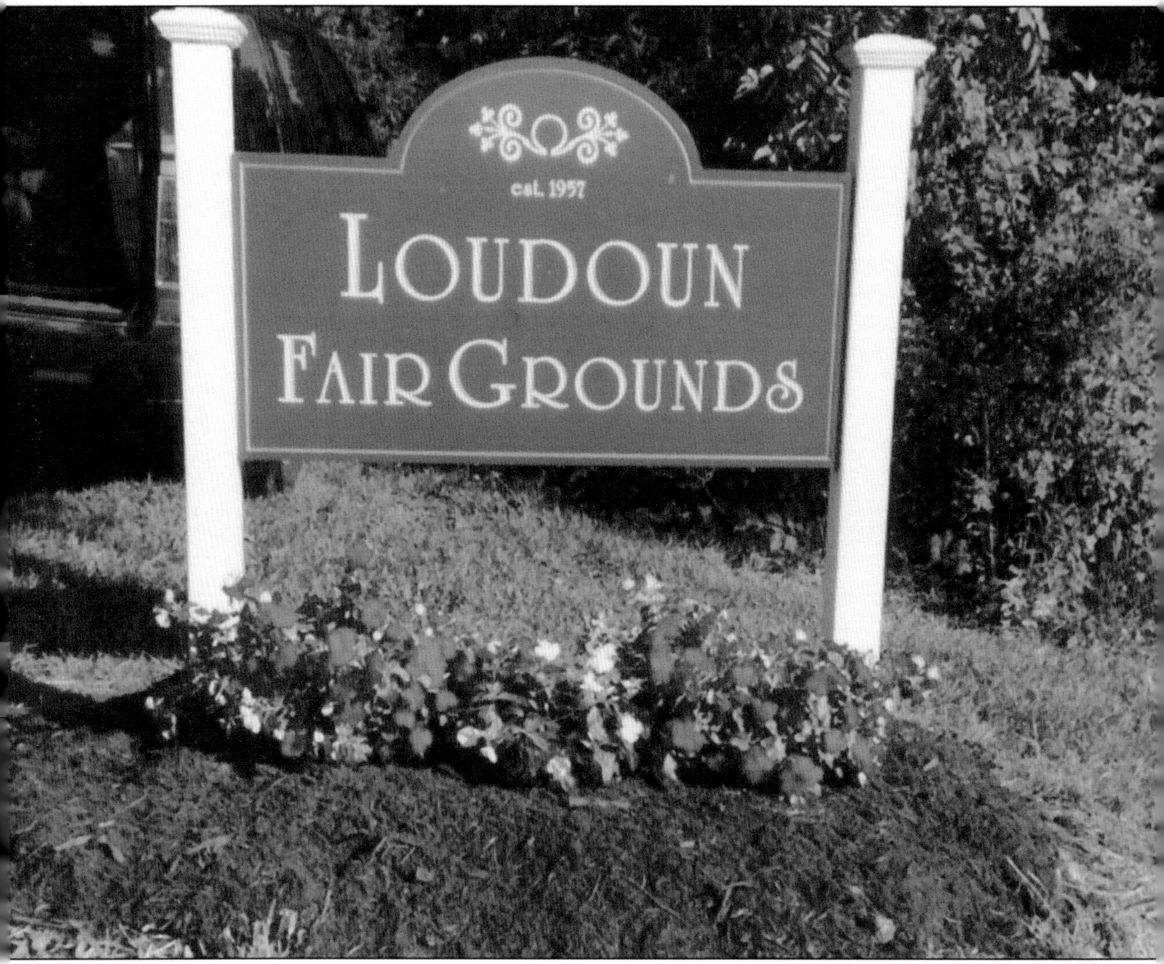

This sign, located at the entrance to the Loudoun County fairgrounds, welcomes visitors as they come to enjoy the spirit of the fair and other events held on the grounds. At the top of the sign is the year in which the grounds were dedicated as the permanent location of the fair. (Author's collection.)

On the Cover: The boys in the cover photograph are baby beef exhibitors at the Purcellville fairgrounds in September 1936 or 1937. Baby beef projects were started in Loudoun in 1921, prior to the Loudoun County 4-H Fair, under the supervision of J.R. Lintner. Baby beef is a young animal between the ages of 12 and 20 months. (Courtesy of Carol Stowers McComb.)

IMAGES
of America

LOUDOUN COUNTY FAIR

Stephanie Briley Fidler

ARCADIA
PUBLISHING

ISBN 978-1-4671-2356-3

Published by Arcadia Publishing
Charleston, South Carolina

Printed in the United States of America

Library of Congress Control Number: 2014957234

For all general information, please contact Arcadia Publishing:
Telephone 843-853-2070
Fax 843-853-0044
E-mail sales@arcadiapublishing.com
For customer service and orders:
Toll-Free 1-888-313-2665

Visit us on the Internet at www.arcadiapublishing.com

This book is dedicated to Doug and Cassidy. I love you both.

Contents

Acknowledgments	6
Introduction	7
1. It All Started with 4-H	9
2. Home Economics	21
3. All about Dairy	31
4. Animals around the Grounds	51
5. Fun at the Fair	67
6. The Grand Parade	101
7. Scenes from Today	111
Index	126
About the Organization	127

ACKNOWLEDGMENTS

In the 80 years of the Loudoun County 4-H Fair, there have been many dedicated volunteers who contribute to the success of the event. I have had the honor of speaking with some of these wonderful people in preparation of this book. Thank you to Kitty Ashby, Barbara Cockerill, Will Cockerill, Jim Colbert, Nancy Colbert, Lynn Conger, Henry Cole, Bill Harrison, Frank Keesling, Carroll Laycock, Hank McCall, Jane McCall, Carol McComb, Kim Monroe, Winnie Morgan, Reece Murray, Tommy Payne, Charles Poland Jr., Eddie Potts, Marty Potts, and Edgar Tillett. The time and resources you have provided for me are invaluable. The support of the Loudoun County Fair Committee is greatly appreciated. Special thanks to Randy Badura, Katie Cockerill, Jackie McClintic, and Richi Norman. Doug, your patience and guidance are immeasurable. Cassidy, I'm glad I had you to sit with late at night while writing. You have very good suggestions. Thanks to both of you for your input and guidance throughout this project. It was a team effort! Last but not least, I am grateful for all of those who have come before me and those to come after me at the fair. Without you, we would not have the fabulous event that we all look forward to and enjoy.

Introduction

In the mid-1930s, a man had an idea that the 4-H youth of Loudoun County needed an event of their own to showcase their hard work. This man, J.R. Lintner, started the Loudoun County 4-H Fair. Without his vision and the help of William H. Cockerill and Karle Bundy, the fair would look much different today. Lintner wrote about the beginning of the fair in an article, "A Brief History of Loudoun County 4-H Work," for the 1949 catalog. In this article, he writes:

> Project club work was begun in Loudoun about 1916. Boys had some corn clubs under the supervision of E.M. Hunter who was then County Agent. Miss Hallie Hughes was Home Agent, and conducted girls' canning clubs. Boys and girls exhibited their work at the annual Loudoun County Fair. This plan of club work was carried on through the period of the First World War.
>
> Organized club work began in 1922 and continued with boys and girls in community clubs until the arrival of the great drought in 1930. With the many demands on the time of one County Agent, club work was not maintained until 1934 when an assistant agent was ushered in. From this year on, individual club and county organization came into being, in line with the state plan for the county club work, and this program has continued to date.
>
> About 14 years ago, after the Loudoun County Fair ceased to function, the Extension Agents then in the county tried a strictly County 4-H Fair which has continued to operate without interruption to this time. Popular support of this Fair has made it a very useful and interesting annual occasion. It has served well as the farm "Show Window" and for development of team work among the county 4-H members themselves.

Once the fair moved to its permanent home in the Clarke's Gap area of Loudoun County, just west of Leesburg, the Loudoun County 4-H Fair and Associates, Inc., was formed. This group consisted of 15 board members and their associates. The associates were the 4-H, the Future Farmers of America, the Future Homemakers of America, the Home Demonstration Club, and the Young Farmers Club. The Home Demonstration Club was a group of ladies who taught others how to cook and clean house, and the Young Farmers was an organization of young men who were too old to be a part of 4-H but wanted to share with others good farming practices.

In 1947, there were sixteen 4-H clubs in the county with 215 girls and 141 boys. The clubs were Aldie, Arcola, Ashburn, Bluemont, Hamilton, Hillsboro, Leesburg Junior, Leesburg Senior, Lincoln Junior, Lincoln Senior, Lovettsville, Lucketts, Purcellville, Round Hill, Sterling, and Waterford. A club was added in 1948, and Lovettsville became separate junior and senior clubs. Today, the clubs are divided by what the 4-H participants show: beef, dairy, horse, rabbit, swine, goat, sheep, and poultry. There is also a cooking and sewing club, an outdoor adventure club, a shooting club, a community club, and a newly formed forage club. Including the special interest clubs and the Cloverbuds (ages five to eight), there are a total of 26 clubs.

The 4-H has always been an important part of the fair; if it were not for the organization, the fair would not exist. In 1994, the Virginia Cooperative Extension Office and the Loudoun County 4-H Fair separated. With this separation, the 4-H was an individual entity from the fair and was no longer the sole purpose of putting on this event. The 4-H name was removed from the fair title as well as from the Loudoun County 4-H Fair and Associates, Inc. Even though this divide occurred, the 4-H has continued to be an integral part of the fair. The kids never stopped showing at the fair and are the reason many of the adults volunteer their time. Throughout this book, I have used the names Loudoun County 4-H Fair and Loudoun County Fair interchangeably.

Many improvements have been made to the fairgrounds since 1957. There are now 13 structures, including barns, pavilions, sheds, and a house built for a caretaker to help watch over the facilities. An addition to Sykes Hall was constructed, which included larger restrooms. A water tank was installed, and much grading has been done to make the grounds more accessible. The Loudoun Fair and Associates, Inc. (LFA), rents the grounds and the buildings to outside groups throughout the year.

In 1966, after a dairy show on the grounds, the barns were cleaned and the manure disposed of in the pit outside. A soda bottle was left beside the manure pit, which was mixed with hay. The sun reflected on the bottle, and the manure pile caught fire, engulfing both cattle barns. This disaster took place just prior to the annual fair. Volunteers pulled together and erected new barns in time for the fair events to start. The men worked to construct the buildings, and the women prepared the meals for everyone. This is one example of the giving nature of the fair volunteers.

In 2003, a tornado destroyed two different livestock barns. The LFA had already been considering how to make the existing structures better support the growing needs of the fair when nature stepped in. Again, the volunteers and community pulled together and rebuilt. A larger steel-enclosed structure was constructed, allowing for year-round use.

A large celebration was held for the 50th annual fair in 1985, which included burying a time capsule in the house on the grounds that contained money from the year, fair catalogs, and other items from the time. The intention is to open this time capsule at the 100th annual fair. A second time capsule is also buried on the grounds near the show pavilion.

As we mark the 80th annual Loudoun County Fair, it is a time for those who have volunteered, showed, or attended the fair to reflect. What were your experiences with the fair? How did the fair impact your life? How did the people you shared the experience with affect you?

The images in this book are a small piece of what comprises the Loudoun County Fair. They tell the story of the small beginnings of a one-day show to a seven-day fair event that draws people from miles around. The fair is an annual educational event for the citizens of Loudoun (and beyond), young and old, to enjoy.

Volunteers, 4-H'ers, and the community rally together to put on an event the whole family can experience. The next time you find yourself in Virginia, head over to Loudoun County and join us at the fair.

One

It All Started with 4-H

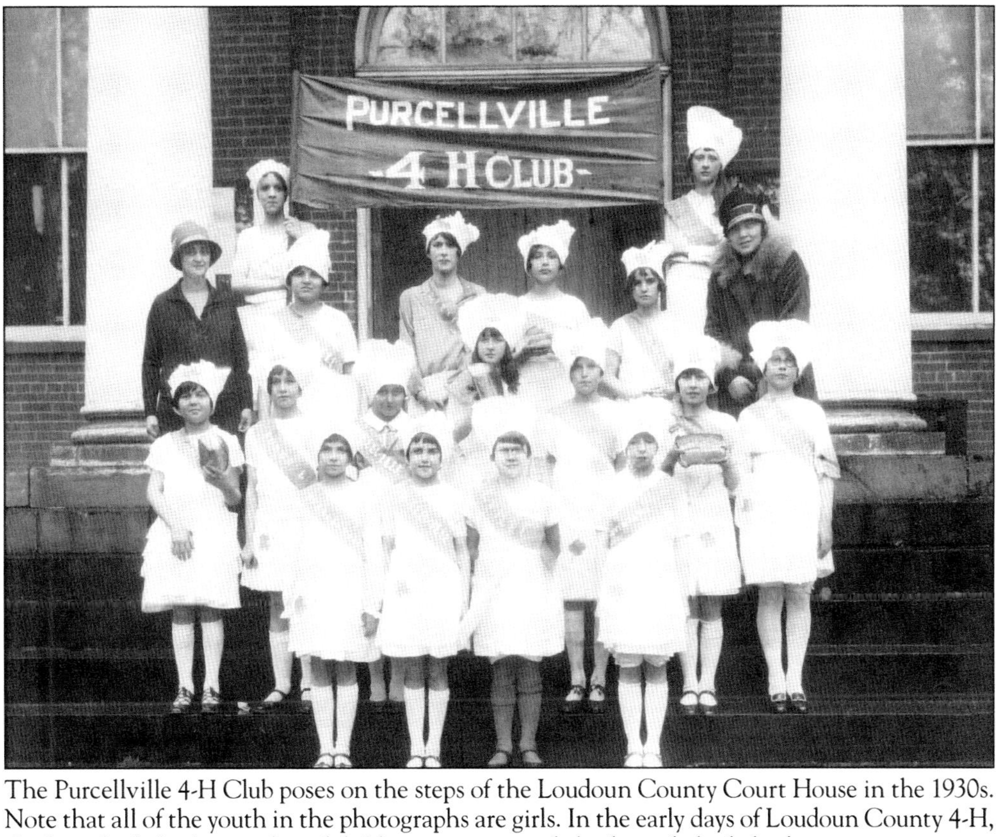

The Purcellville 4-H Club poses on the steps of the Loudoun County Court House in the 1930s. Note that all of the youth in the photographs are girls. In the early days of Loudoun County 4-H, the boys had the livestock and field-crop projects while the girls had the home-improvement, canning, and flower-arranging projects. (Courtesy of William Harrison.)

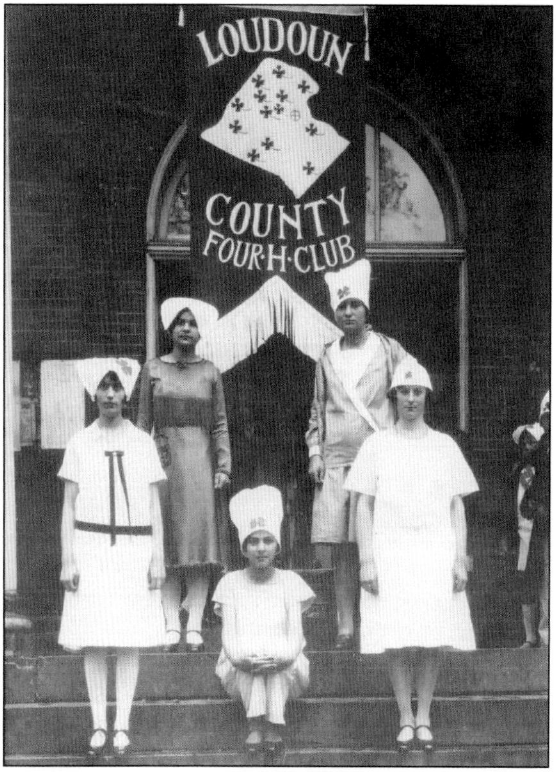

In the photograph at left, the Loudoun County 4-H Club poses on the steps of the courthouse in the 1930s. In the photograph below is the Lucketts 4-H club. In the early days of Loudoun's 4-H, the organization was divided into community clubs instead of by showing animal or home economics. A general livestock club was created first, eventually branching out to focus on separate areas such as dairy, sheep, beef cows, and swine. The clubs were consolidated so the 4-H'ers could study their animals more thoroughly—the feeding, care, and showing. (Left, courtesy of William Harrison; below, courtesy of the William H. Cockerill family.)

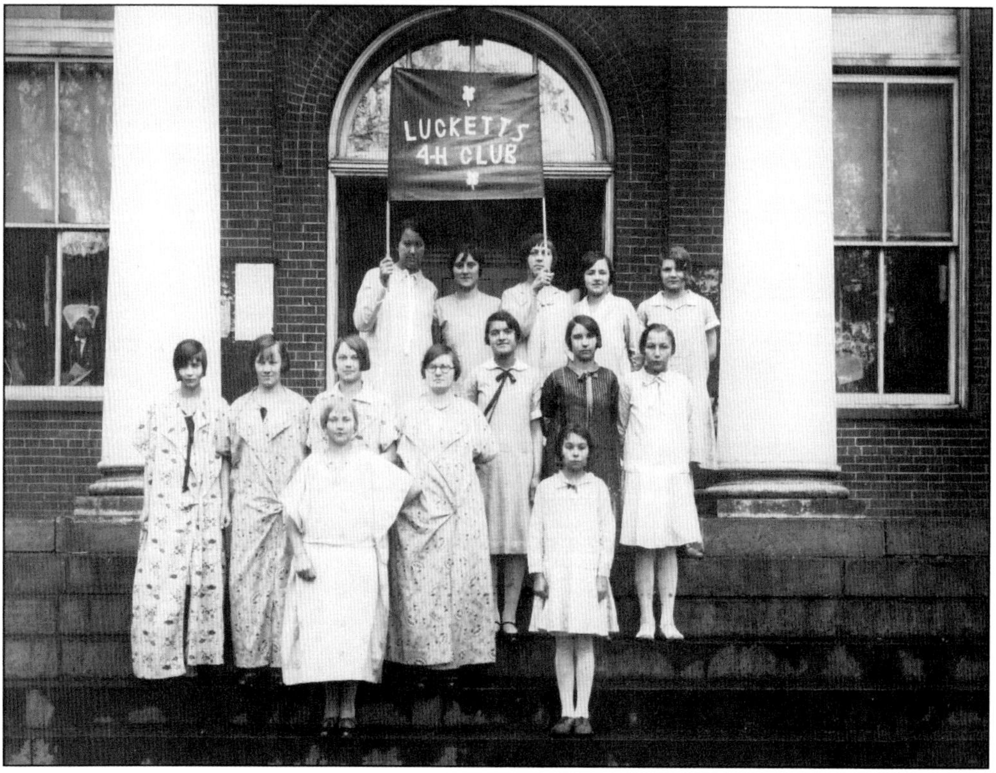

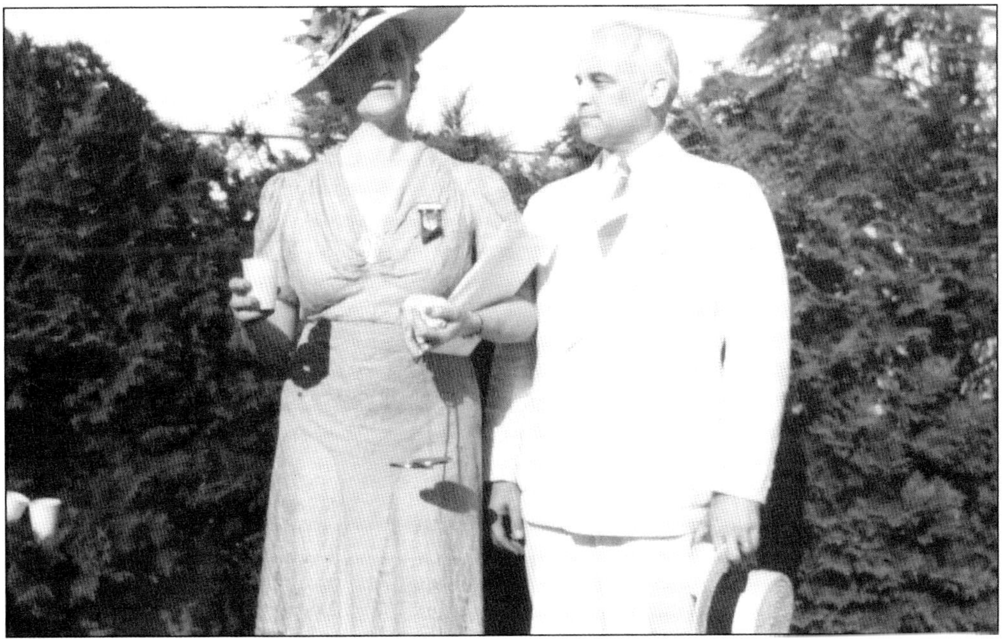

William H. "Bill" Cockerill took the state 4-H poultry judging team to Cleveland in 1939 for a contest. The 45th mayor of Cleveland, Ohio, Harold Hitz Burton, is pictured here with his wife, Selma Florence Smith. He was photographed during the 4-H trip. (Courtesy of the William H. Cockerill family.)

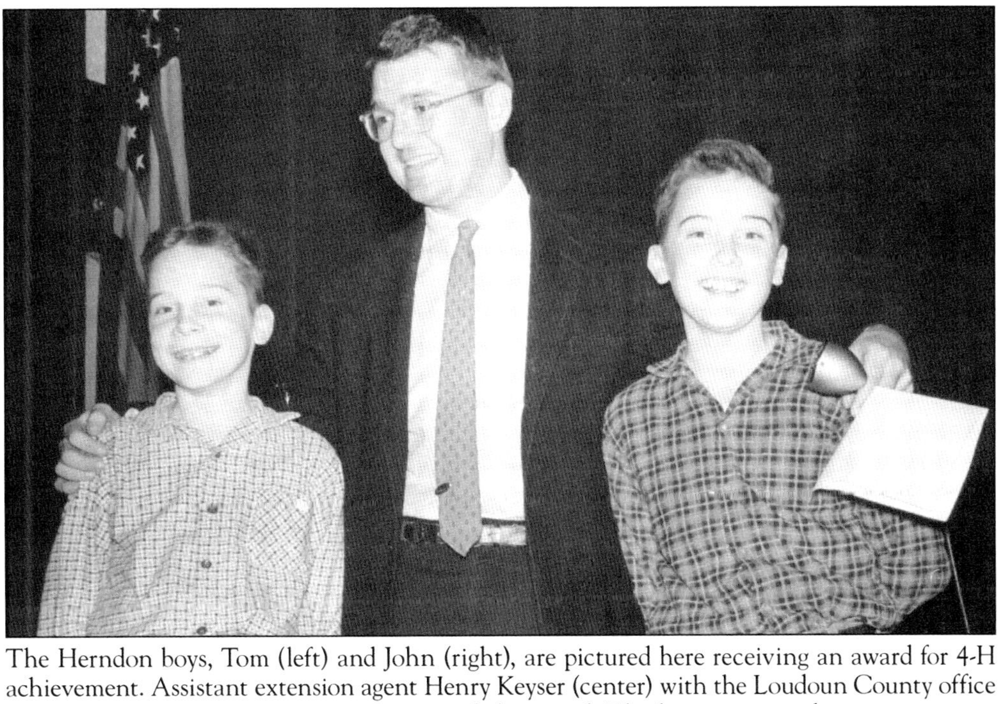

The Herndon boys, Tom (left) and John (right), are pictured here receiving an award for 4-H achievement. Assistant extension agent Henry Keyser (center) with the Loudoun County office of Virginia Cooperative Extension presented the award. The boys continued to participate in 4-H into their high school years. (Photograph by John Eisenhard; courtesy of the William H. Cockerill family.)

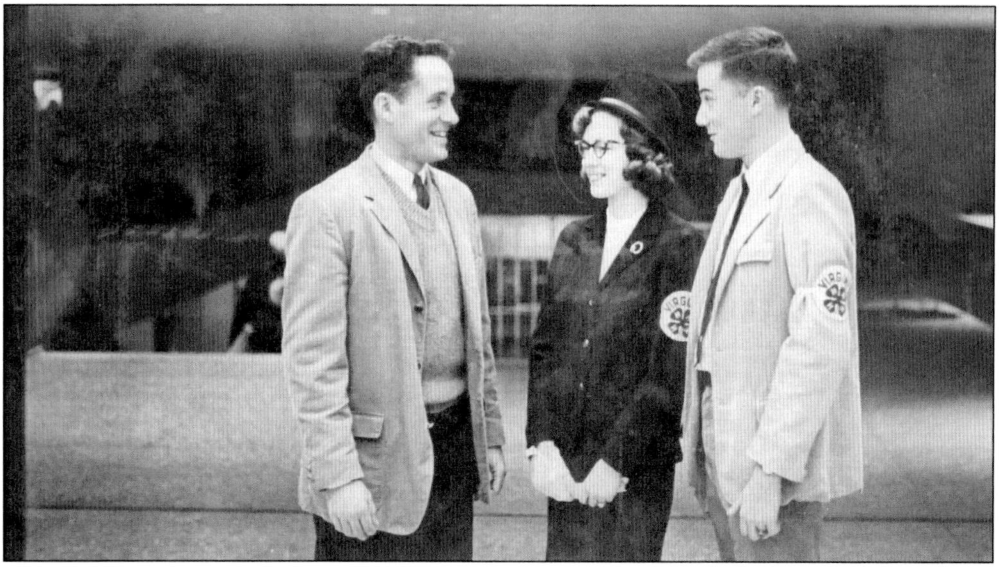

William "Bill" Harrison (left), Loudoun County assistant extension agent, is pictured here with Barbara Fletcher and Tommy Herndon. Barbara and Tommy were active in 4-H and with the fair for many years. Harrison took groups of 4-H youth to events, including local and state contests as well as national-level conferences. (Courtesy of the William H. Cockerill family.)

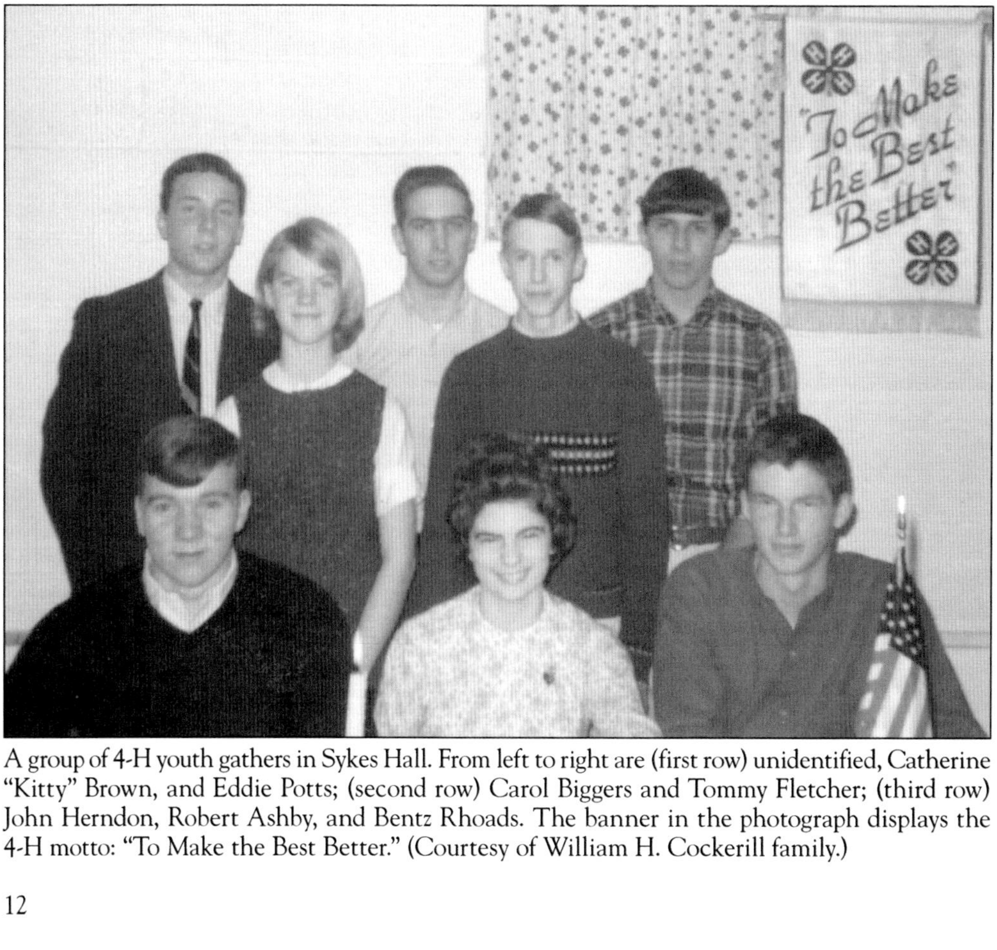

A group of 4-H youth gathers in Sykes Hall. From left to right are (first row) unidentified, Catherine "Kitty" Brown, and Eddie Potts; (second row) Carol Biggers and Tommy Fletcher; (third row) John Herndon, Robert Ashby, and Bentz Rhoads. The banner in the photograph displays the 4-H motto: "To Make the Best Better." (Courtesy of William H. Cockerill family.)

The group pictured here in the 1960s won a state dairy award. From left to right are Tommy Fletcher, unidentified, and Jimmy Williamson. Williamson is from Washington County, and in later years, he worked for the Southeast Dairyman's Association. At the state level, youth may be on a competition team with others who are not within their county, as was the case here. (Courtesy of the William H. Cockerill family.)

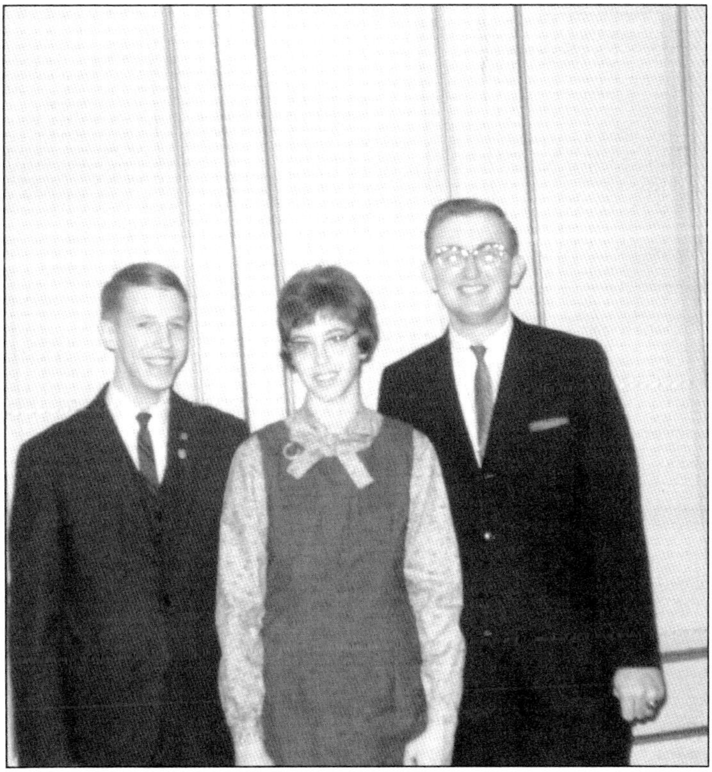

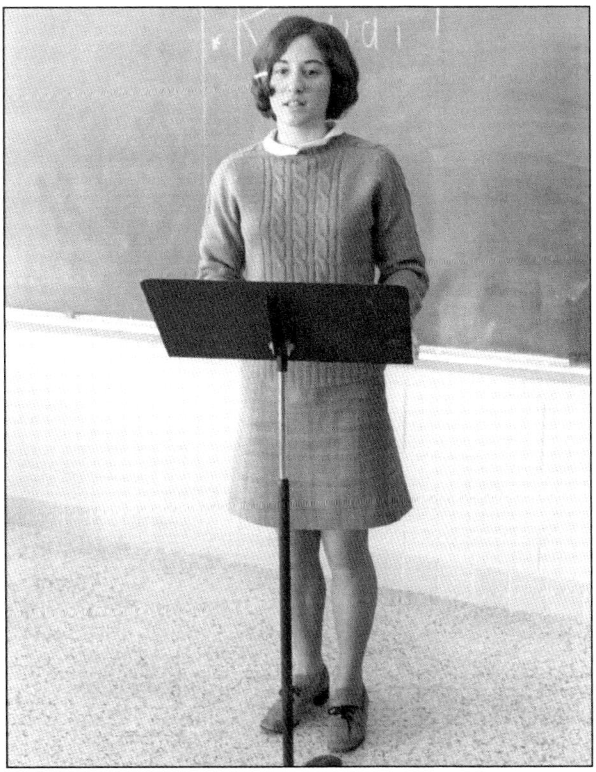

As a part of 4-H, the youth give presentations and complete projects. In this photograph, Dee Dee Stout is giving a presentation. Stout is the daughter of 4-H'er Peggy Anne Benedum and niece of Mary Jane Benedum, both of whom showed at the 4-H fair. (Courtesy of the William H. Cockerill family.)

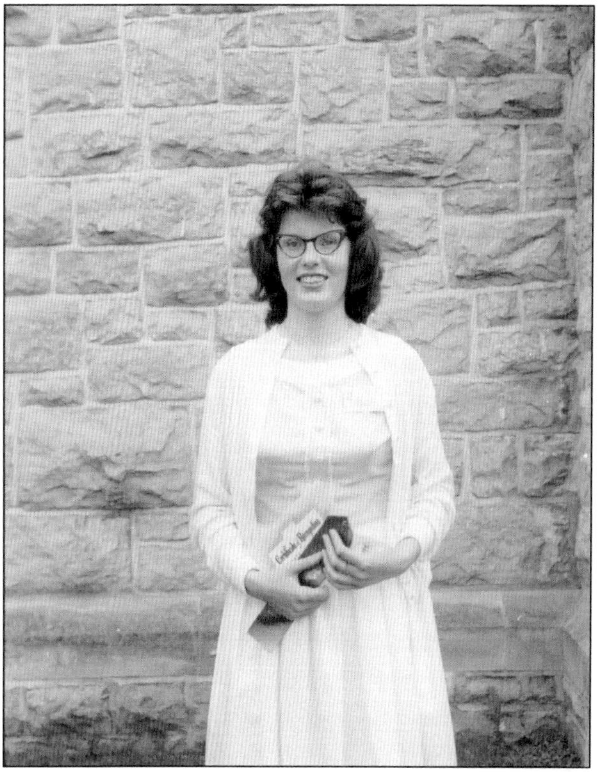

Jane Virts is pictured here at Virginia Polytechnic Institute and State University (VPI, later known as Virginia Tech) in Blacksburg, Virginia. Virts, holding her first-place ribbon in poultry judging, attended the 4-H Club Congress as a Virginia 4-H All Stars in 1960. She also attended Club Congress in 1959 for home demonstration and in 1961 for livestock judging. (Courtesy of the William H. Cockerill family.)

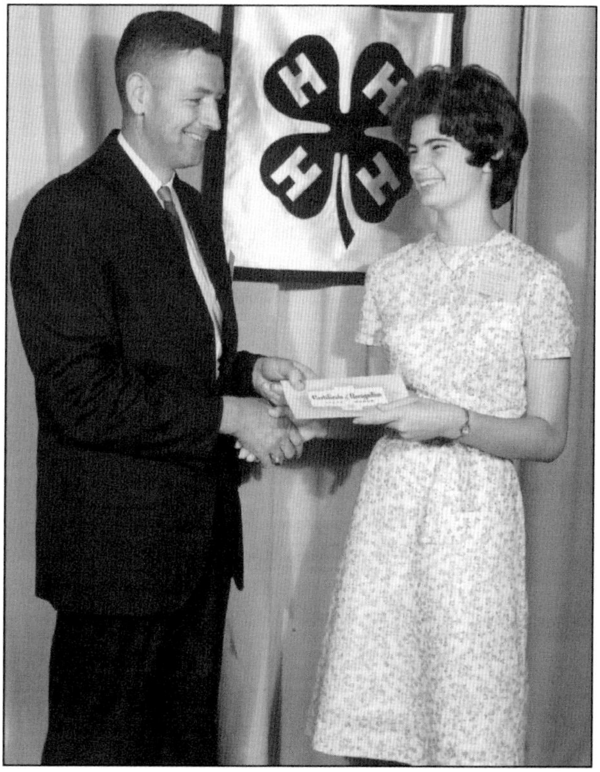

Catherine "Kitty" Brown, later a longtime commissioner of revenue for Loudoun County, receives a certificate of recognition from Harold Roller, a Loudoun County extension agent. A commissioner of revenue is an elected representative of the people responsible for the just administration of local taxes levied by the government. (Courtesy of the William H. Cockerill family.)

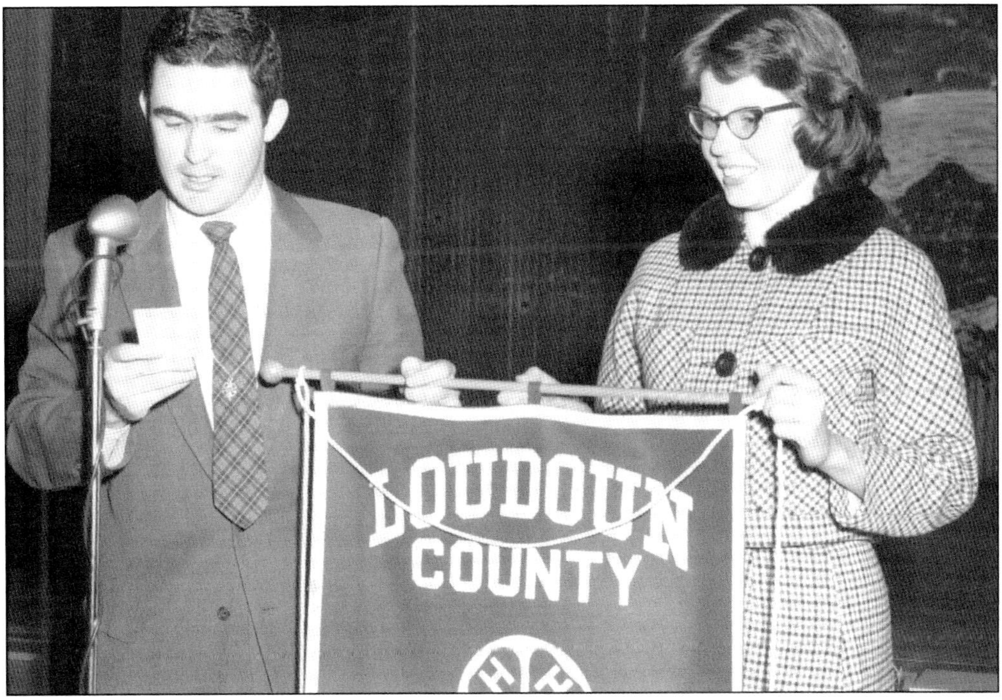

Jane Virts, a member of the Lovettsville Senior Club, is receiving the Champion Senior 4-H Club Banner on behalf of her club. John Garber, assistant county agent, is presenting the banner, a coveted, hard-earned achievement. Club members earn points for project books, presentations, attending meetings, and leadership activities, and the club with the most points earns the banner for the year. (Courtesy of the William H. Cockerill family.)

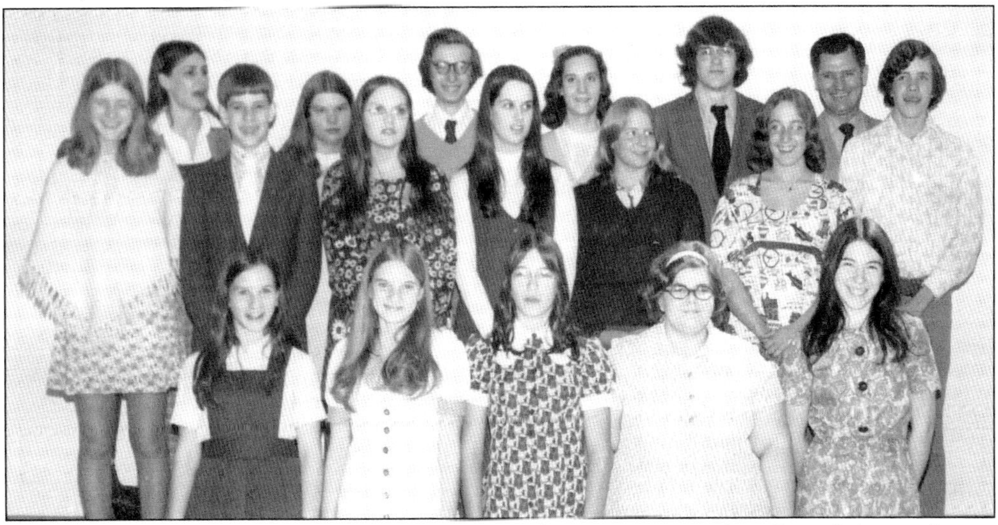

In Sykes Hall, a group of outstanding youth pose for a picture together. From left to right are (first row) Bonnie Shoemaker, Cathy Campbell, Carol Baird, Cathy Frye, and Dody Welch; (second row) Cindy Johnson, Glynn Moreland, Pat Biship, Martha Arnold, Patty Mothes, Beth Gallagher, and Tom Dukes; (third row) Winnie Peele (county agent), Vanessa Moss, Henry Cole, Carol Saunders, Mike McDonald, and Robert Haston (county agent). (Courtesy of the William H. Cockerill family.)

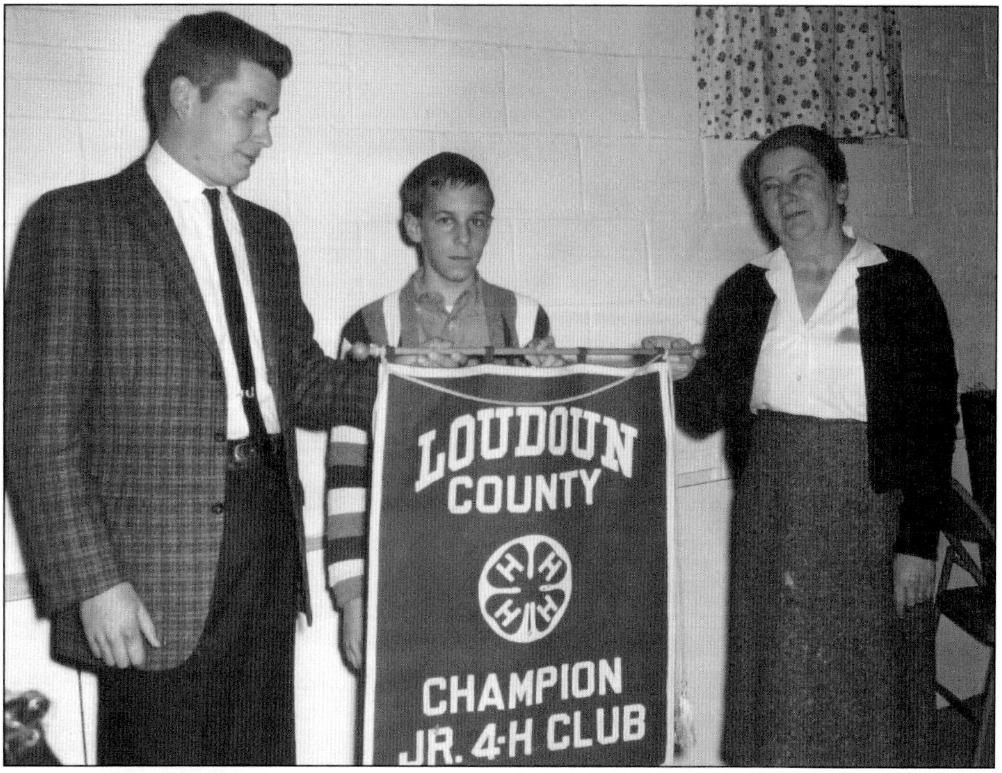

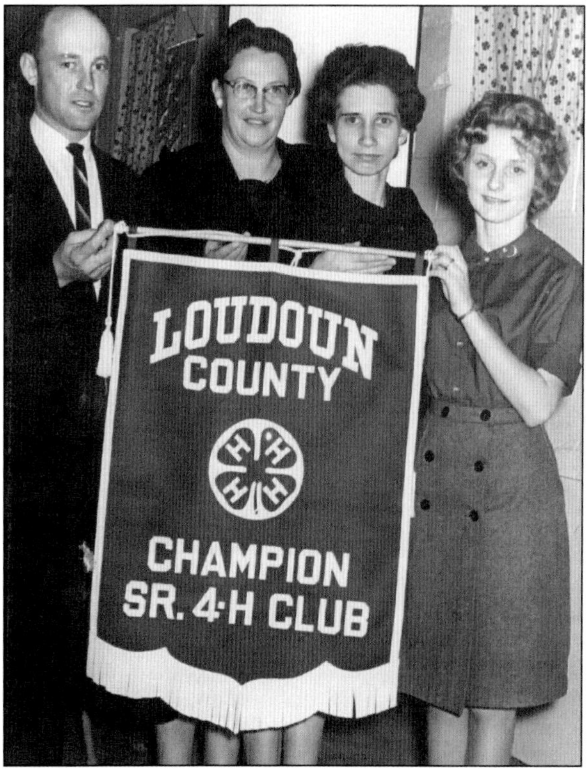

From left to right, Tommy Hoff, Ronnie Blake, and leader Ellen Stowers, all of the Waterford Club, received the Champion Junior 4-H Club Banner. Stowers was affectionately called "Granny" by all who knew her, and the nickname even appeared in the annual fair catalogs. The club that kept the banner for the year was referred to as the banner club. (Courtesy of Sykes Hall Archives.)

The Champion Senior 4-H Club Banner went to the Lovettsville Senior Club many times. Once a club earned the banner four times, the banner was kept by that club and a new one was bought to present the following year. The members of the Lovettsville Senior Club pictured here are, from left to right, Frank Keesling (leader), Kay Kreiger (leader), Treeva Utterback, and Cathy Smith. (Courtesy of the William H. Cockerill family.)

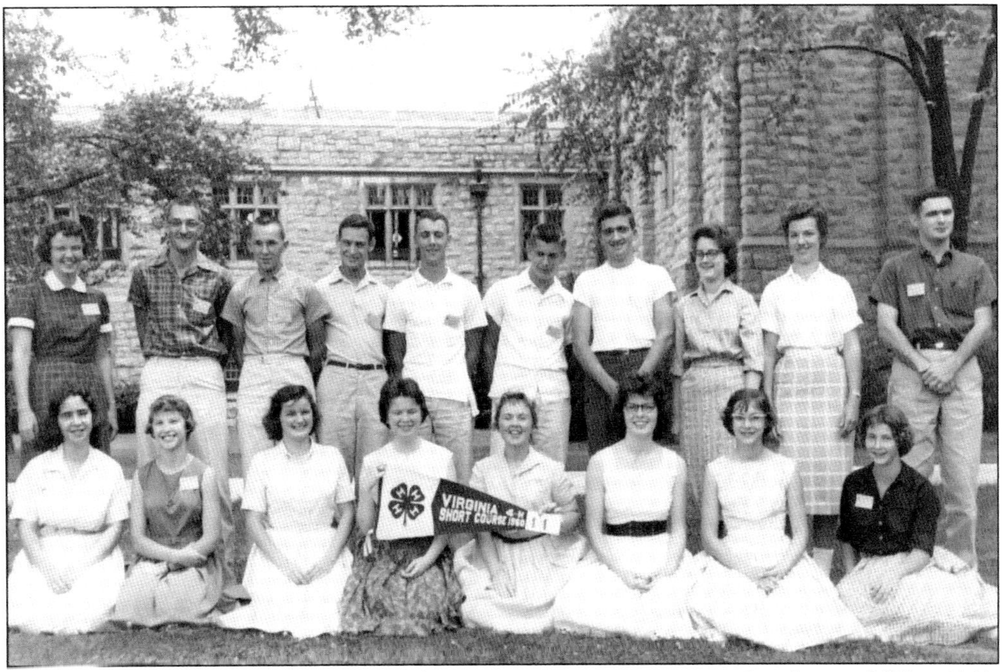

This group of teenagers is the Virginia Short Course team representing Loudoun at VPI in 1960. Above, from left to right are (first row) Josephine Terminella, Beth Welch, Rachel Norman, Charlotte Cook, Ruth Brown, Jane Virts, Jo Ann Bailey, and Mary Florence Piggott; (second row) Jane Norman, Shirley Myers, Charlie Hope, James "Jimmy" Colbert, Ralph Fields Jr., Tommy Hoff, Claude Stowers (VPI student), Emily Gill, Bonnie Jo Dillon, and John Garber (assistant county agent). The 1961 Short Course Team includes, from left to right, (first row) Mildred Crawford, Beth Welch, Ruth Brown, Rachel Norman, Roberta James, Josephine Terminella, and Jane Virts; (second row) Connie Smith, Sam Welch, Leroy Cullen, Jimmy Colbert, Tommy Huff, Bill Brown, Bill McKimmy, and Jim Biggers. (Above, courtesy of the William H. Cockerill family; below, courtesy of Sykes Hall Archives.)

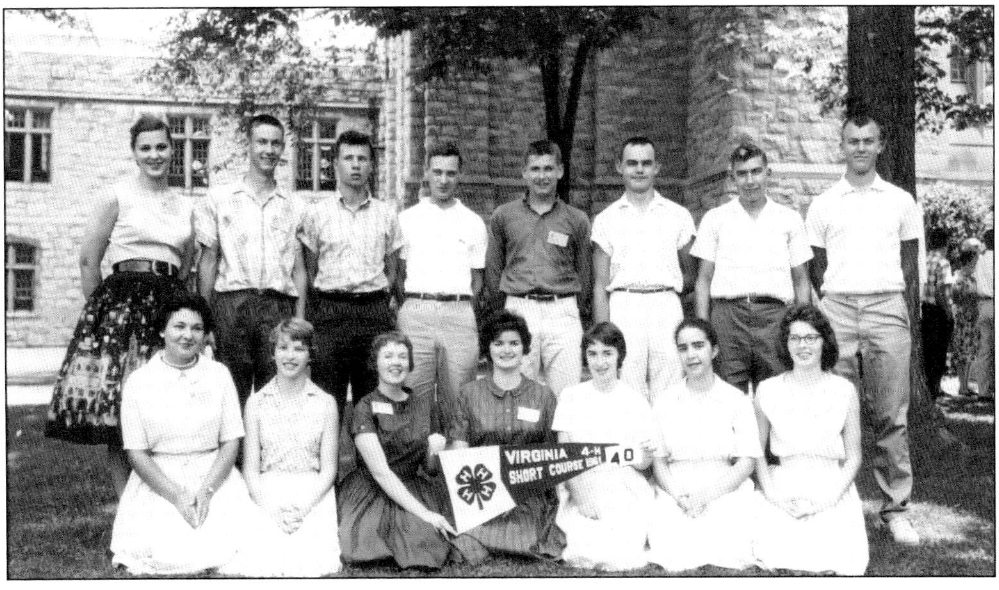

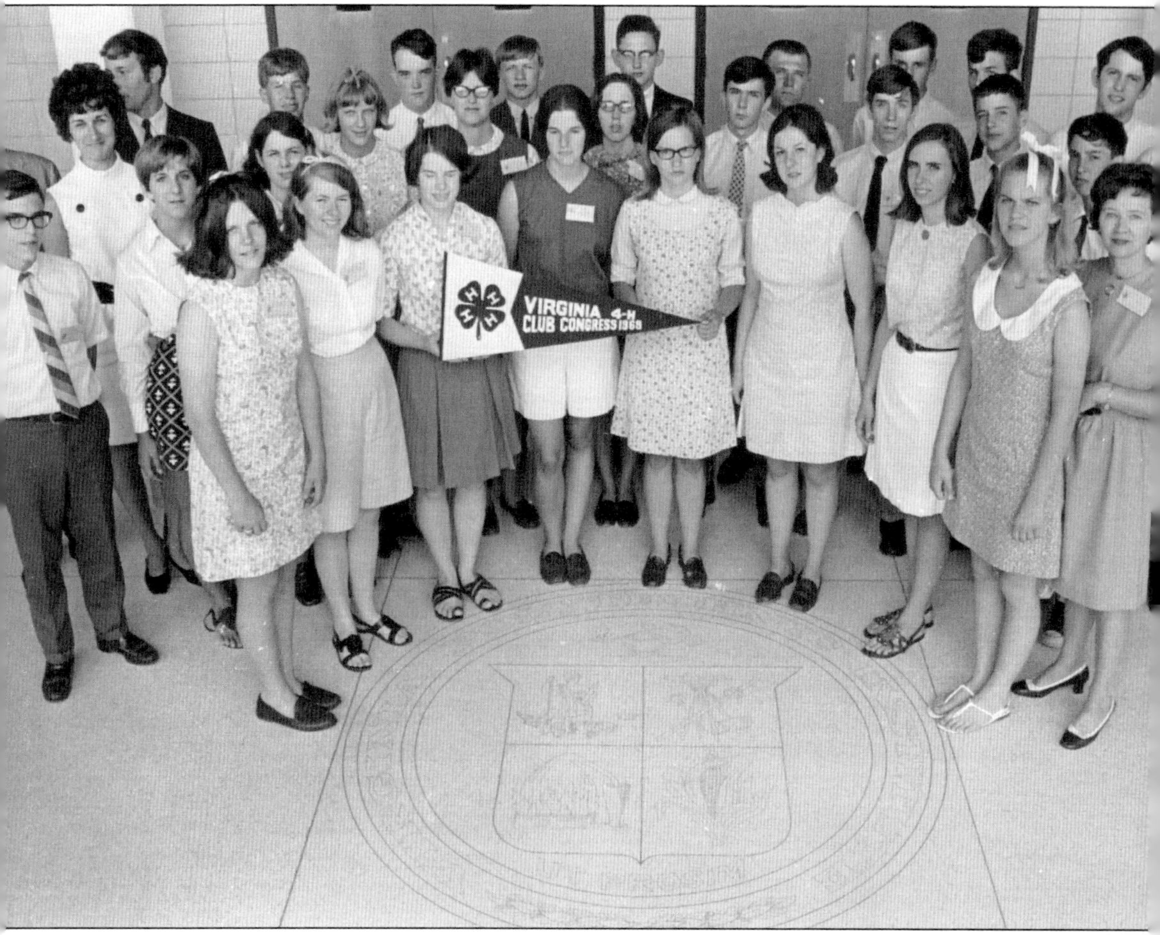

The Club Congress 4-H'ers attended VPI in 1969 for the annual state convention. From left to right are (first row) Mary Beth Muir, unidentified, Sarah Potts, Ann Cole, JoAnn Shoemaker, Sandra Greenfield, Lynn Divine, Carol Biggers, and Gertrude Fletcher; (second row) Robbie Thompson, unidentified, ? Potts, Terry Kushner, unidentified, Carolyn Potts, Carroll Laycock, and four unidentified individuals; (third row) William Harrison (county extension agent), two unidentified individuals, Charlie Cockerill, Henry Creel, Joe Stowers, Arthur Krieger, Reggie Sanbower, Daryl Arnold, Morris Nix, Allen Rollins, and one unidentified individual. The State Club Congress was an opportunity for Virginia 4-H All Stars to gather together to exchange ideas and receive recognition for individual accomplishments and community service. (Courtesy of the William H. Cockerill family.)

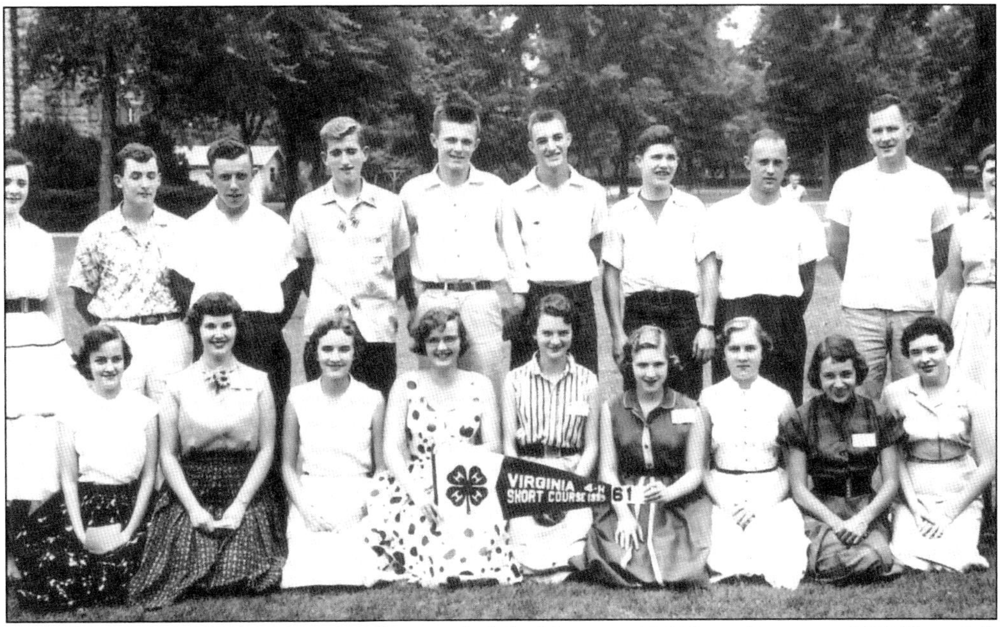

In 1959, the group in this photograph attended the Virginia 4-H Short Course at VPI. From left to right are (first row) Eleanor Gill, unidentified, Ann Cole, Jane Norman, three unidentified girls, Mary Jane Benedum, and ? Brown; (second row) Anna Mae Fields, Bill Thomas, Edwin Utterback, Gunter Buse, Don Virts, Shirley Myers, Scott Forsyth, Frank Keesling, Jack Brown (county agent), and unidentified. (Courtesy of Carol Stowers McComb.)

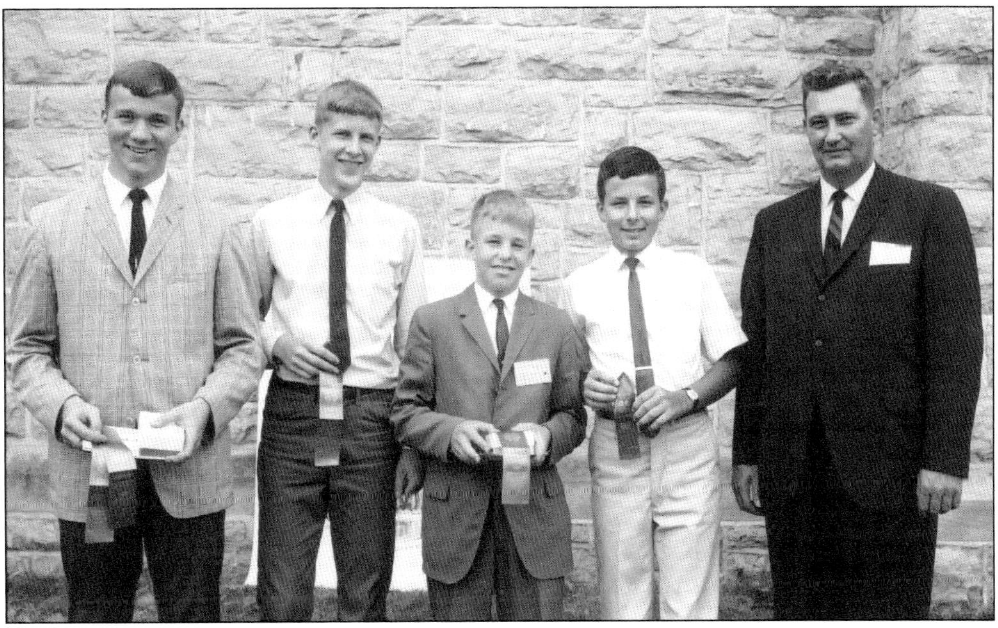
Land appreciation and soils judging consisted of 4-H'ers learning the function and characteristics of soil, human accountability, and environmental decision making as well as conservation. The team consisting of, from left to right, Robert McEwan, Jimmy Cole, Charlie Cockerill, Morris Nix, and Lowell Coffelt (leader) won the state contest in soils judging in 1966. (Courtesy of the William H. Cockerill family.)

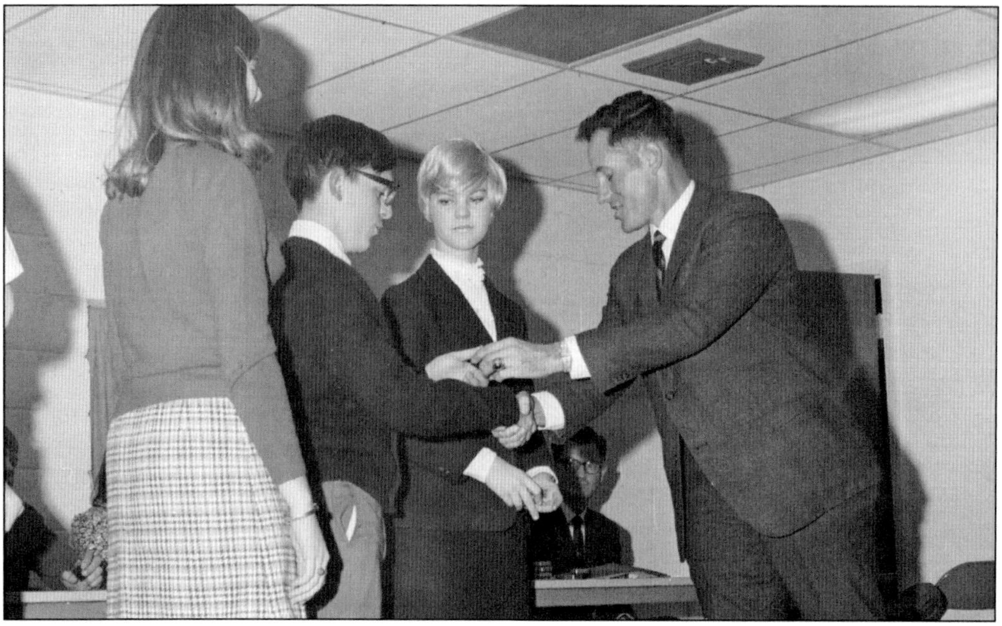

Achievement Night for 4-H is the time when 4-H'ers come together to celebrate their accomplishments for the year. Lapel pins were given to the participants for projects, leadership, and overall achievement. In this photograph, from left to right, Lynn Divine, Robbie Thompson, and Carol Biggers receive their pins from county extension agent William Harrison. (Courtesy of the William H. Cockerill family.)

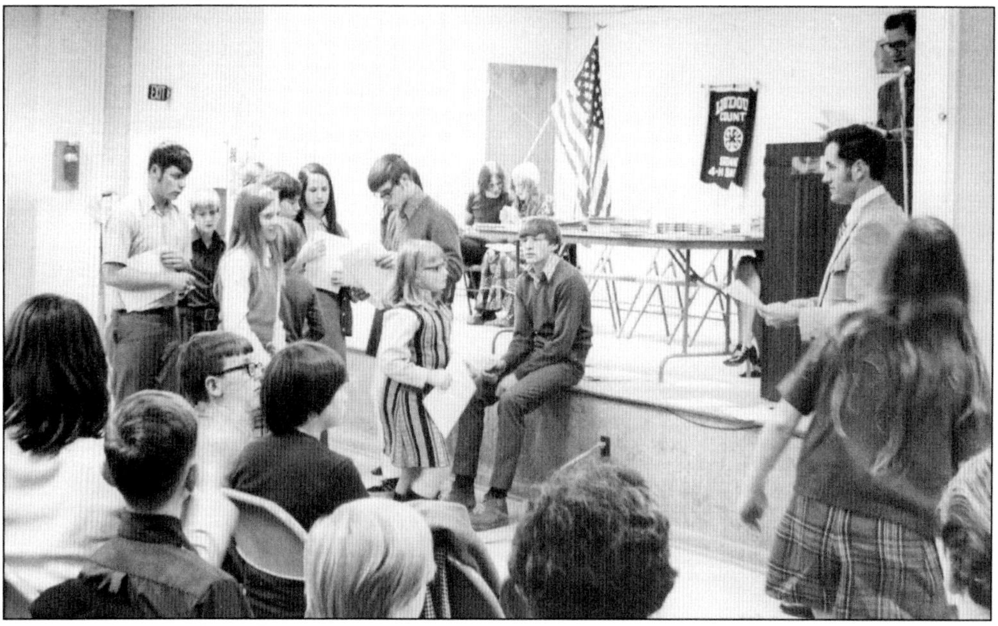

Sykes Hall, located on the fairgrounds, has been the setting for Achievement Night since it was built in 1960. Receiving awards on this night are, from left to right in front of the stage, Jeff Flippo, unidentified, Terra Moreland, unidentified, Martha Arnold, Gray Price, Rebecca Sanbower, Joe Stowers, and county extension agent William Harrison. (Courtesy of the William H. Cockerill family.)

Two

HOME ECONOMICS

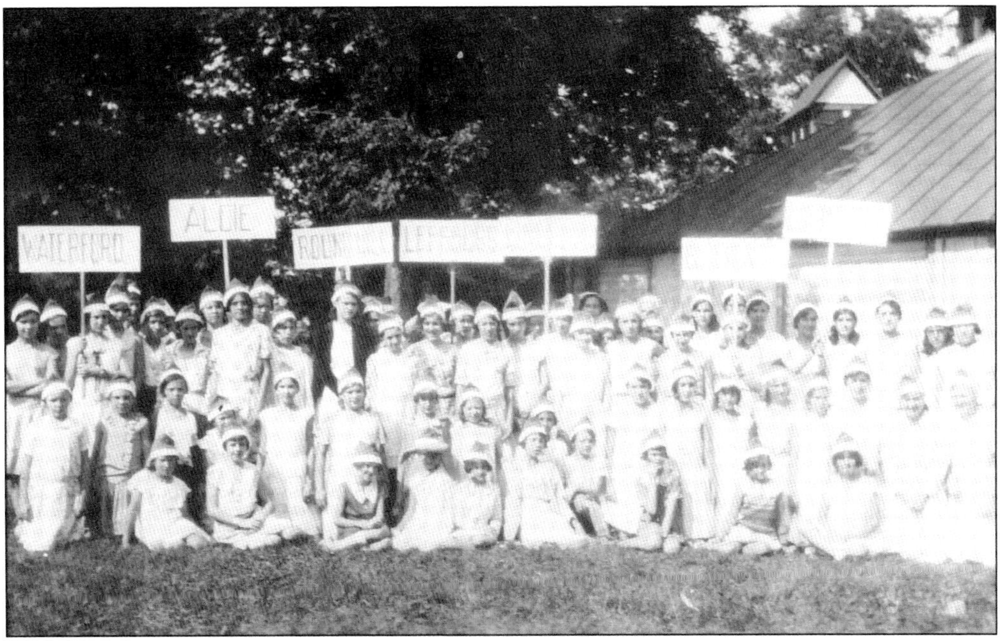

This group of girls representing the community clubs of Waterford, Aldie, Round Hill, Leesburg, Lincoln, Bluemont, and Lucketts is gathered in front of the Bush Tabernacle Auditorium on the grounds of the first fair in 1936. The Loudoun County 4-H Fair was held in this location through 1952. (Courtesy of the William H. Cockerill family.)

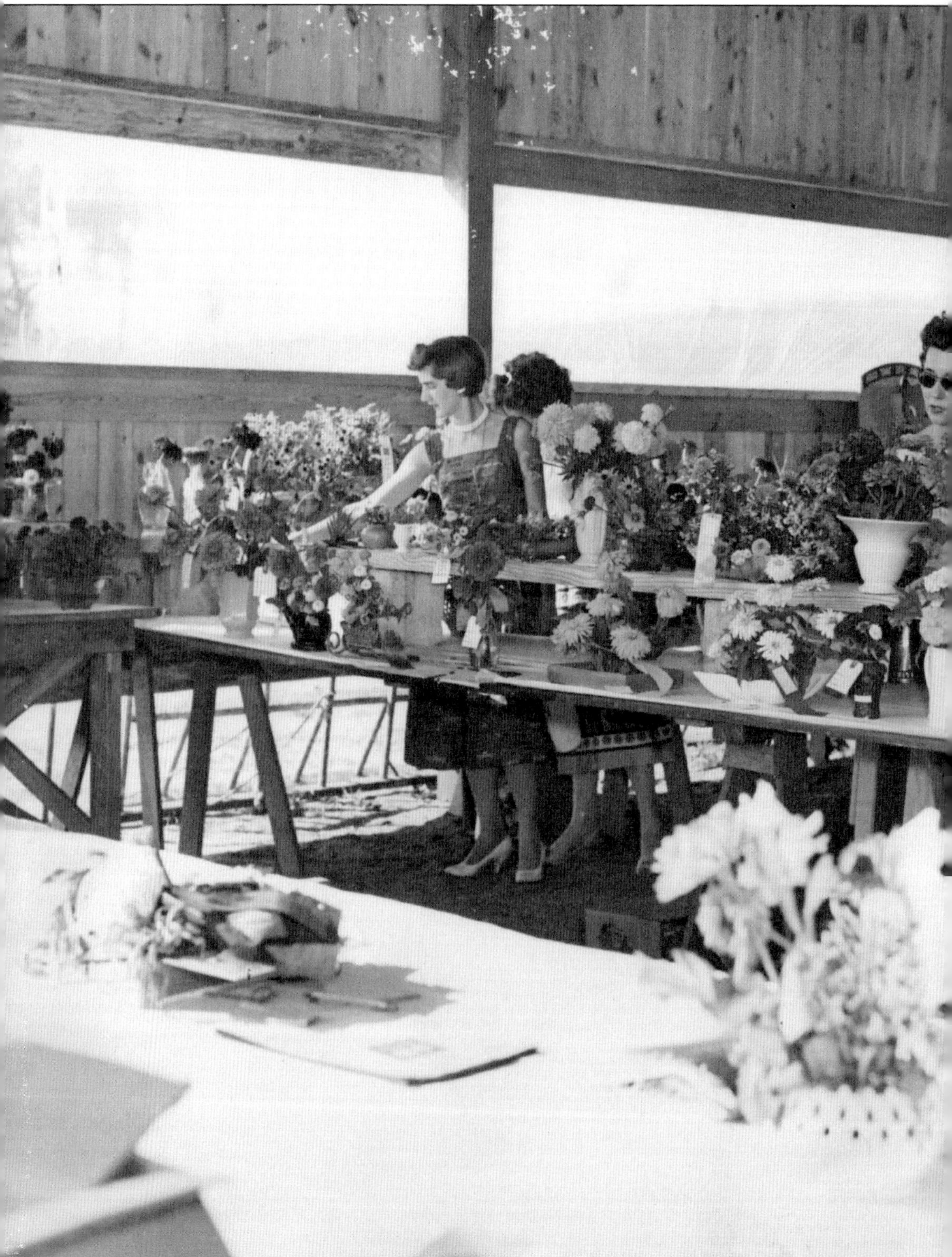

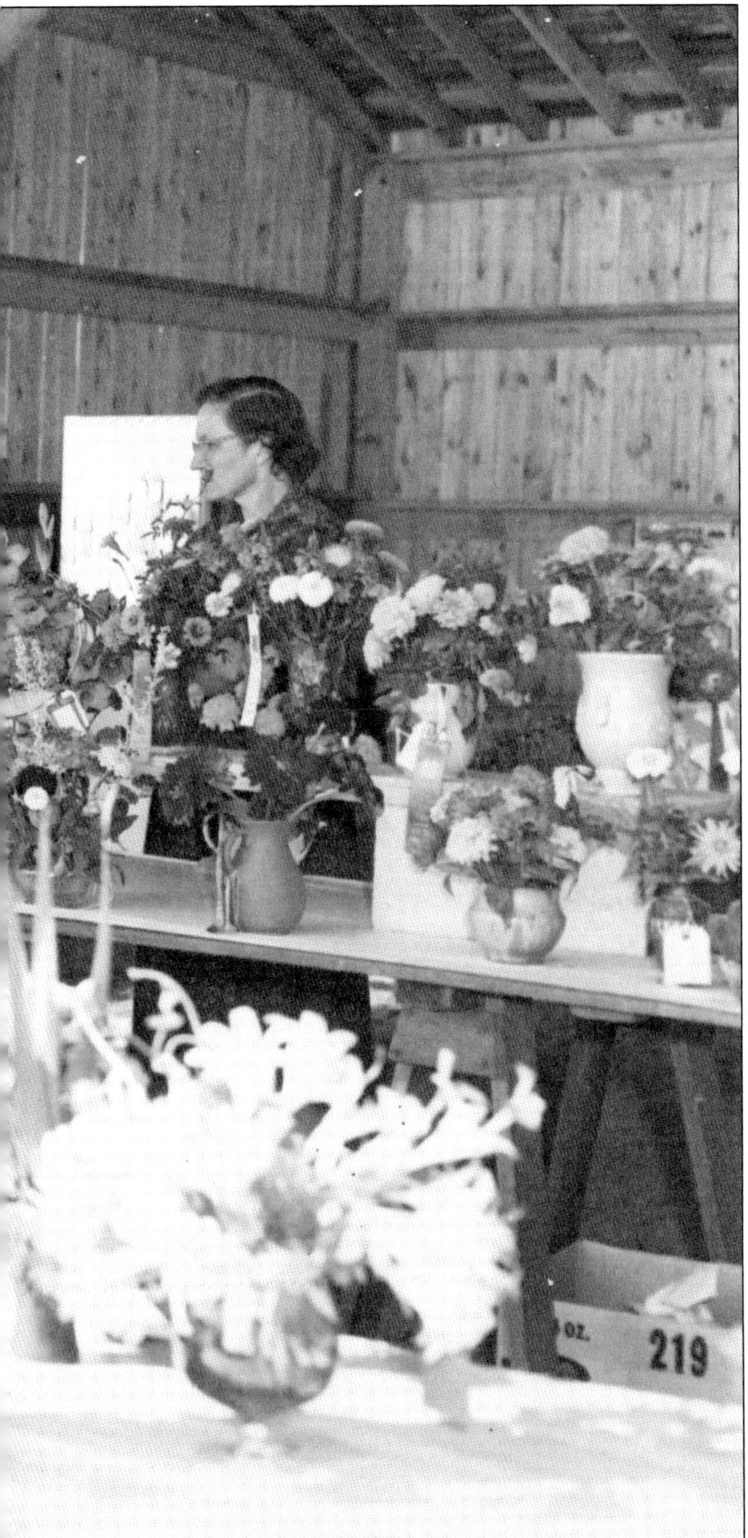

These flower exhibits were on display in the show pavilion in 1957. The first day of the fair, the home economics exhibits were on display; after that day, they were removed in order for the livestock to use the pavilion for their showing. Prior to 1960, when the Sykes Hall auditorium was constructed, there was no other place on the grounds that could accommodate the home economics and field exhibits. The women viewing the displays from left to right are unidentified, Dorothy Kelly Hill, and Isabelle Grant. (Photograph by Stanley J. Wortman; courtesy of the William H. Cockerill family.)

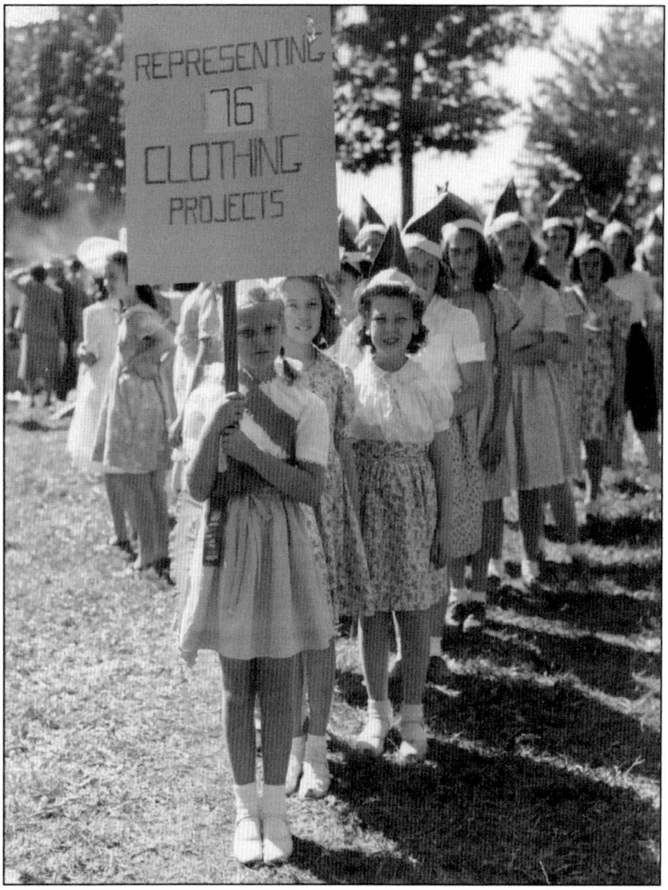

The 4-H girls in this photograph are representing 76 clothing projects by modeling the items they made. The girl in the front is wearing the ribbon she won for her project. The photograph was taken on the grounds of the fair location in Purcellville. (Courtesy of the William H. Cockerill family.)

When the girls in the 4-H home economics clubs sewed dresses for judging, they wore them to demonstrate what they had made. The dresses were judged while being worn, and two girls in the front proudly wear the ribbons they won for the dresses. In the second row at center is Ann Coffey, who later became a teacher in Loudoun County public schools. (Courtesy of the William H. Cockerill family.)

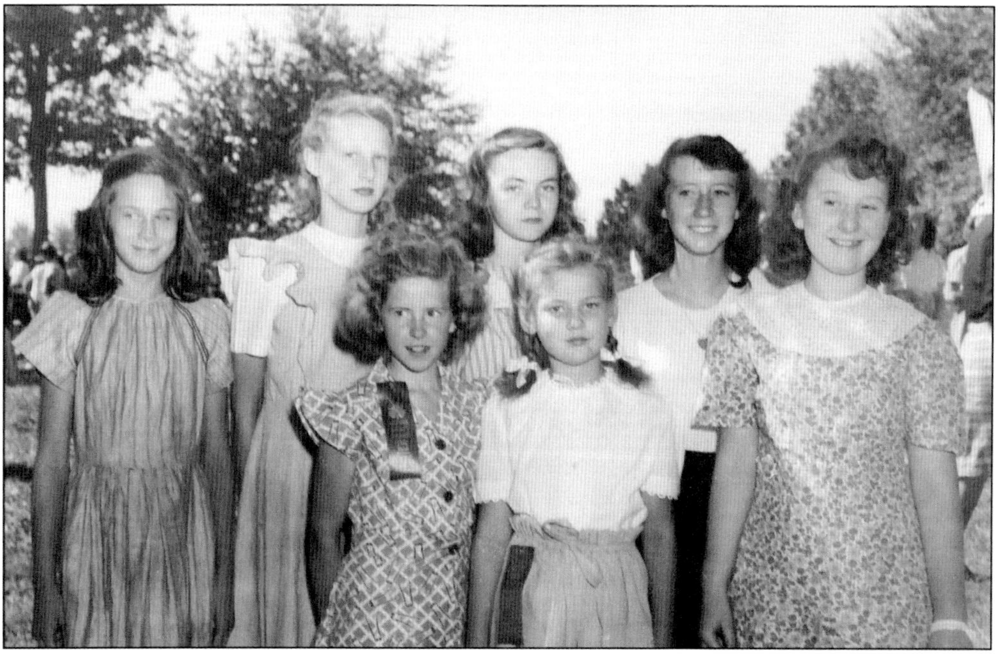

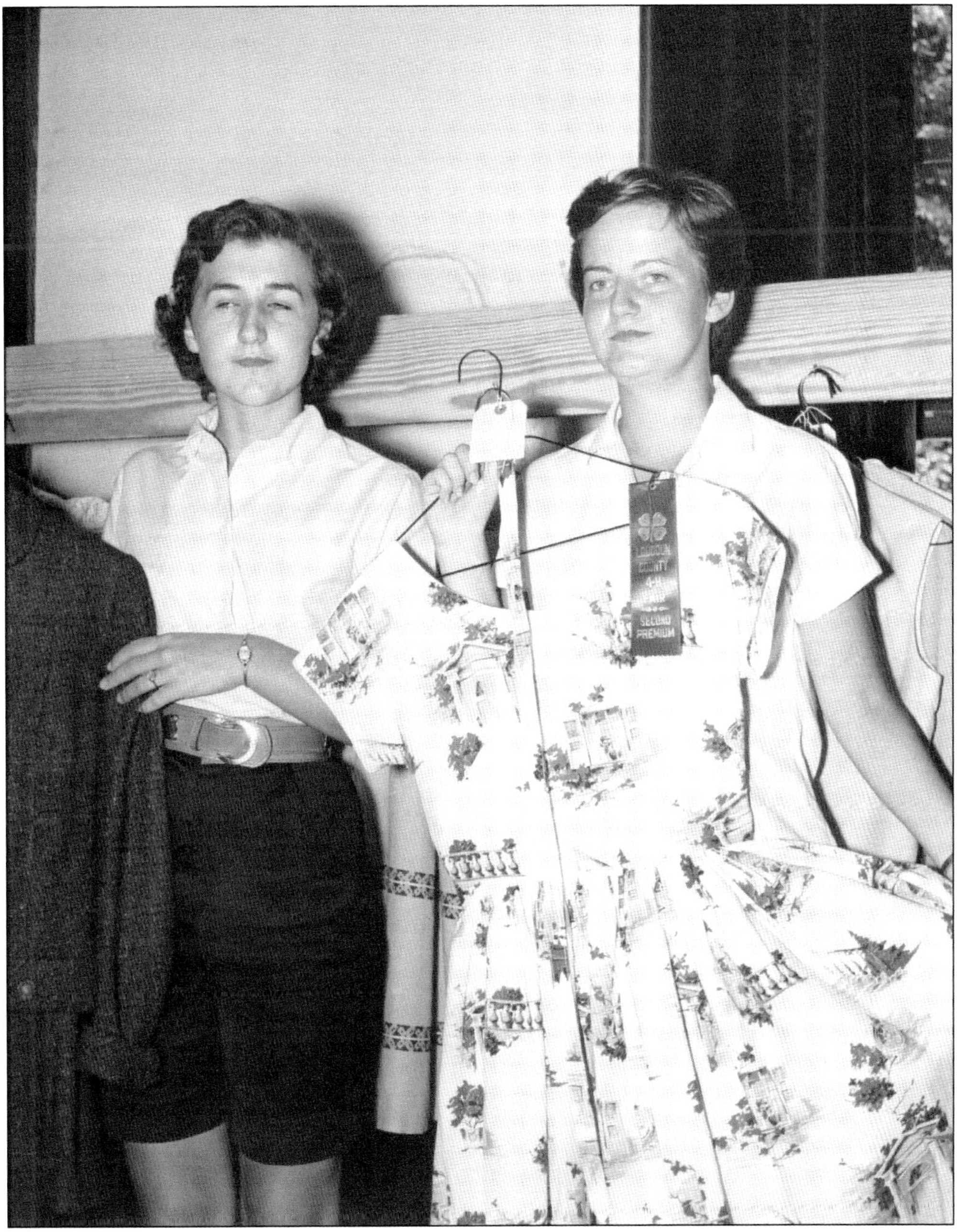

Mary Hope Stowers (left) and Eleanor Gill (right) are showing off their winning clothing entries at the 1956 4-H fair. The dress Eleanor is holding reflects the style of the 1950s. Clothing classes were open to juniors and seniors and consisted of pieces such as a cotton skirt, a tailored suit or dress, and a pair of pajamas. Other classes had judging on best garment made from feed bags, best active-sports outfit, best housecoat, and best dress-up dress. The 1956 clothing judges were Mrs. Harry Burke and Mrs. Henry Thompson. In addition to the clothing construction projects, there was also a division titled "So You'd Like to Sew." These classes were for junior girls and were designed to showcase items that beginning seamstresses could create. Items they made include a laundry bag, an apron, a stuffed toy, a handkerchief, and a towel. (Courtesy of Carol Stowers McComb.)

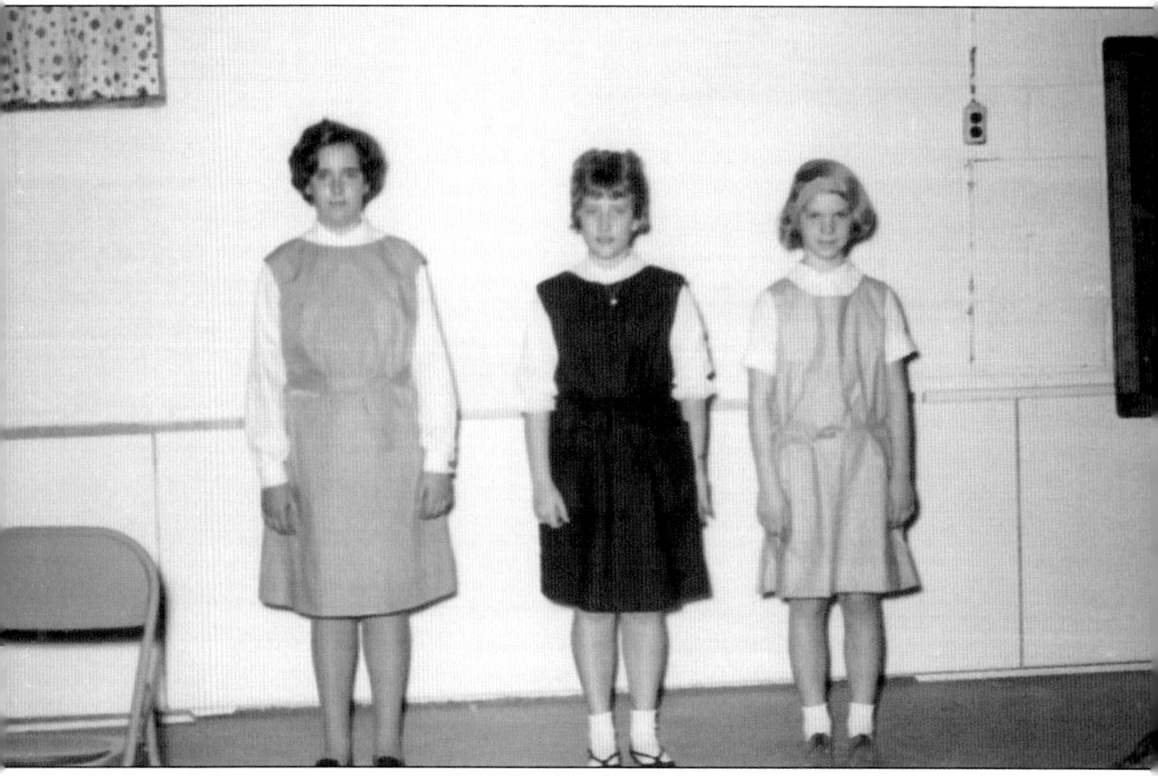

The 4-H clothing projects allowed the youth to learn about and explore clothing. They learned how to use the tools needed to create clothing. The fashion dress review is a time when the 4-H'ers were able to show off the clothes they made. In the photograph are, from left to right, Lynn Divine, unidentified, and Carol Biggers. (Courtesy of the William H. Cockerill family.)

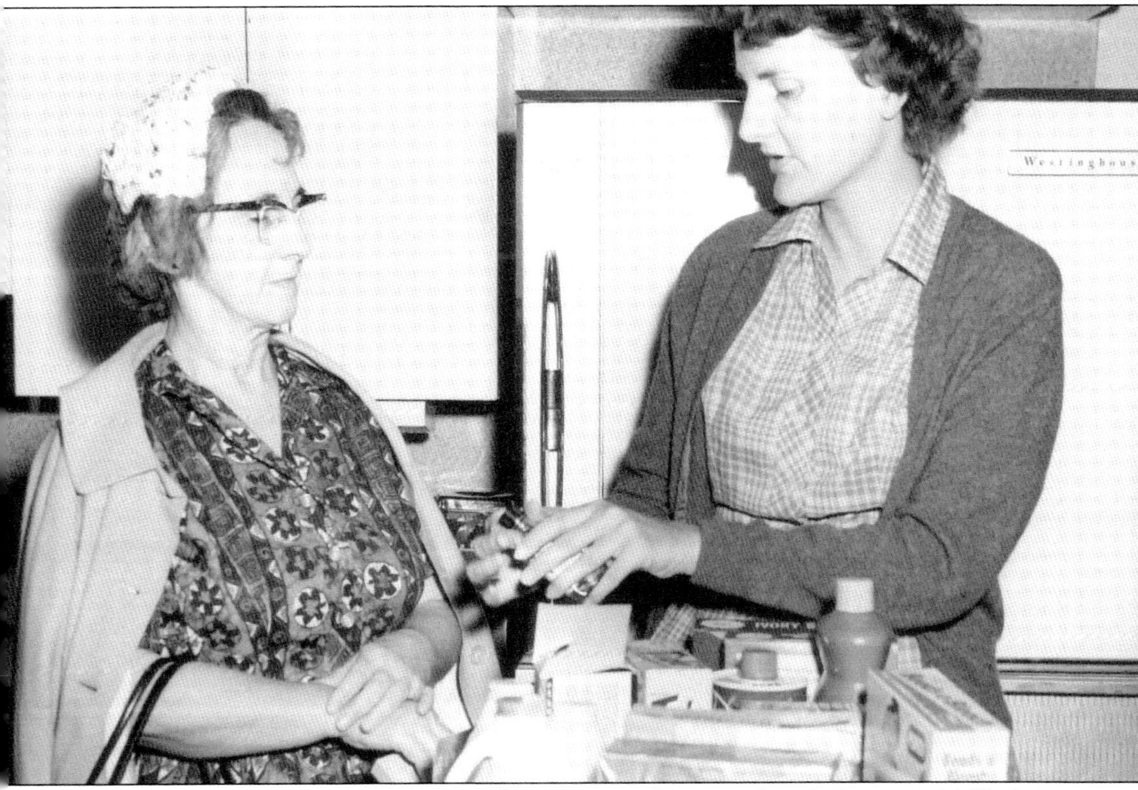

Louise McKinley is performing a cooking demonstration for an unidentified woman. McKinley was a representative for the Virginia Electric and Power Company as a home economist, whose role was to share home economic developments. She would go to homes and demonstrate cooking, clothing, and food-preservation tips. McKinley would also educate the community on the safety and saving of electricity in addition to teaching home economics and cosponsoring Future Homemakers of America. (Courtesy of the William H. Cockerill family.)

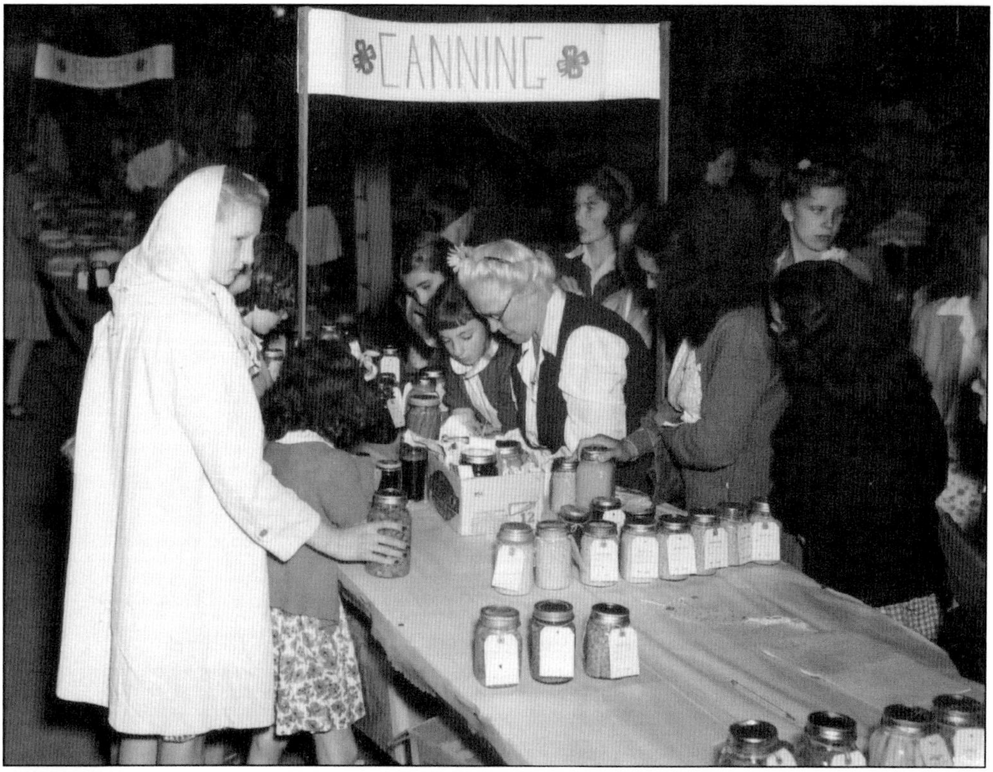

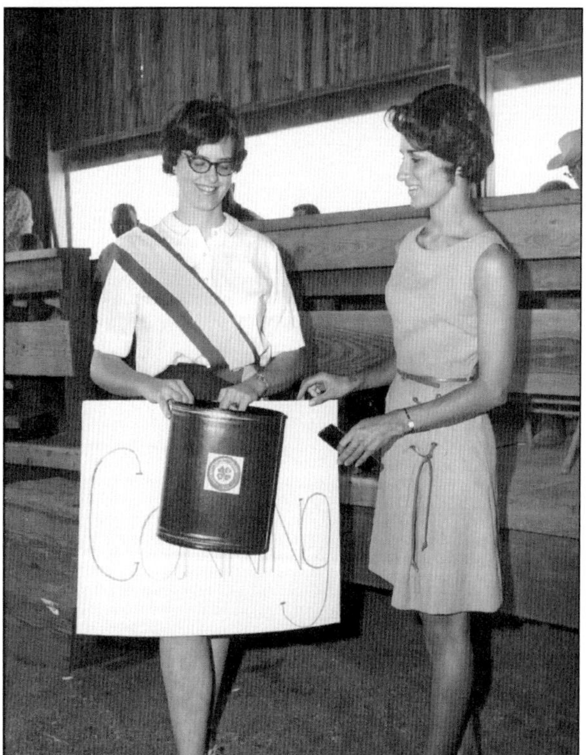

Many projects fall under the umbrella of home economics. Pictured here are canning and bread items. The 4-H'ers took their home economics projects very seriously, and they were fastidious in preparing the items for show. Not only were the products being judged on taste, but also on appearance. When preparing the food for canning, great detail was placed in having the items the same size, shape, and color, and food was put in the jars in a strategic manner. No seeds were permitted. In the photograph at left, Carolyn Potts (left) and Betty Unger (right) showcase canning, an important part of the fair. (Above, courtesy of the William H. Cockerill family; left, courtesy of Loudoun County Fair and Associates Collection, Rust Archive, Thomas Balch Library.)

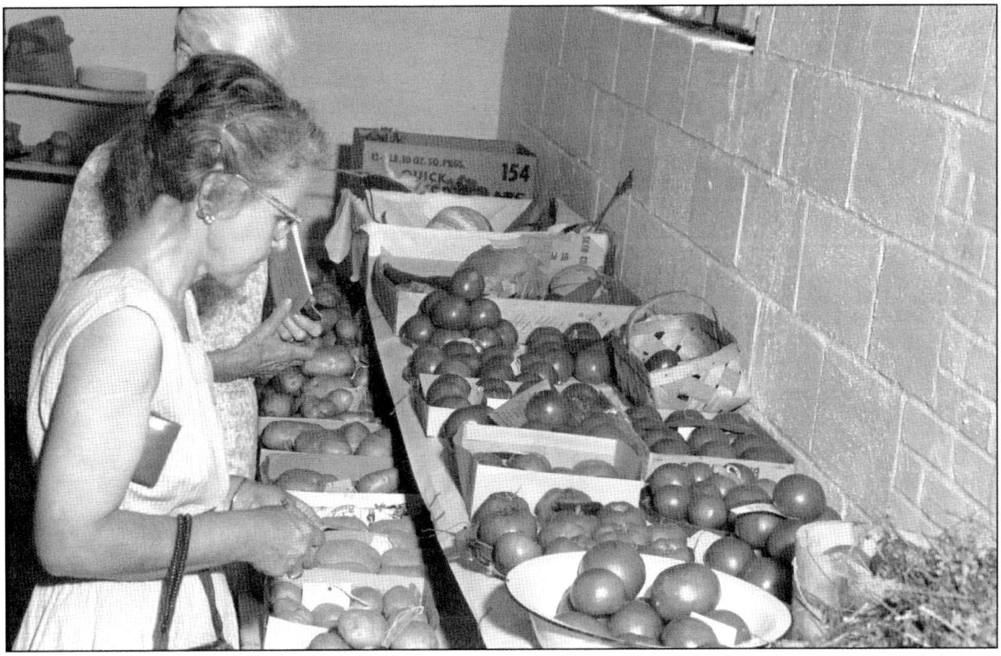

Martha Cockerille is viewing the vegetables on display as part of the home economic exhibit in Sykes Hall during the 1961 4-H fair. The large room on the second floor of Sykes Hall would be full with the home economics exhibits, many of them which were fresh-grown fruits and vegetables. (Courtesy of Carol Stowers McComb.)

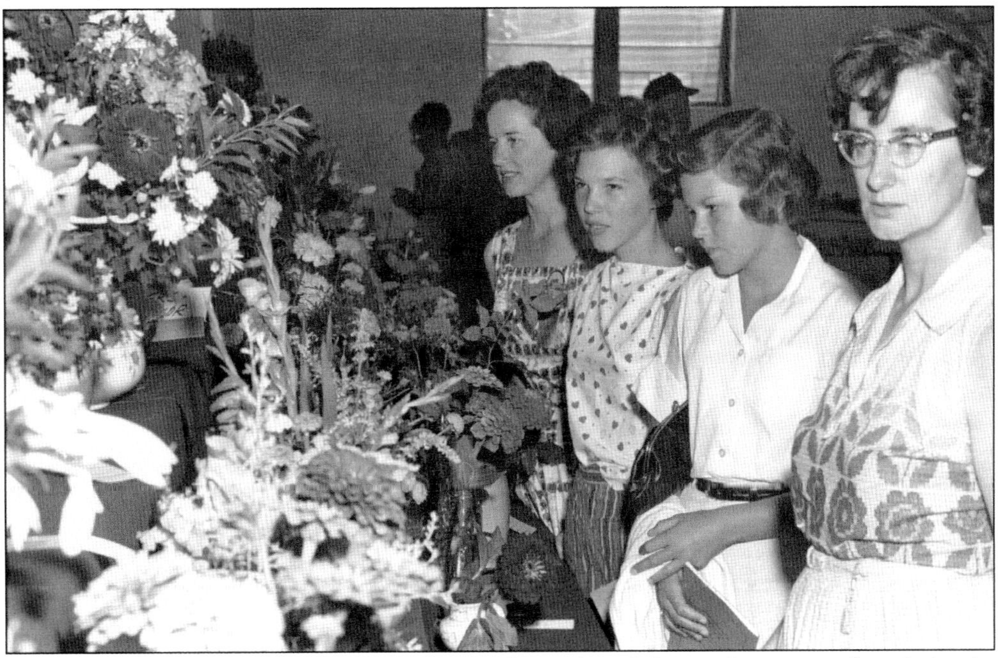

Gazing at the flower arrangements in Sykes Hall are, from left to right, two unidentified girls, Jean Daniel, and Eleanor Colbert. The flowers were always freshly picked from the gardens of the exhibitor and arranged in a perfect display. In the 1960s, the Sykes Hall exhibits were always a popular place for people to go. (Courtesy of the William H. Cockerill family.)

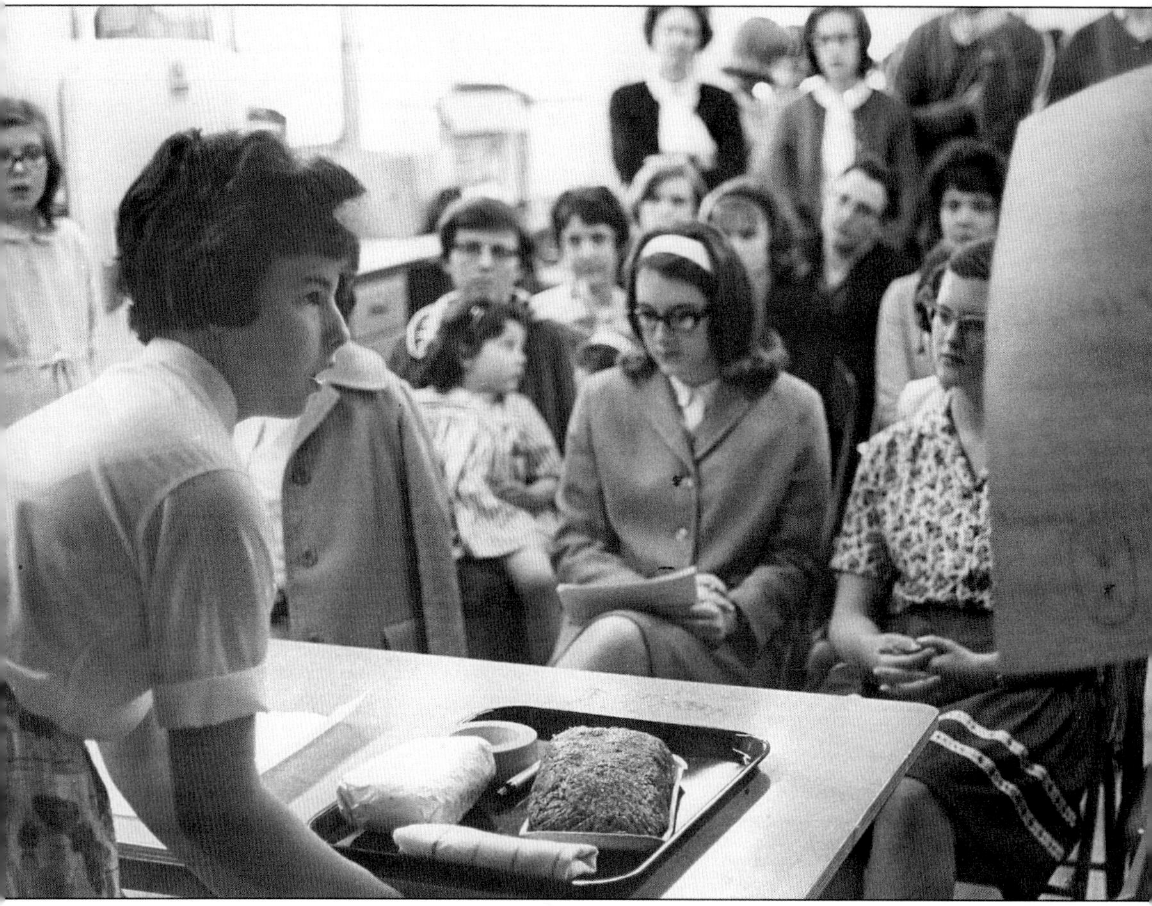

Evelyn Cook is showing off a baking project on Demonstration Day in the early 1960s. Evelyn's father was Clinton Cook, a longtime 4-H leader. On Demonstration Day, youth showed their family, friends, and judges what they had learned from their project. Some baked a cake, some made bread, and others may have planted flowers. In the audience in the center is Linda James and on the right is Carolyn Potts. (Courtesy of the William H. Cockerill family.)

Three

ALL ABOUT DAIRY

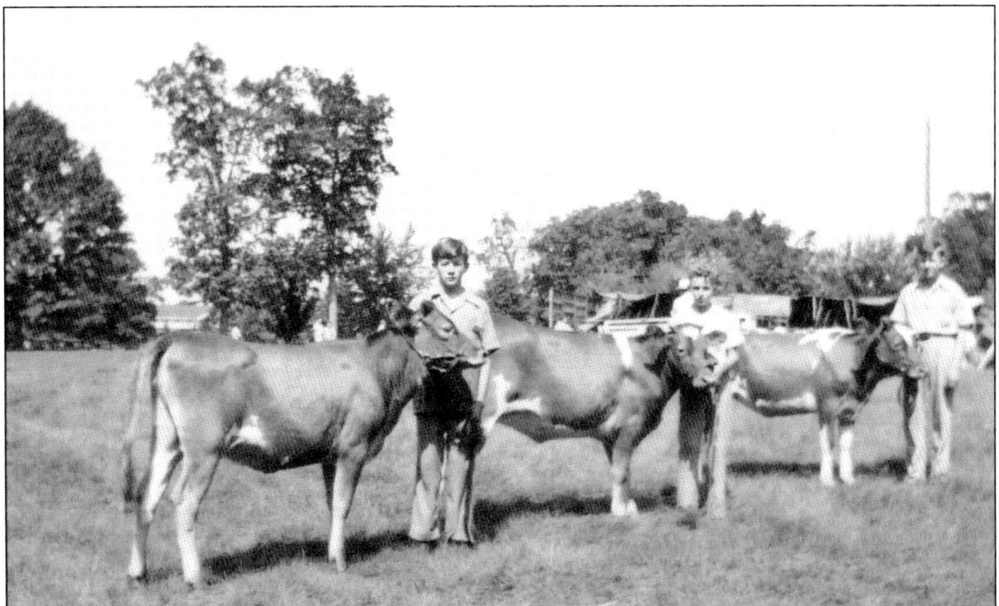

Dairy cows were a large part of the Loudoun County Fair in the early years, reflecting the dairy industry in Loudoun at the time. In this photograph, three boys pose with their dairy cows in September 1942, preparing for the show. (Courtesy of the William H. Cockerill family.)

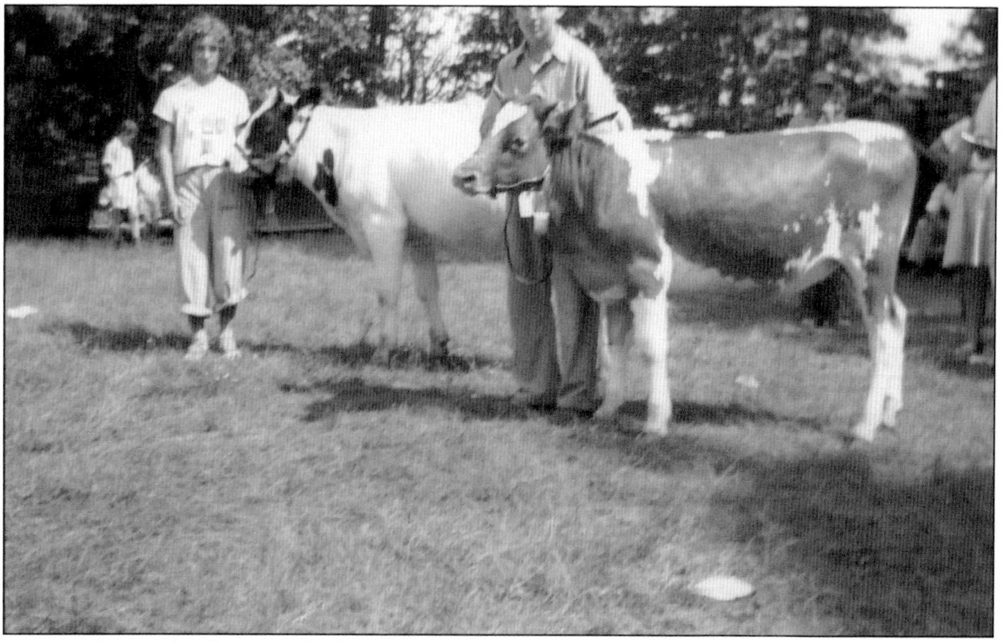

A young boy and girl pose with their dairy cows in September 1942. Without the standard white show attire, the youth were likely training and preparing for the fair. During this time, the fair was held in Purcellville at what was known as the Bush Meeting Grounds. (Courtesy of the William H. Cockerill family.)

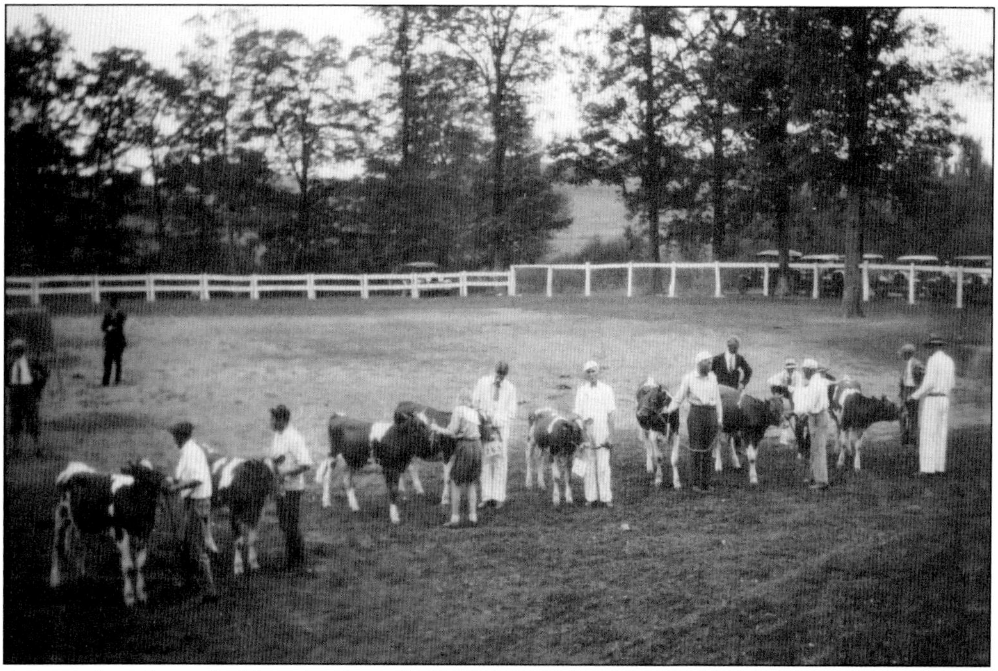

A dairy show being held at the Purcellville fairgrounds is pictured here. The exhibitors stand in line waiting to be judged; they would be judged on the animal's frame, udders, rear feet and legs, and dairy strength. The exhibitors in this photograph are senior 4-H'ers. (Courtesy of William Harrison.)

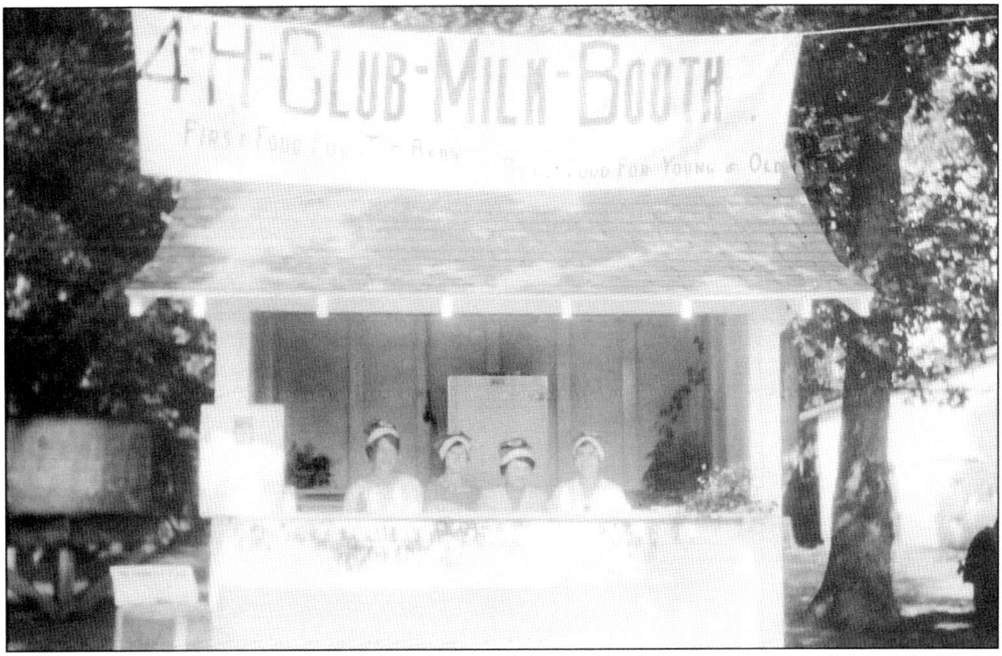

As part of the first fairs, clubs had booths that displayed their projects. One of the clubs had a dairy booth displaying and selling milk, advertised as the "First Food For the Baby, Best Food For Young and Old." This booth was located at the Purcellville fairgrounds. (Courtesy of the William H. Cockerill family.)

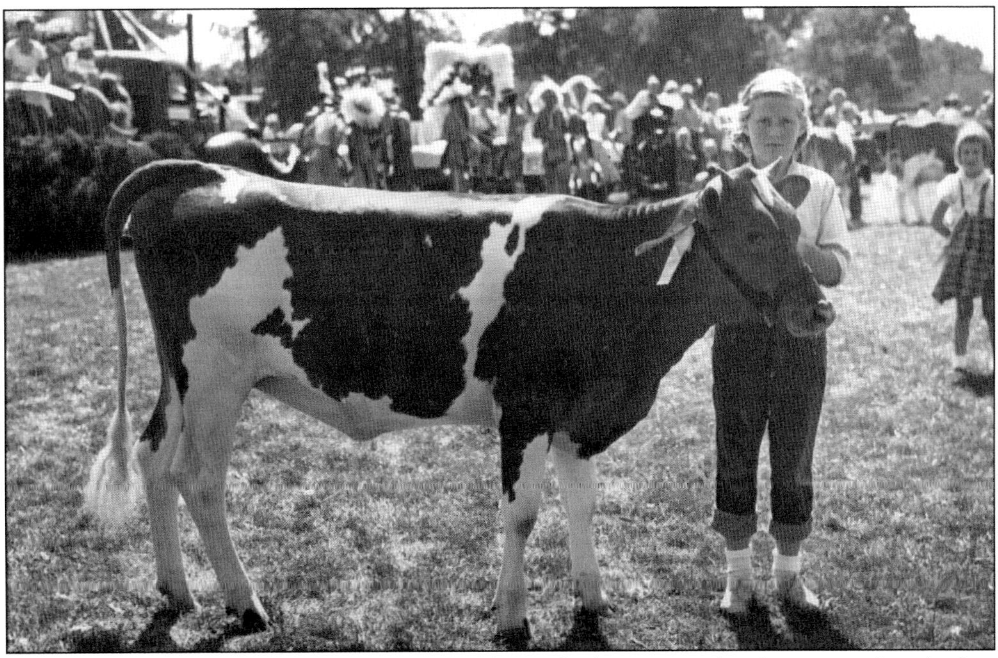

This photograph is of Patricia Godfrey, daughter of television and radio personality Arthur Godfrey of Waterford. Patricia and her Holstein won first place in fitting and showing at the 1954 fair in Middleburg. Patricia was an active participant in the fair for several years. (Courtesy of Carol Stowers McComb.)

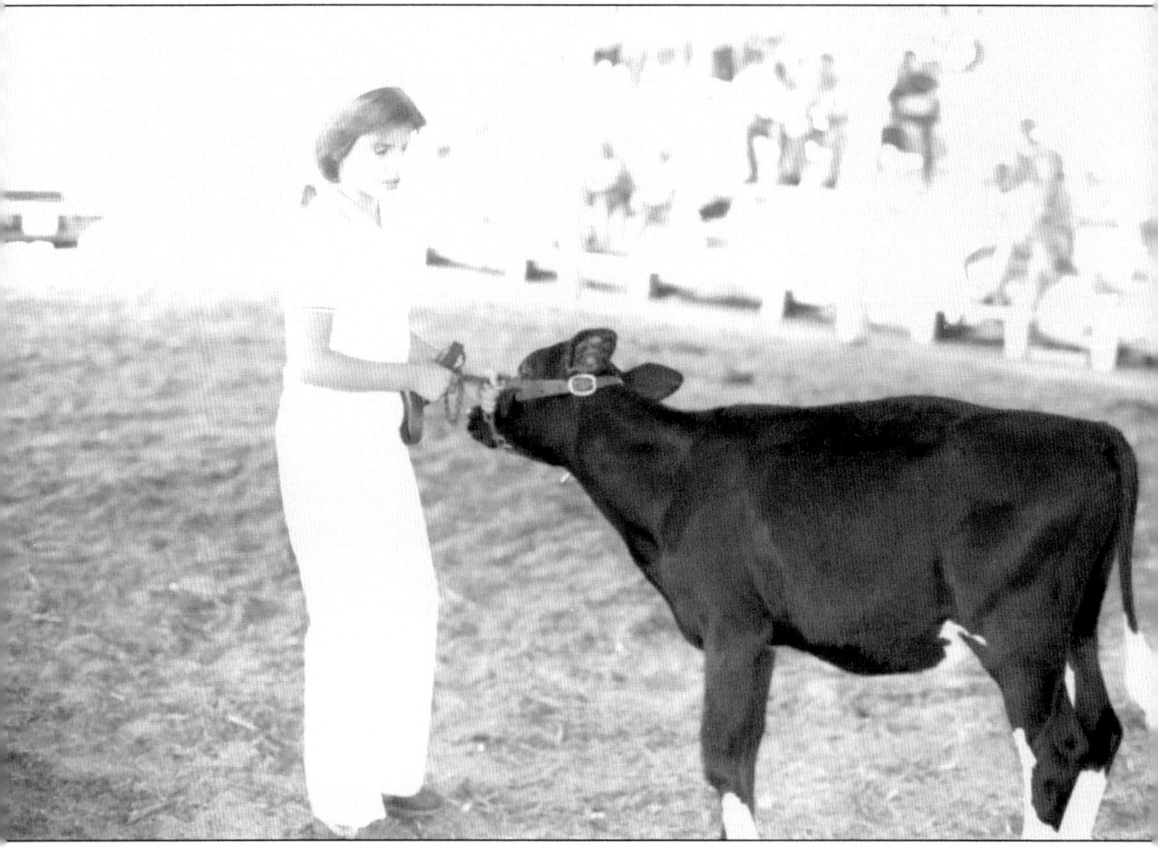

The girl in this photograph is in traditional dairy attire while she parades her calf in the show pavilion. This Holstein calf in is in the beginning stages of showing, having only recently begun to wear a halter. (Courtesy of Loudoun County Fair and Associates Collection, Rust Archive, Thomas Balch Library.)

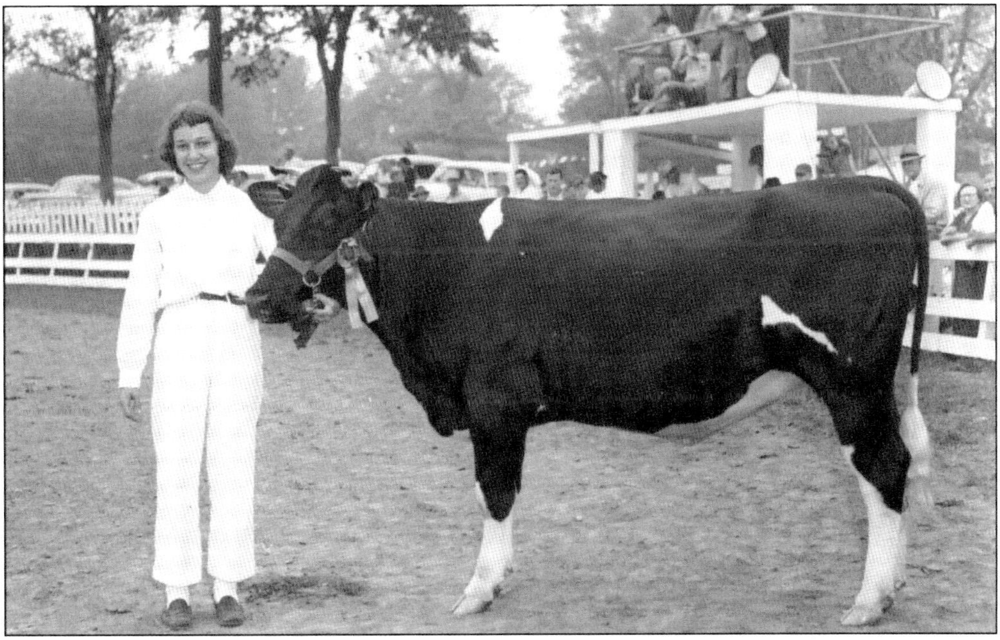

Mary Jane Benedum stands at the halter of her champion Holstein at the 1955 fair in Middleburg. Frank Ellmore of Virginia Polytechnic Institute and State University was the judge of the dairy cattle event during this fair. The superintendents were Norvel Lowry and Randy Rust. (Courtesy of Carol Stowers McComb.)

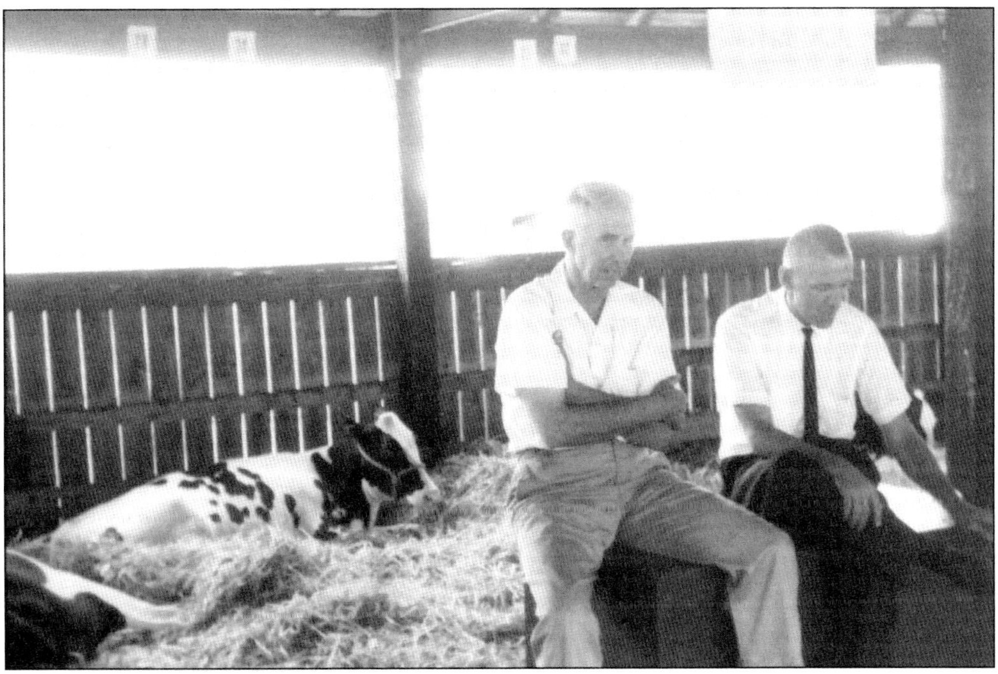

William H. Cockerill (left) and an unidentified man take a rare moment to relax in the dairy barn at the fair in 1957, the first year it was located in the Clarke's Gap area of Loudoun County. The men, as well as the dairy cows in the background, would have had a full day of working and showing. (Courtesy of William H. Cockerill Jr.)

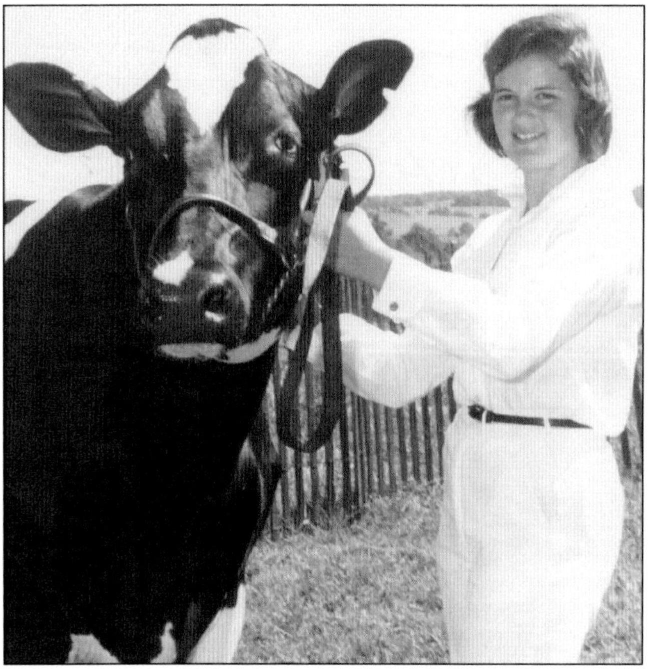

Rachel Norman of Purcellville holds her champion Holstein in 1958. During her 4-H years, Norman was a Virginia 4-H All Star and later became a dairy princess. Along with her husband, she owns a lodge in the mountains of Virginia where they have hosted many 4-H events, including Virginia 4-H All Stars picnics and conferences. (Courtesy of Carol Stowers McComb.)

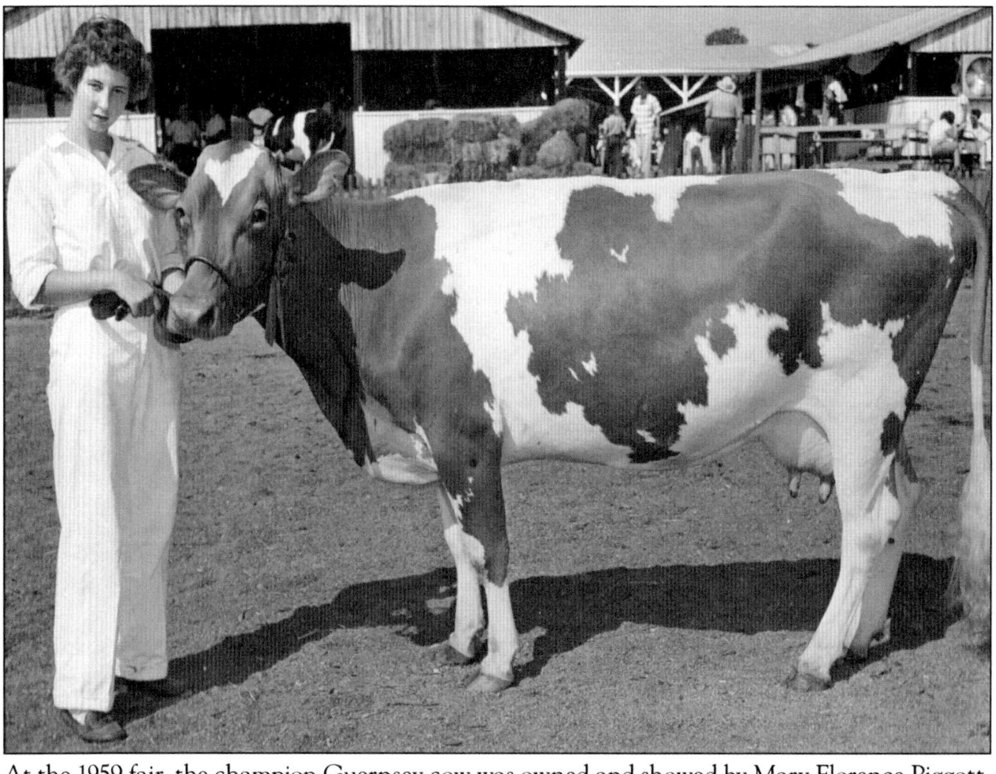

At the 1959 fair, the champion Guernsey cow was owned and showed by Mary Florence Piggott. Piggott was an active 4-H'er with the dairy club and at the Loudoun County Fair. Note the cow's fluffy tail, traditional grooming completed in preparation for showing. (Courtesy of Carol Stowers McComb.)

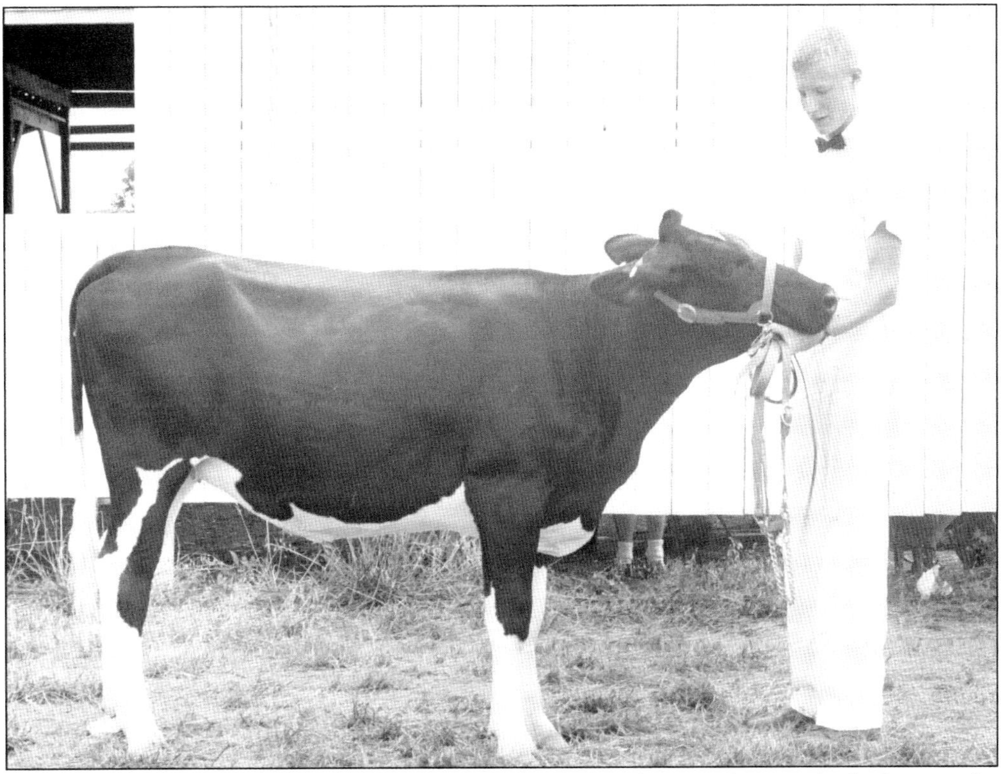

Bill Cole of Purcellville is shown here with his Holstein at the 1961 fair, at which the prize for first place was $5, and second place garnered $4. The fair at this time would have spanned two days—a Friday and Saturday. Cole would have shown his dairy cow on Friday in the show pavilion. (Courtesy of Carol Stowers McComb.)

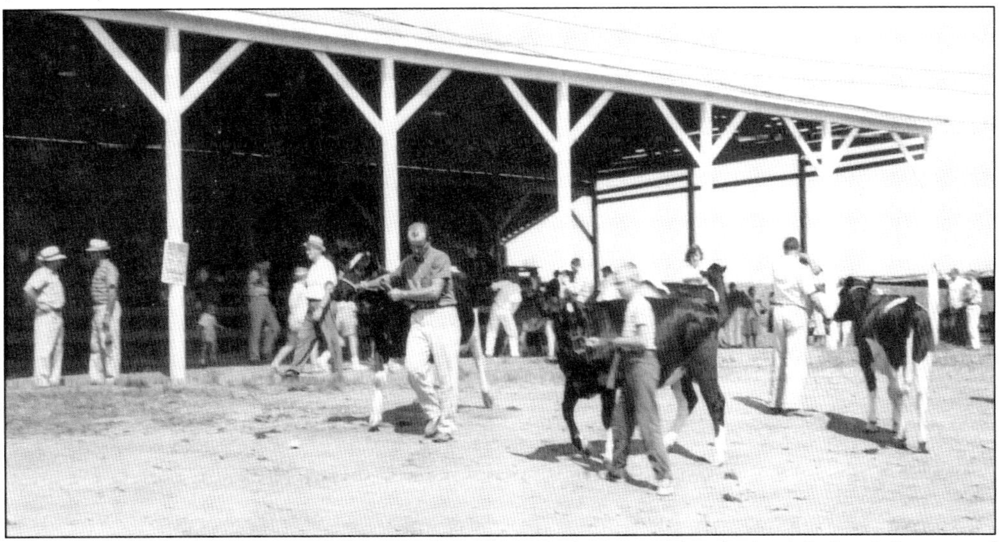

Bob McComb (holding the cow on the left) and Rachel Norman (in the back behind the second cow, facing the camera) walk their cattle prior to the start of the dairy show in the early 1960s. The show pavilion on the 4-H fairgrounds outside of Leesburg is in the background. This is the building where the dairy shows took place. (Courtesy of the William H. Cockerill family.)

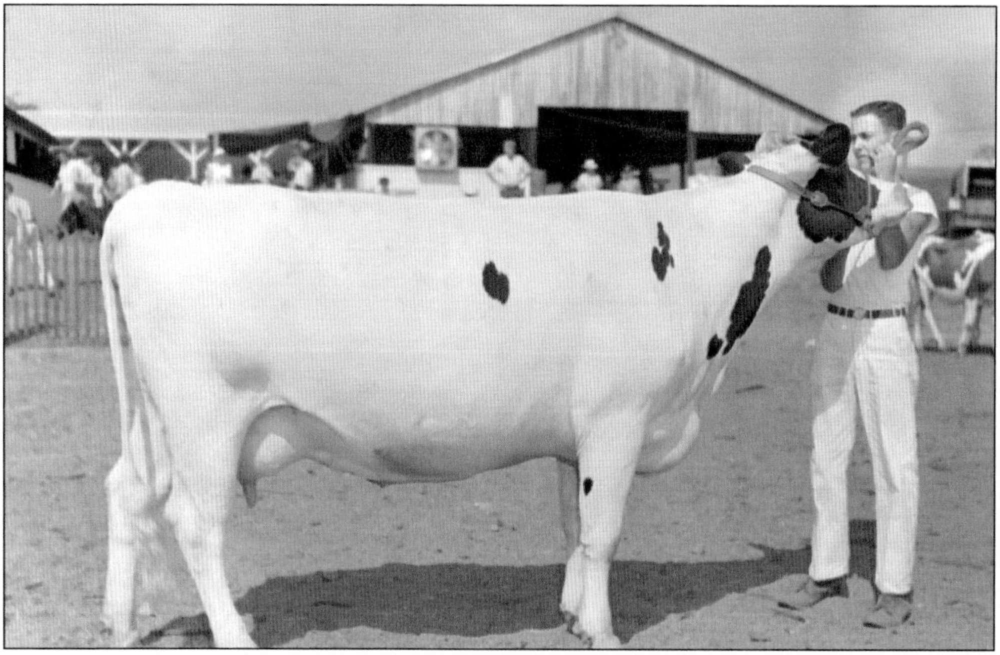

Ralph Fields is pictured here with his Holstein in front of the dairy barn. Preparing for a dairy show requires much time and effort; keeping an animal immaculate, especially one with so much white, would have been even more challenging. Fields's family farm continues to be a working farm in Purcellville, and the original springhouse still stands on the property. (Courtesy of Sykes Hall Archives.)

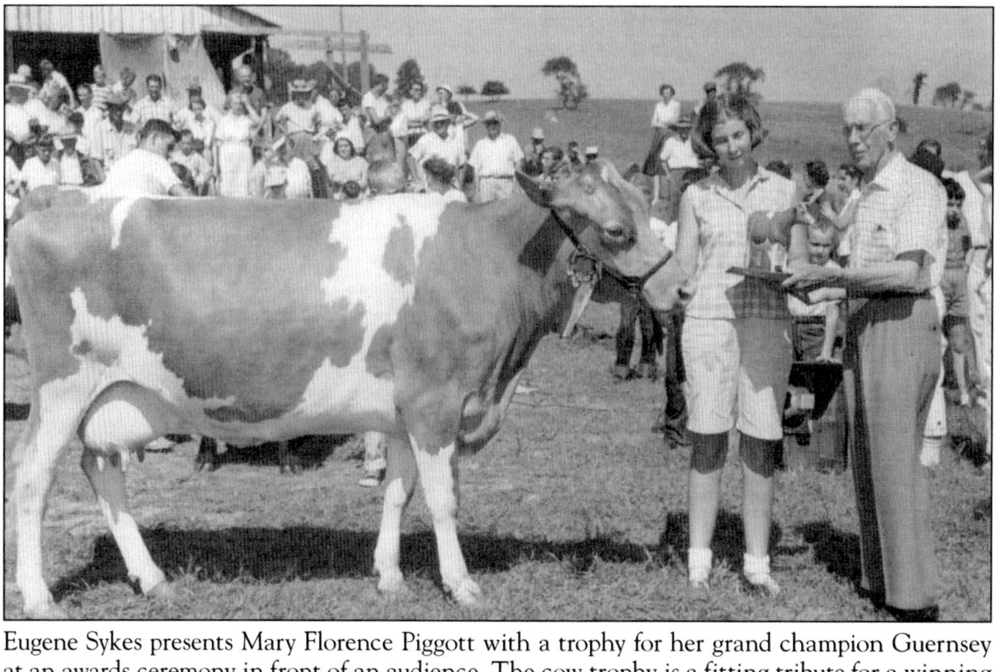

Eugene Sykes presents Mary Florence Piggott with a trophy for her grand champion Guernsey at an awards ceremony in front of an audience. The cow trophy is a fitting tribute for a winning dairy animal. In the background is one of the livestock barns on the fairgrounds. (Courtesy of William Harrrison.)

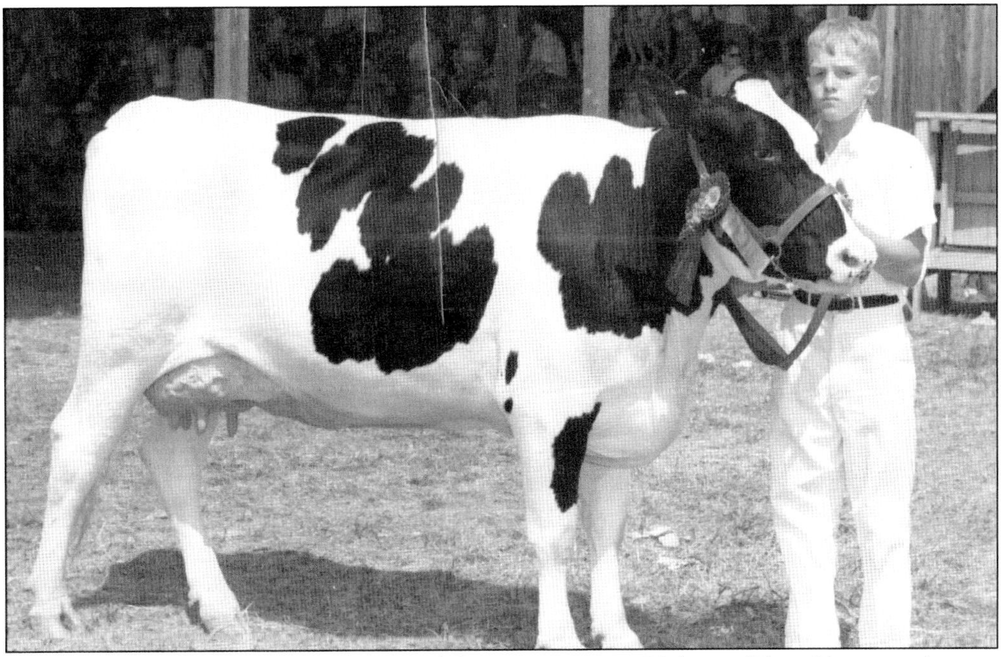

Thomas "Tommy" Cockerill is posing with his prize-winning Holstein. The ribbons on the cow are for winning the class and being overall champion. Tommy is the son of William and Nancy Cockerill, both of whom worked with the extension office and were active fair supporters. (Courtesy of the William H. Cockerill family.)

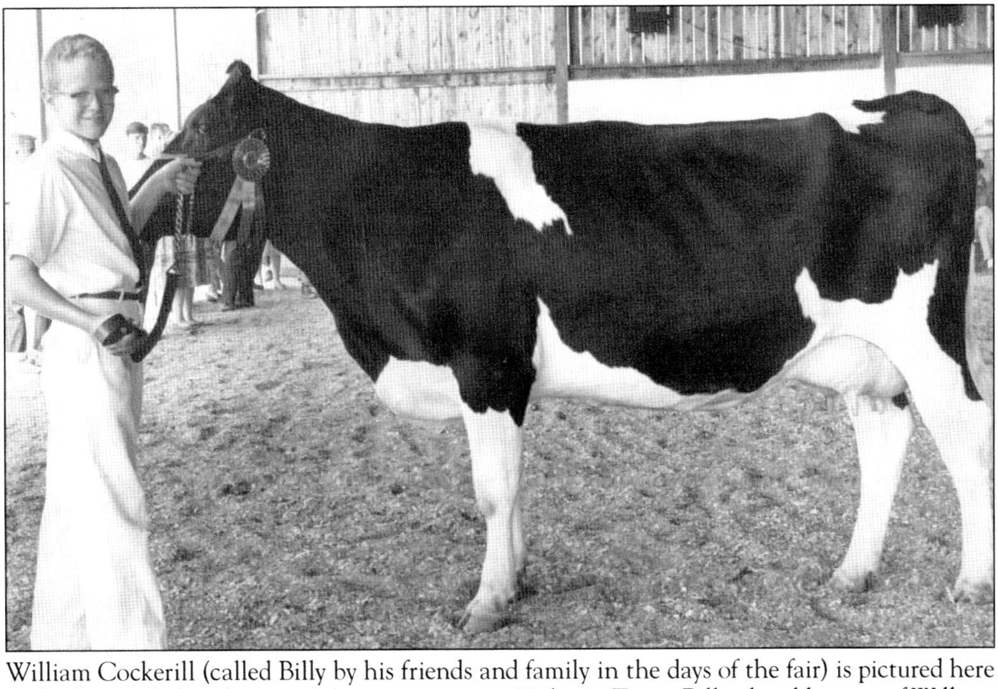

William Cockerill (called Billy by his friends and family in the days of the fair) is pictured here in the livestock show barn with his prize-winning Holstein Topsy. Billy, the oldest son of William and Nancy Cockerill, showed dairy cattle for many years at the fair. (Courtesy of the William H. Cockerill family.)

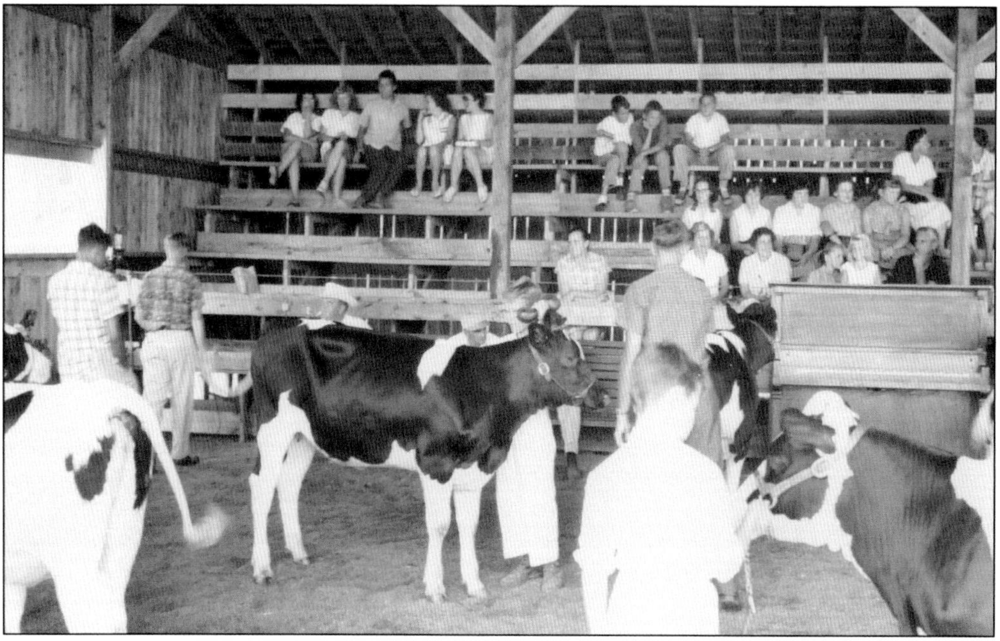

In the above photograph, Billy Cockerill is showing his Holstein, Topsy, in the livestock show barn at the fair in the 1960s. Note the audience in the bleachers. These bleacher seats were erected by volunteers in the spring of 1959 and are still in use today. In the photograph below, the dairy class is standing, waiting to be judged. The boy in the bow tie is Billy Cockerill. To the right is Gerald James, and at far right is Billy's sister Anne. Oftentimes, a crowd comes and goes throughout a show as an event progresses; the crowd in the image below is much larger. (Both, courtesy of the William H. Cockerill family.)

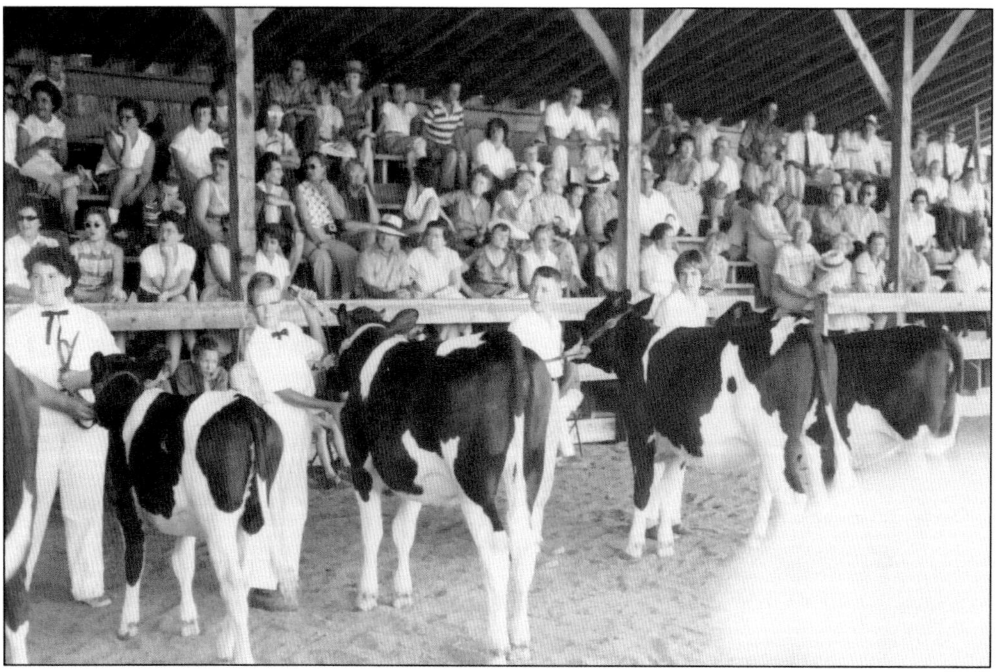

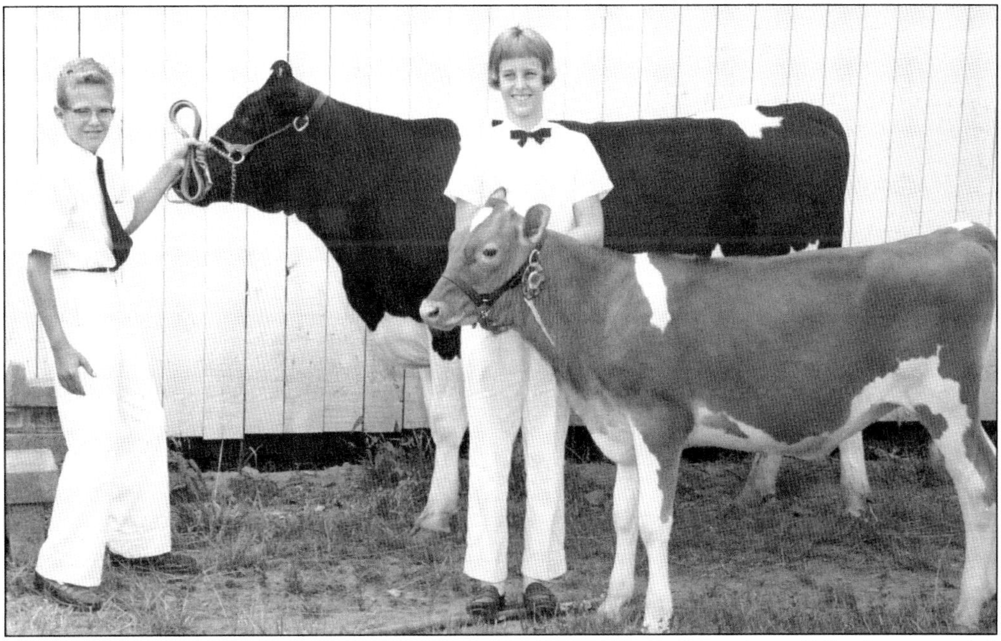

Billy with Topsy and Anne Cockerill with her Guernsey cow are shown here. Billy always tended to show Holsteins, while Anne, the oldest of the Cockerill children, preferred Guernseys. When showing dairy cattle, 4-H'ers wore all an all-white uniform with a black tie. (Courtesy of the William H. Cockerill family.)

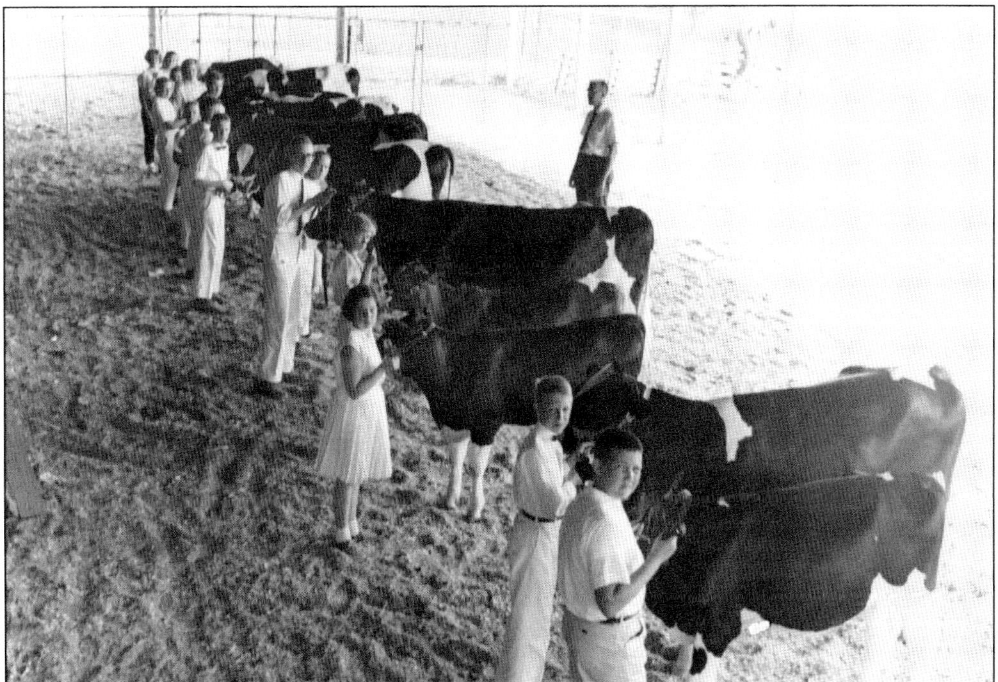

There were many youth who showed dairy cows in the early days of the fair. This group is being judged on their animals in the livestock show pavilion. When showing, the girls could wear pants or a dress as seen in this photograph. (Courtesy of the William H. Cockerill family.)

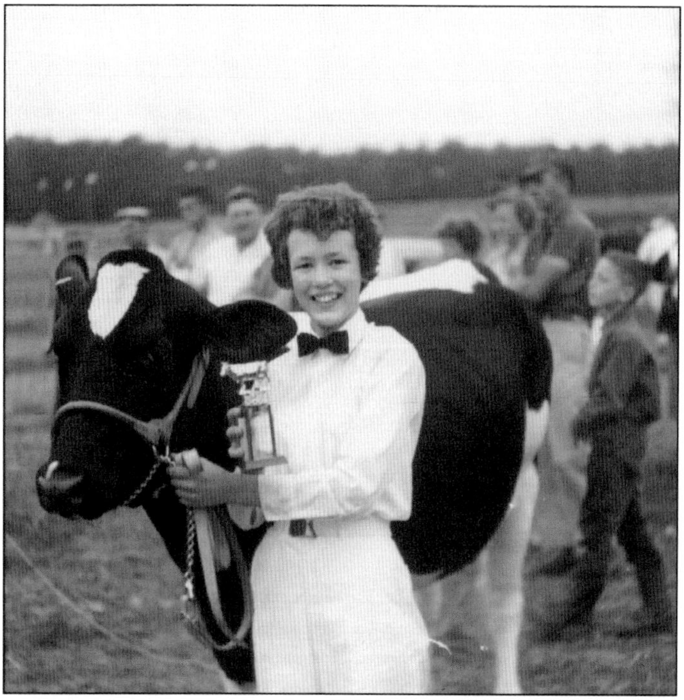

Barbara Fletcher shows off the trophy she won with her winning Holstein. Fletcher was an active 4-H'er who showed in the dairy club for multiple years and was a Virginia 4-H All Star in high school. Barbara and her brother Tommy both showed at the Loudoun County Fair. (Courtesy of the William H. Cockerill family.)

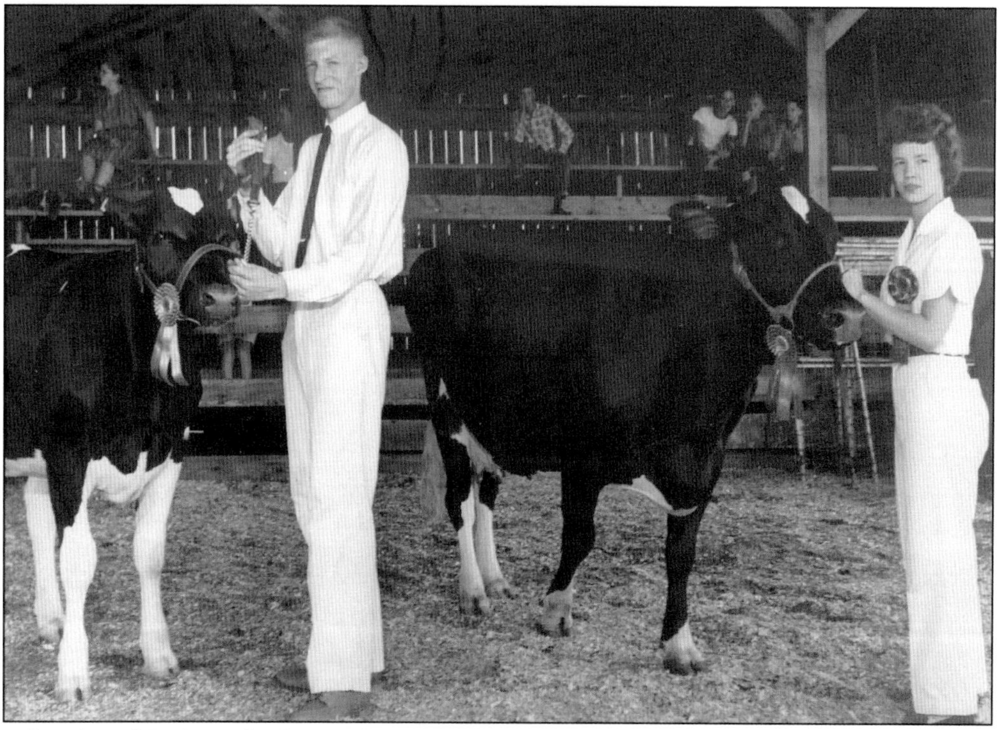

Bill Cole and Barbara Fletcher are both holding their prize-winning dairy cows. The back of the original photograph indicates that the image was captured by Hugh Grubbs, who recorded many events at the Loudoun County Fair. Both Bill and Barbara had families that were very active with the 4-H and fair. (Courtesy of the William H. Cockerill family.)

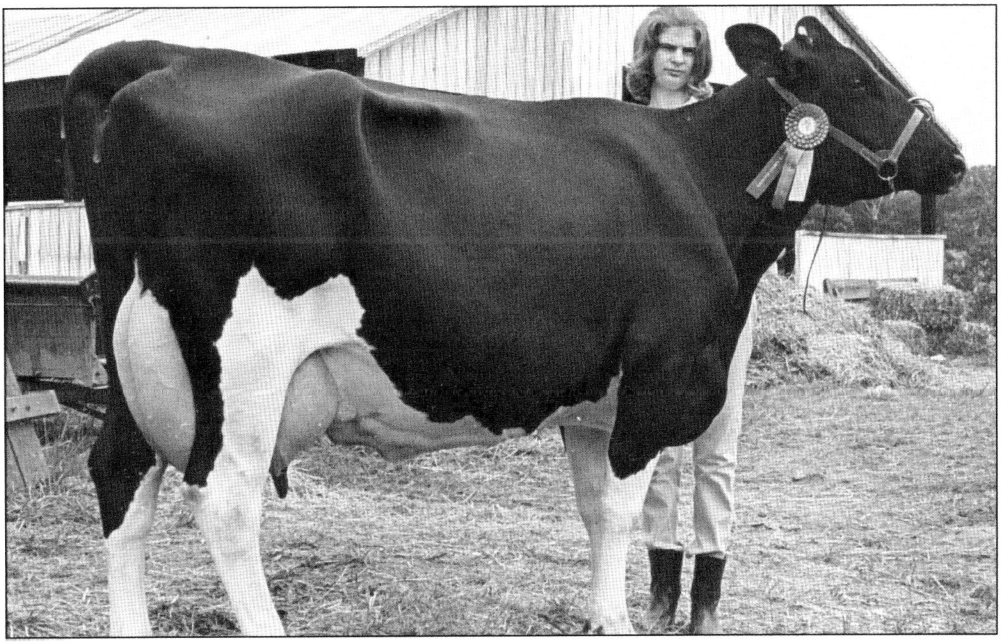

Catherine "Kitty" Brown poses with her champion Holstein cow. When showing a dairy cow, the hind leg nearest the judge should be far enough ahead of the opposite leg to allow the judge to see the udders. The udder is important, as it is the main aspect of a dairy cow. (Courtesy of Carol Stowers McComb.)

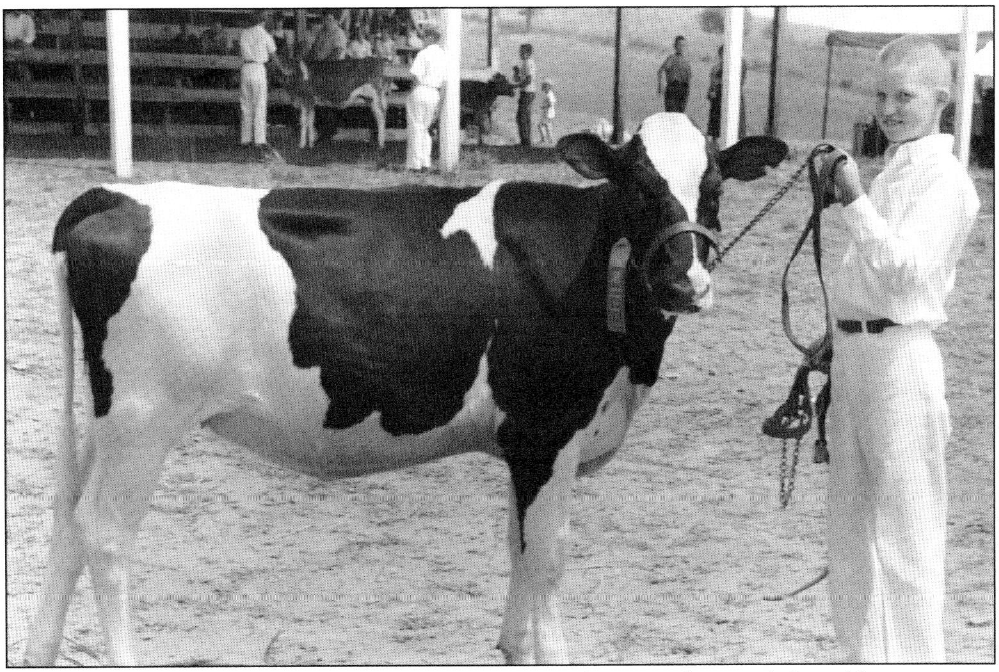

Edwin "Eddie" Potts stands in front of the livestock show pavilion with his ribbon-winning Holstein in 1961. Both Eddie and his cow pose for the camera. Generations of the Potts family have had dairy farms in Loudoun County. The only dairy farm left in the county is owned by Eddie's cousin. (Courtesy of Carol Stowers McComb.)

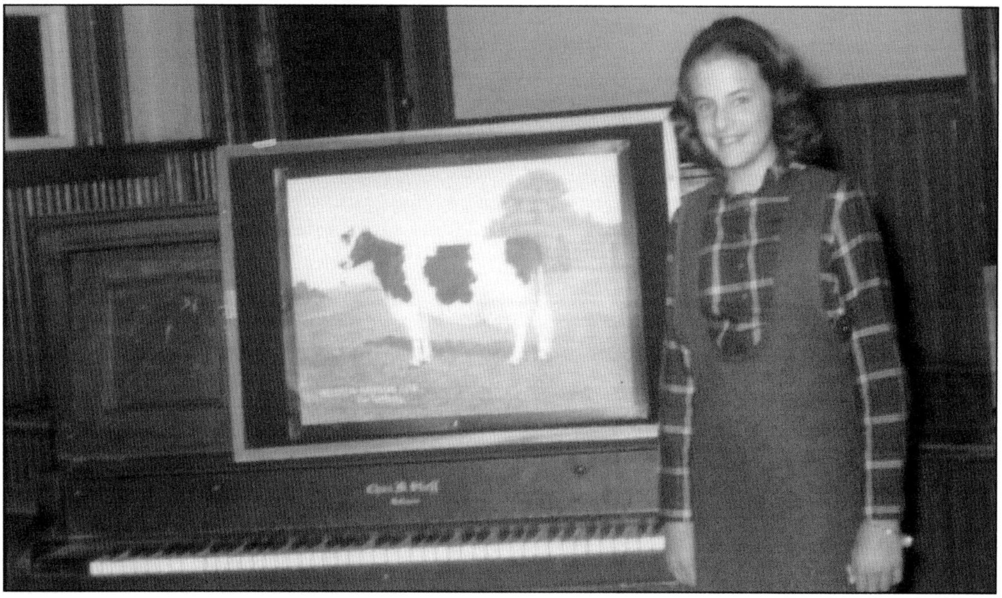

Patricia Cole is in front of a framed photograph of the ideal cow in 1966. Cole's family owned Shadowlawn Farm in Purcellville from 1909 to 2005. Originally 88 acres, it was a thriving dairy operation. Patricia is the daughter of Curtis and Maxine Cole. (Courtesy of the William H. Cockerill family.)

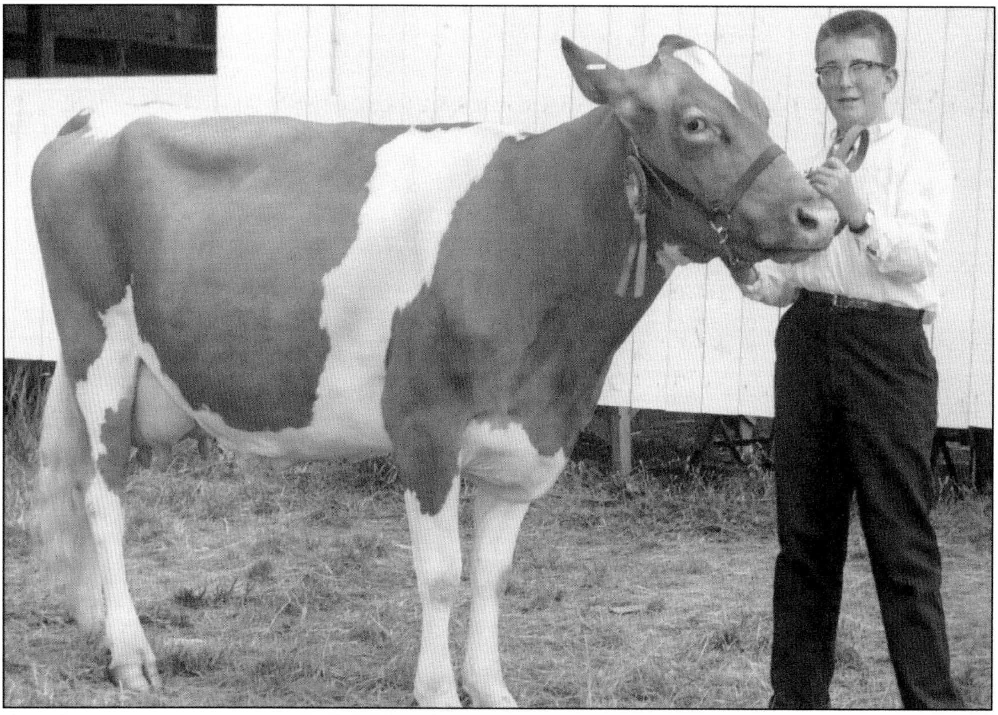

Another prize-winning cow is that of Billy Piggott in 1961. Note the protruding hip bones on the back of the cow. Dairy animals appear to be skinny because they put the calories they ingest into the milk they produce, not in the fat stores like beef cattle. (Courtesy of the William H. Cockerill family.)

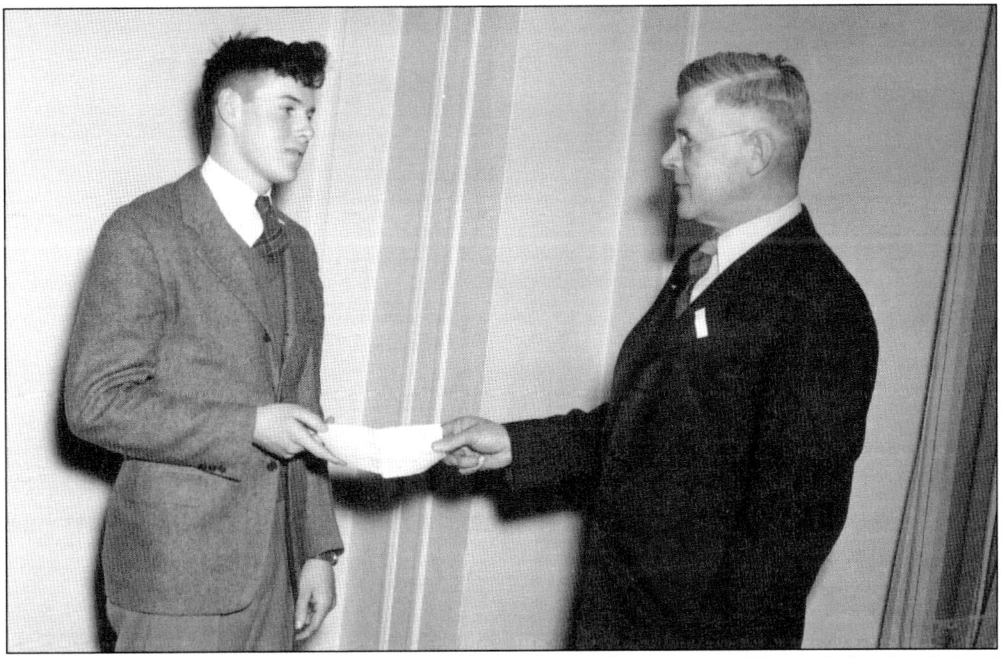

George Miller of Purcellville is receiving a dairy scholarship in 1946. This scholarship helped Miller continue his work with dairy animals. Miller spent his entire life working with the dairy industry, many of those years in Columbus, Ohio, and he worked with 4-H youth into adulthood. (Courtesy of the William H. Cockerill family.)

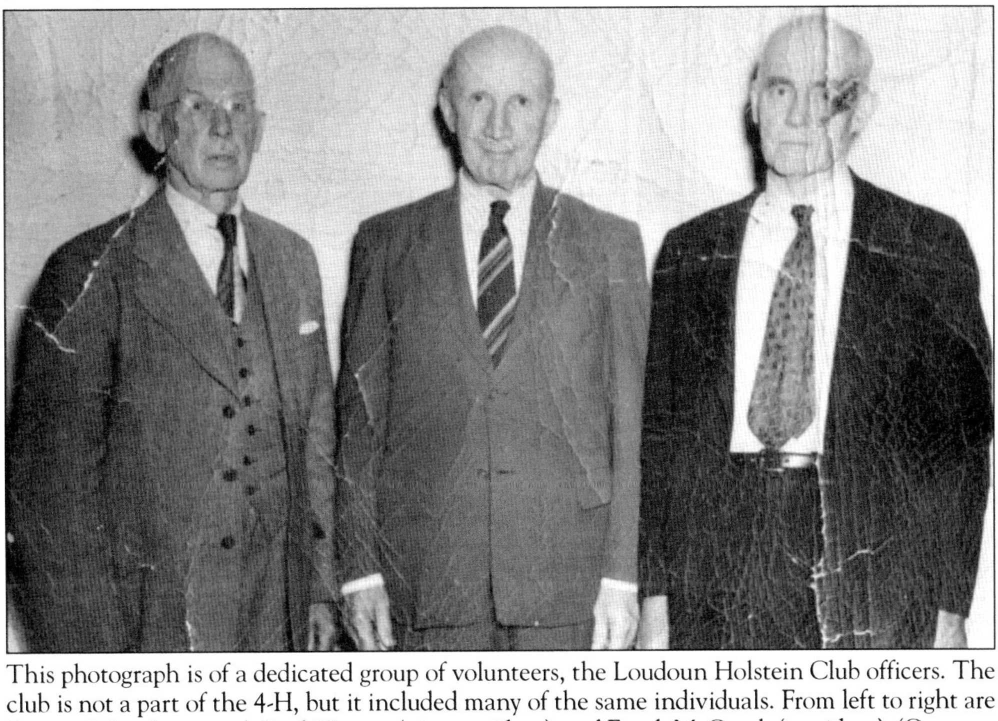

This photograph is of a dedicated group of volunteers, the Loudoun Holstein Club officers. The club is not a part of the 4-H, but it included many of the same individuals. From left to right are Eugene Sykes (treasurer), Paul Warner (vice president), and Frank McComb (president). (Courtesy of the William H. Cockerill family.)

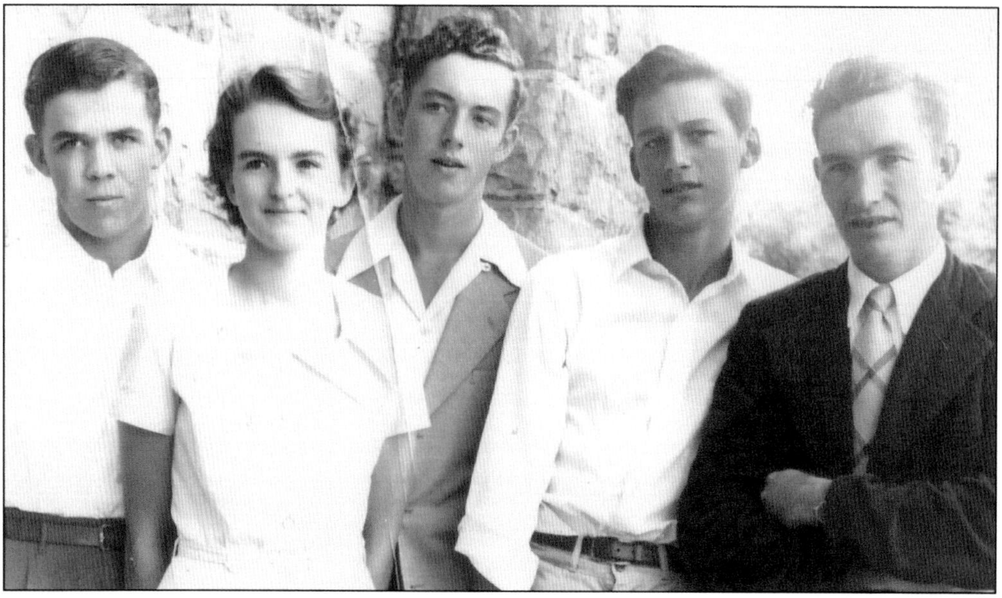

In 1951, the Loudoun 4-H dairy judging team won the state contest. From left to right are Frankie Cornwell, Jean Sprague, Adolph Rose, Randy Rust, and Conner Grimes (coach). Over the years, Loudoun has had many winning dairy judging teams on the local, state, and national levels. (Courtesy of Carol Stowers McComb.)

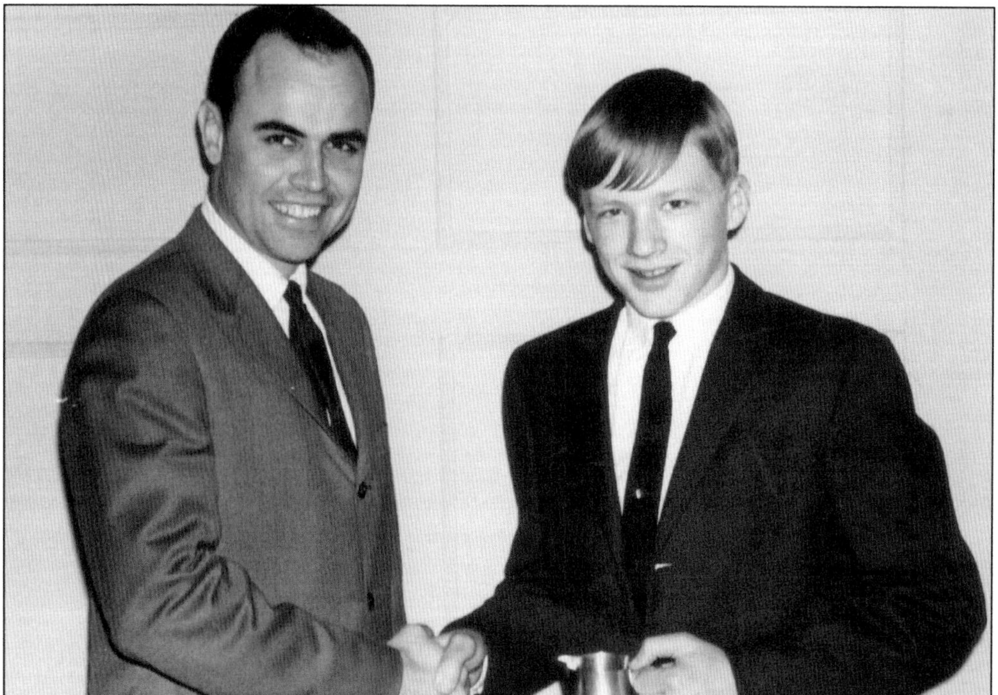

In this photograph, Joe Stowers is receiving a state Holstein award. Presenting the engraved creamer pitcher to Stowers is Doug Childs of Broadnax, Virginia. Stowers's family was very active with the 4-H and the fair. His siblings participated in both, and his mother, Ellen Stowers, was a longtime volunteer. (Courtesy of the William H. Cockerill family.)

Pictured here are, from left to right, Tommy Fletcher, Joe Stowers, Edwin Potts, Barbara Fletcher, and William Harrison. Known to everyone as Bill, Harrison was an assistant agent, later the county extension agent. He began his career in 1963 with the county office as a dairy specialist. As the dairy industry in Loudoun declined, he focused more on horticulture until 1991. (Courtesy of the William H. Cockerill family.)

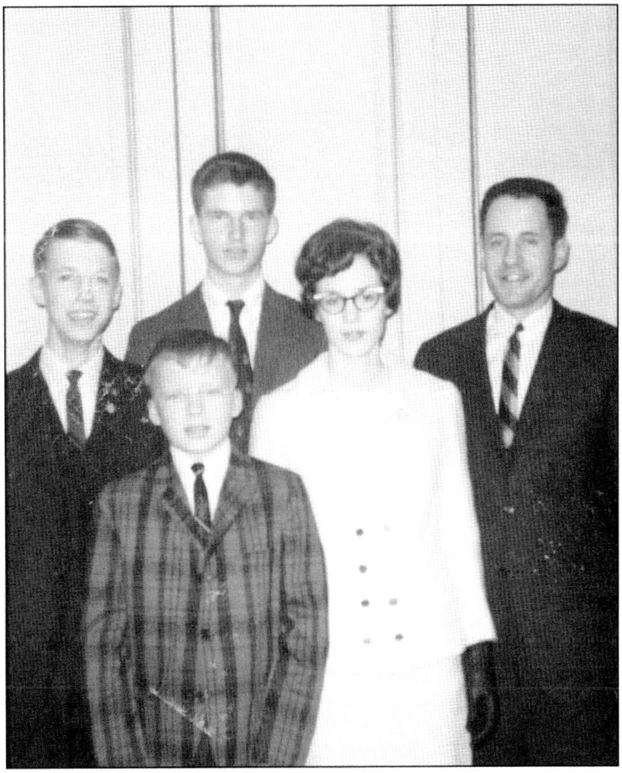

Carol Stowers received an award at the 1961 fair from longtime 4-H leader Dorothy Heasley. Stowers later volunteered many hours with the fair as a member of the board of directors, fair committee member, 4-H dairy entries facilitator, and vice president of awards, to name a few. (Courtesy of Carol Stowers McComb.)

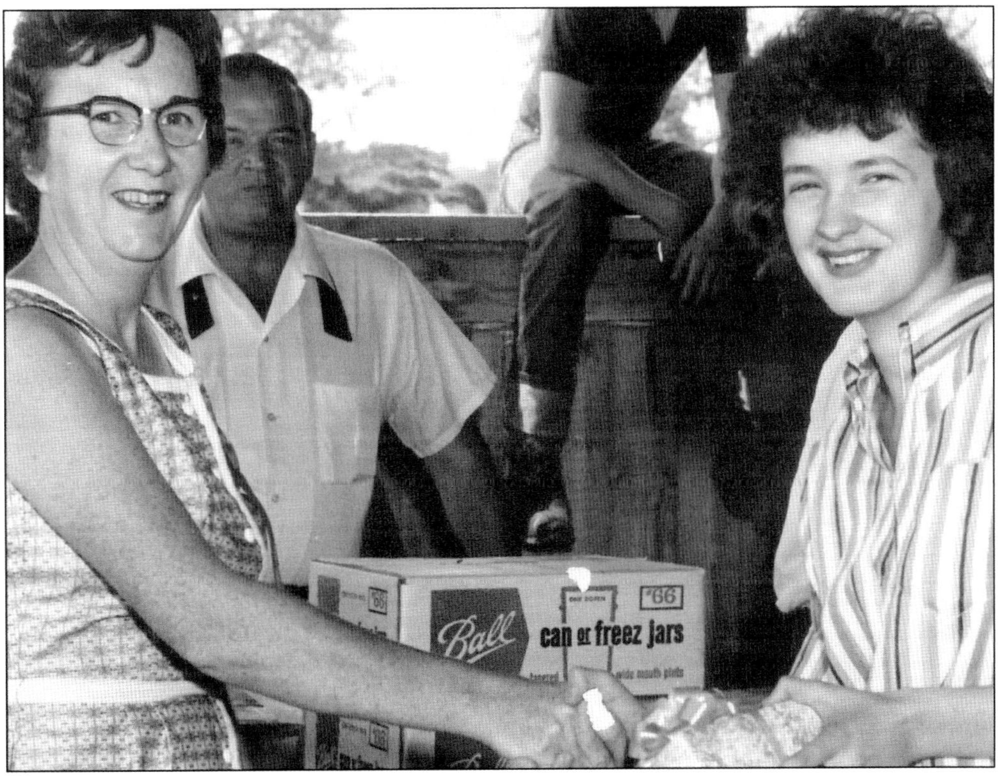

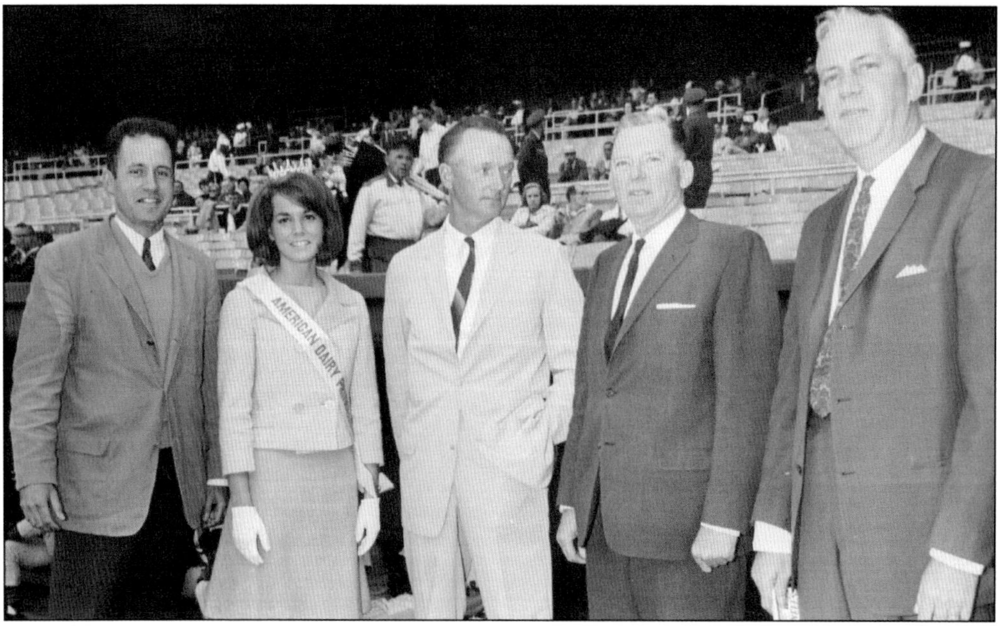

Pictured here during a dairy conference, gentlemen from the Loudoun area pose with the American Dairy princess. From left to right are William Harrison (county agent), unidentified princess, unidentified individual, Ed Norman, and Jim Click. Norman was president of the Maryland and Virginia Milk Producers Association, and Click was the executive director of the same cooperative. (Courtesy of the William H. Cockerill family.)

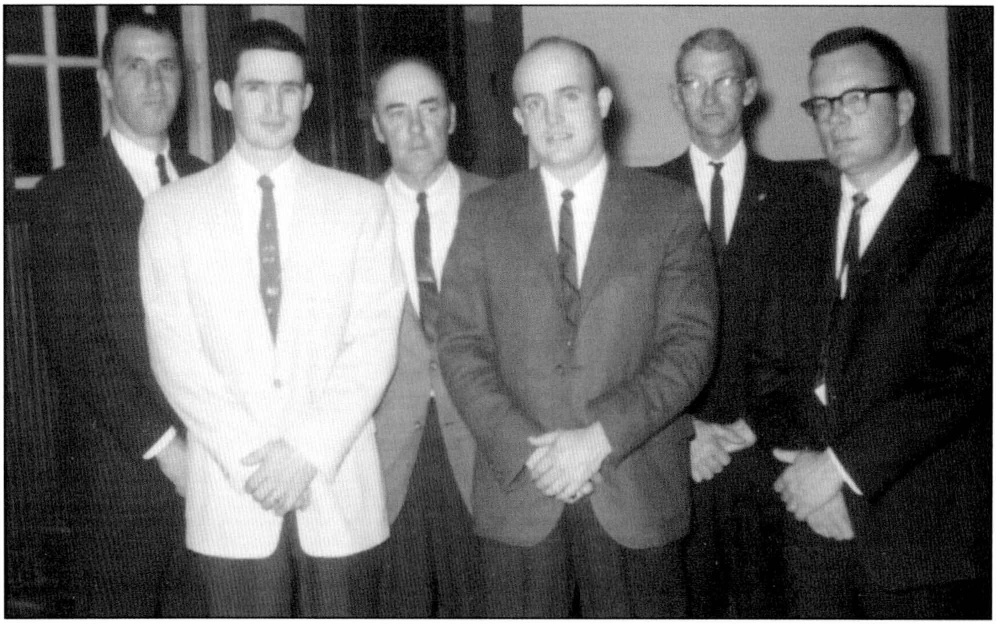

Pictured here are the officers of the Loudoun-Fairfax Holstein Club; from left to right are (first row) John Garber from Purcellville (president), Bob McComb of Purcellville (vice president), and Jerry Michael from Arcola (secretary and treasurer); (second row) Robert K. Reid of Purcellville, H. Ralph Fields of Purcellville, and John D. Peck of Herndon. (Courtesy of the William H. Cockerill family.)

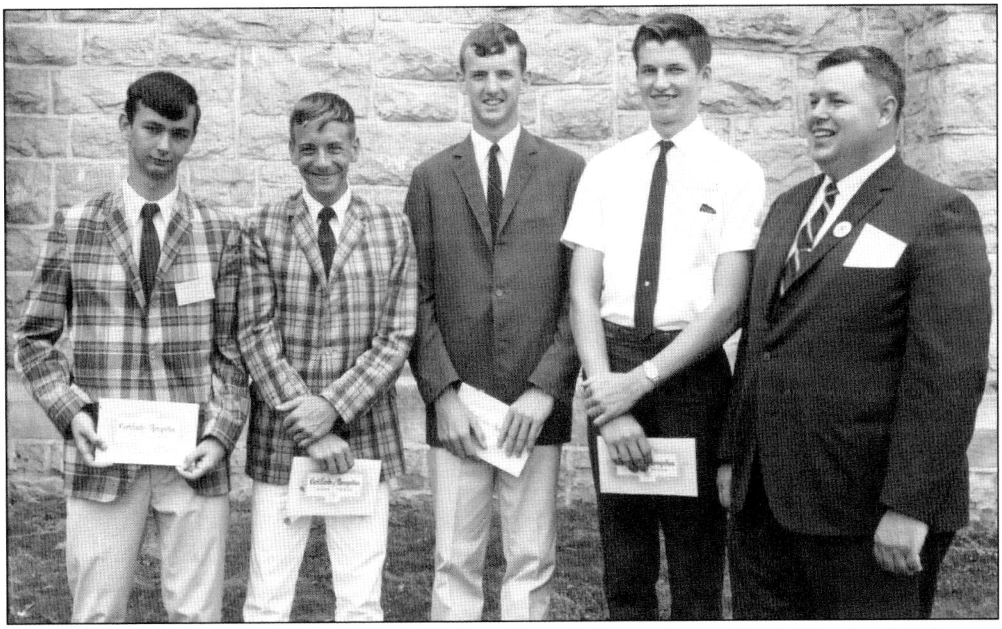

This state dairy judging team won second place. From left to right are Keith Harris of Culpeper, Jimmy Weaver of Culpeper, Charles Hankins of Lunenburg, Edwin Potts of Loudoun, and George Miller. This photograph was taken while at VPI. The building is clearly identified by the Hokie Stone, which is found in the vicinity of the university. (Courtesy of the William H. Cockerill family.)

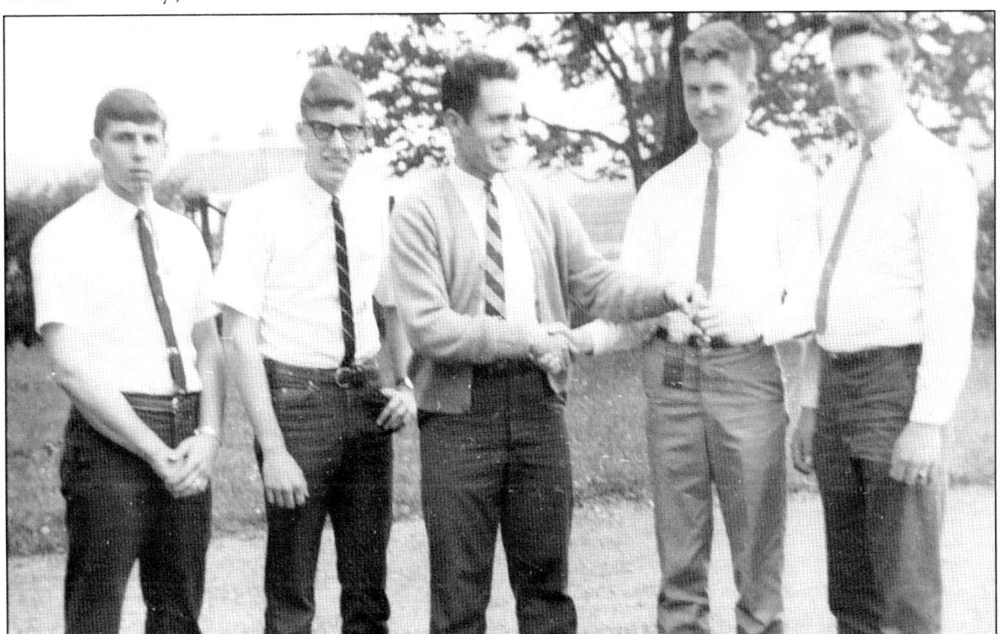

The 1965 Loudoun dairy judging team is pictured here. Members are, from left to right, Bentz Rhoads, Frank Cole, William Harrison (county agent), Edwin Potts, and Robert Ashby. The dairy judging team earned some of the highest honors at the state and national level. (Courtesy of the William H. Cockerill family.)

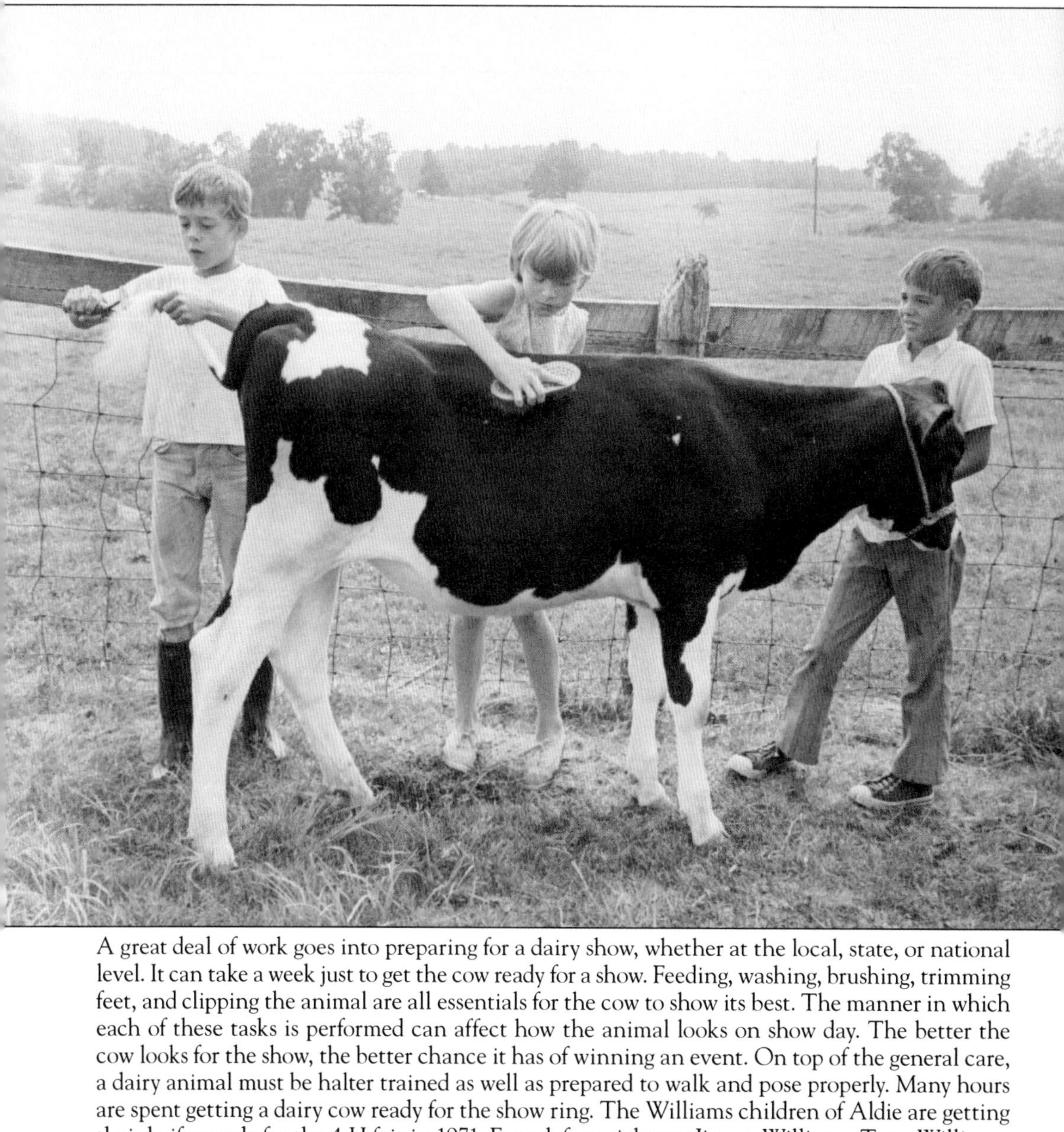

A great deal of work goes into preparing for a dairy show, whether at the local, state, or national level. It can take a week just to get the cow ready for a show. Feeding, washing, brushing, trimming feet, and clipping the animal are all essentials for the cow to show its best. The manner in which each of these tasks is performed can affect how the animal looks on show day. The better the cow looks for the show, the better chance it has of winning an event. On top of the general care, a dairy animal must be halter trained as well as prepared to walk and pose properly. Many hours are spent getting a dairy cow ready for the show ring. The Williams children of Aldie are getting their heifer ready for the 4-H fair in 1971. From left to right are Jimmy Williams, Terry Williams, and Mark Williams. (Courtesy of Carol Stowers McComb.)

Four

Animals around the Grounds

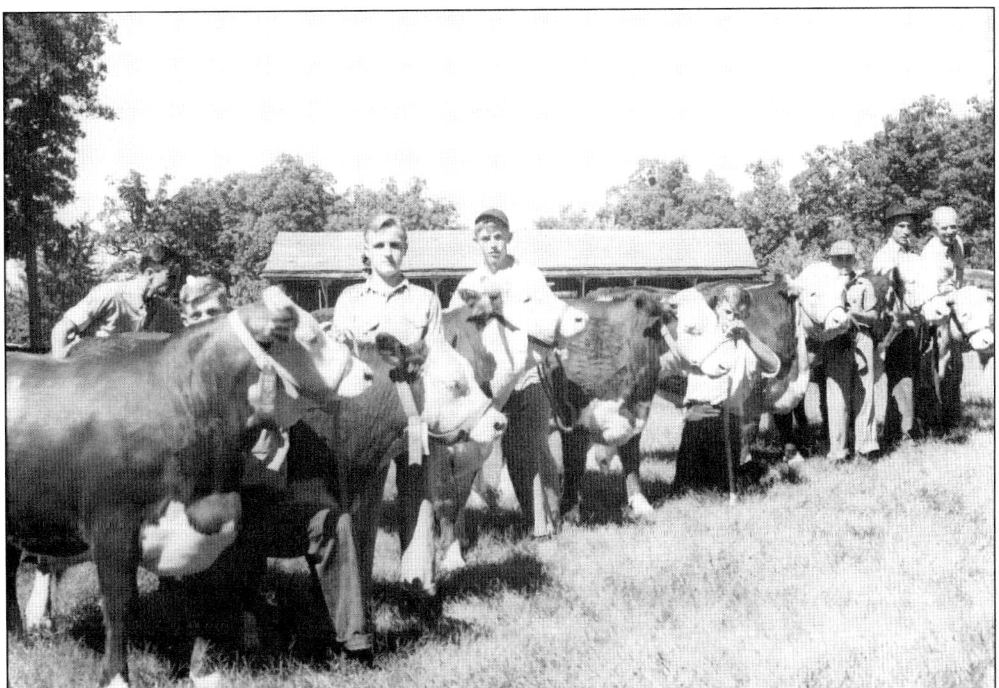

The seven boys in this photograph are showing their steer at the 1936 fair. The Purcellville Fair was held on the Bush Meeting Grounds, which later was called the Purcellville Fireman's Community Center. Fairgoers knew the area as the Purcellville fairgrounds. (Courtesy of the William H. Cockerill family.)

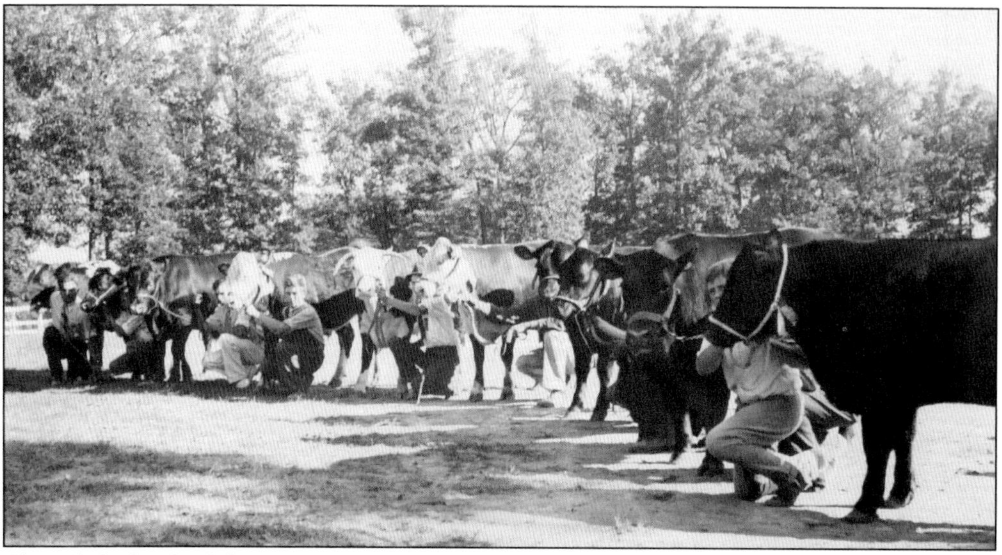

These baby beef exhibitors are at the Purcellville fairgrounds in 1936. It is interesting to note that all of the exhibitors are kneeling beside their Herefords and Angus steer. Kneeling in the show ring is not a practice that has continued today. A large number of 4-H'ers showed steer; the beef club continues to be one of the largest 4-H clubs in Loudoun today. (Courtesy of Carol Stowers McComb.)

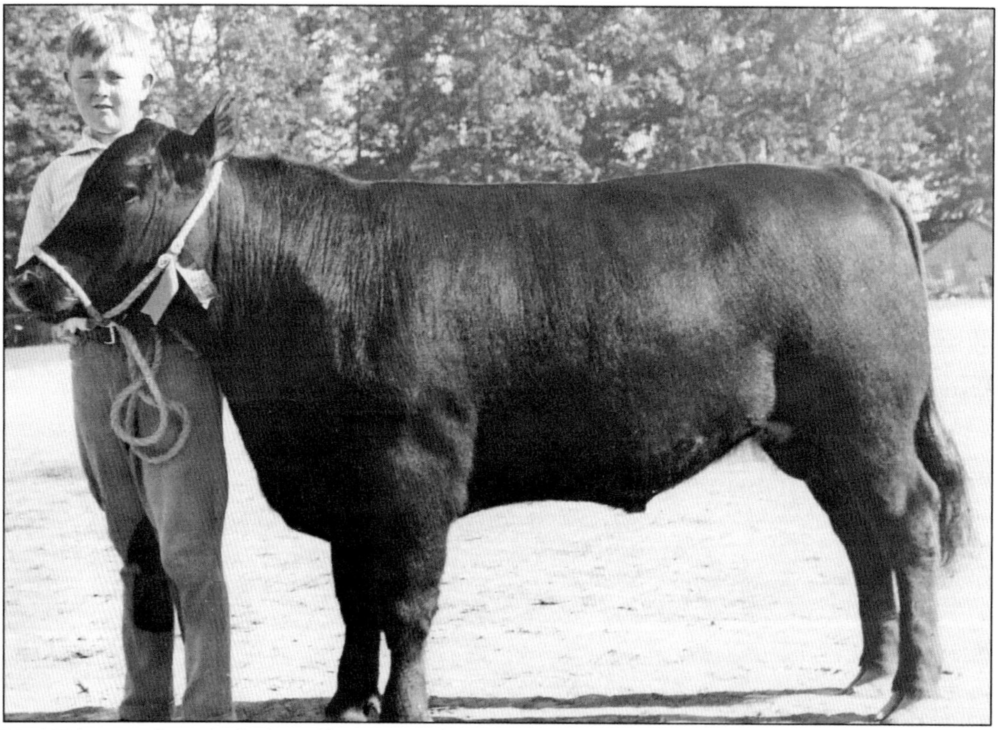

Ned Tyler stands at the halter of his steer. The rope halter was all Tyler needed to guide his animal in the showing area. Tyler was known to have good cattle stock in the Purcellville area, and he and his brother Jim both showed their cattle in the Loudoun County 4-H Fair. (Courtesy of the William H. Cockerill family.)

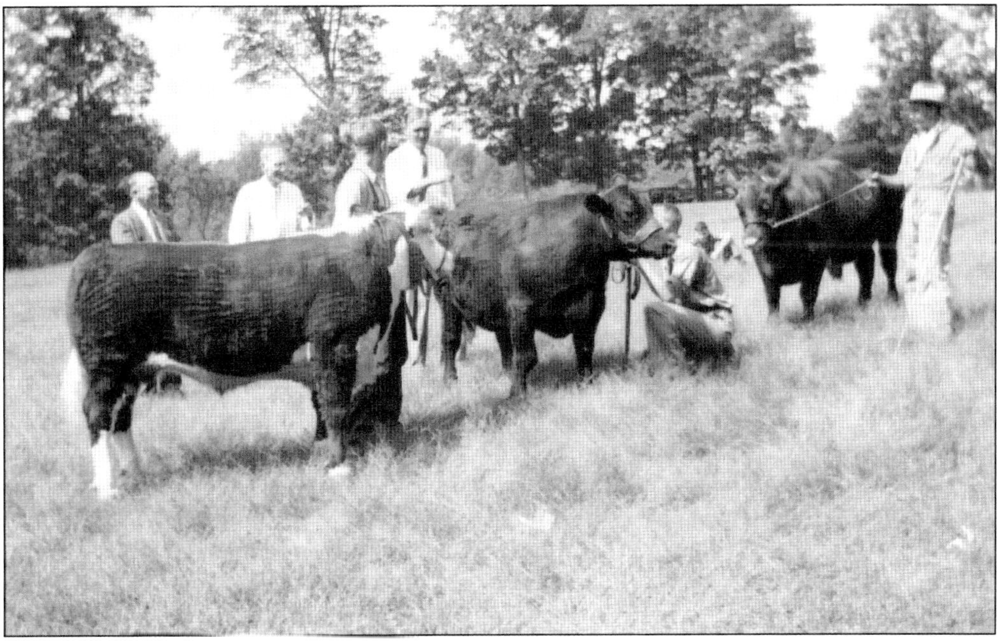

In 1942, judges and spectators observe these cattle at a fair steer show in Purcellville. The Herefords and Angus in these photographs are well groomed for the show; note the comb markings on the side of the animals. Again, in this image, the 4-H'ers are kneeling beside their steer while the judges closely examine the animals. In 4-H, the judges are known to have conversations with the participants after the class to share with them the reasons for their placing both positive and constructive. This is especially the case for showmanship classes where the judging is based on the 4-H'er. (Both, courtesy of the William H. Cockerill family.)

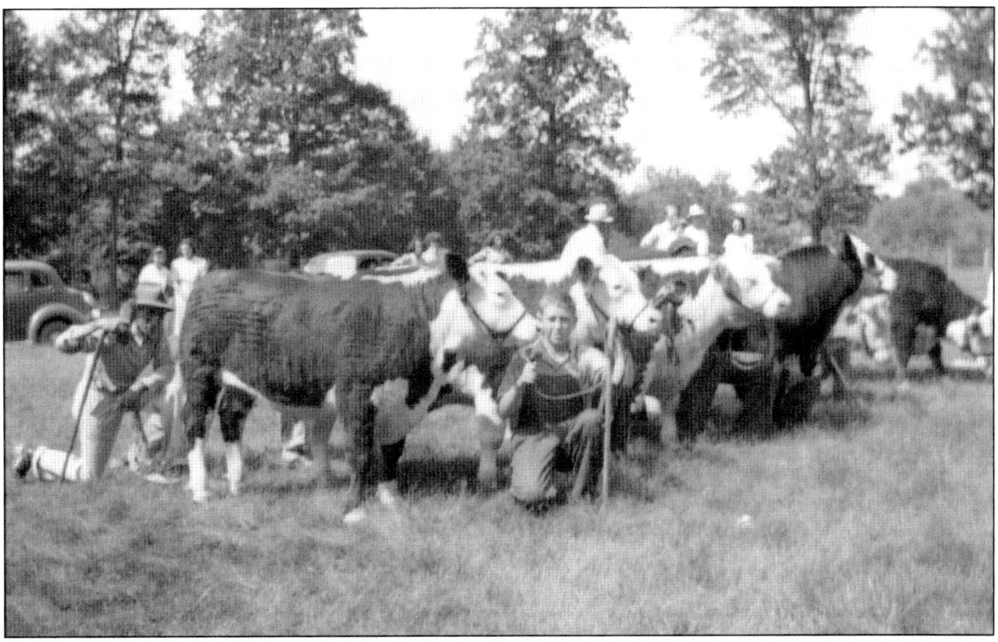

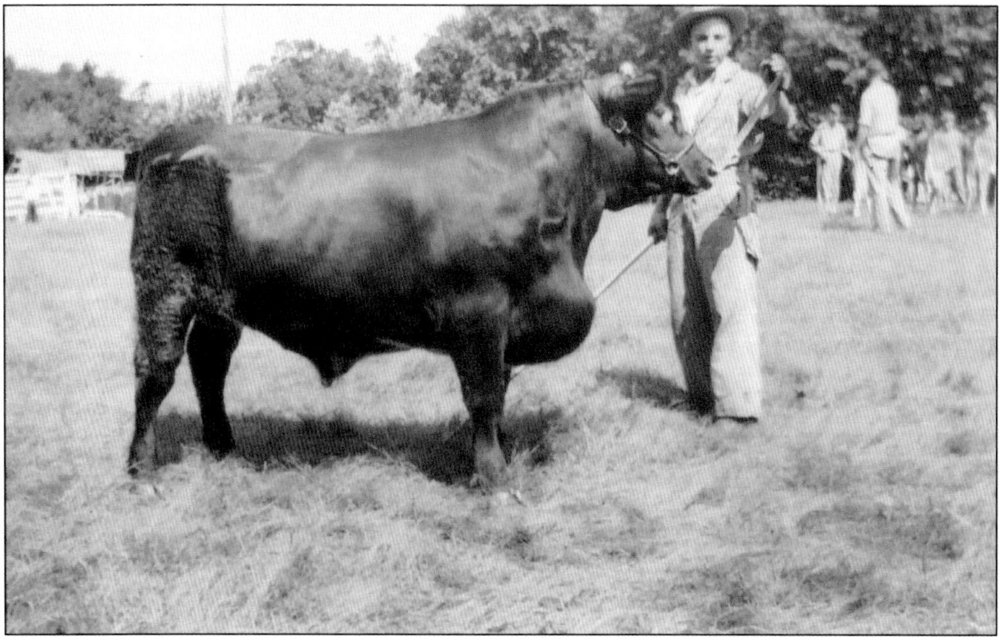

Frank Eppes is showing his Angus steer at the 1942 4-H fair. Note the show stick in Eppes's right hand. The stick is used to guide the steer to stand properly while being judged. Most judges want to see the animal stand with the forefeet and one hind foot directly under him and the other hind foot more forward. (Courtesy of the William H. Cockerill family.)

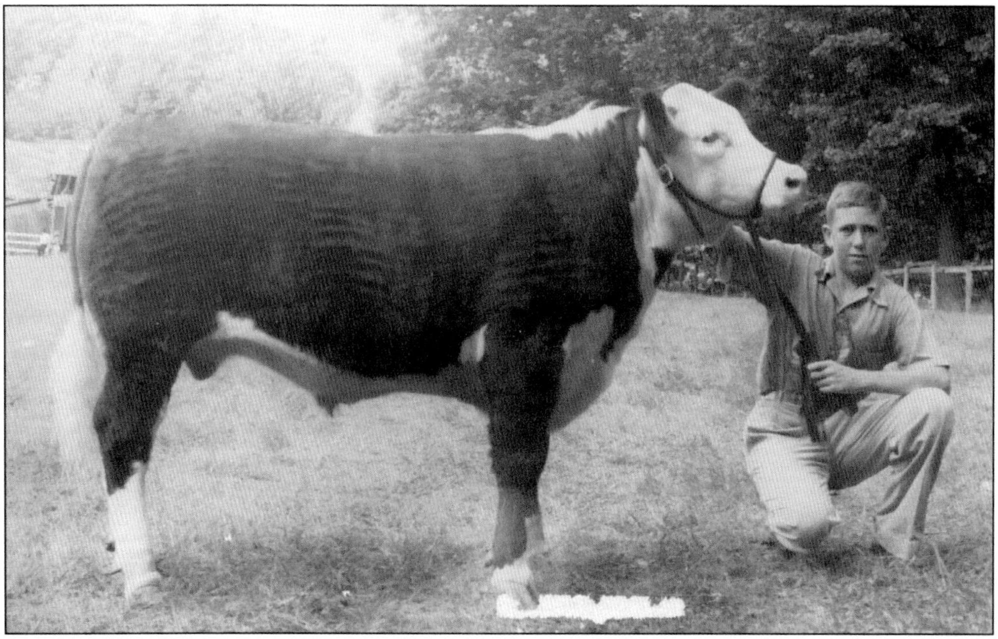

Jim Tyler showed his Hereford at the Loudoun County 4-H Fair in 1945. He won grand champion steer and went on to Richmond, Virginia, and Baltimore, Maryland, to do the same. In Baltimore, he was the grand champion in both 4-H open classes and overall champion of all breeds. (Courtesy of the William H. Cockerill family.)

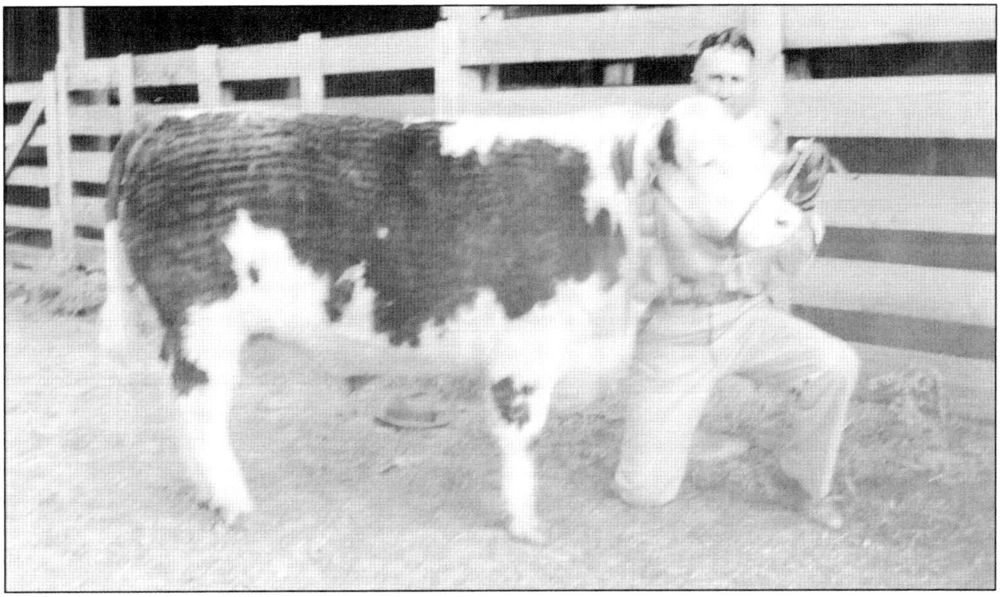

In this photograph, William Cockerill kneels with his Hereford steer. Note the waves in the steer's fur. Some in the steer-showing arena prefer to have a fluffy animal, and the fur on a steer is brushed and trained to stand up straight, then combed into the distinctive patterns. (Courtesy of the William H. Cockerill family.)

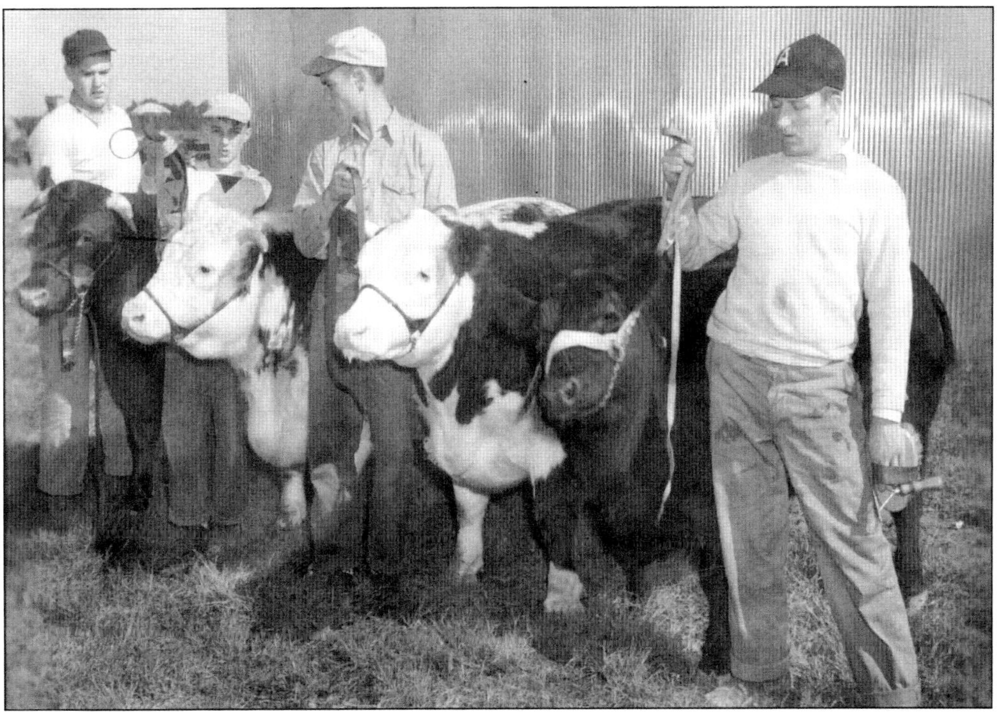

In addition to preparing for and showing at the county fair, many 4-H'ers competed in state- and national-level shows. Many of the Loudoun 4-H'ers showed in a livestock show in Baltimore. In this photograph, from left to right, Tommy Fleming, Edwin Arnold, Jack Arnold, and Edgar Tillett prepare their cattle for show. (Courtesy of the William H. Cockerill family.)

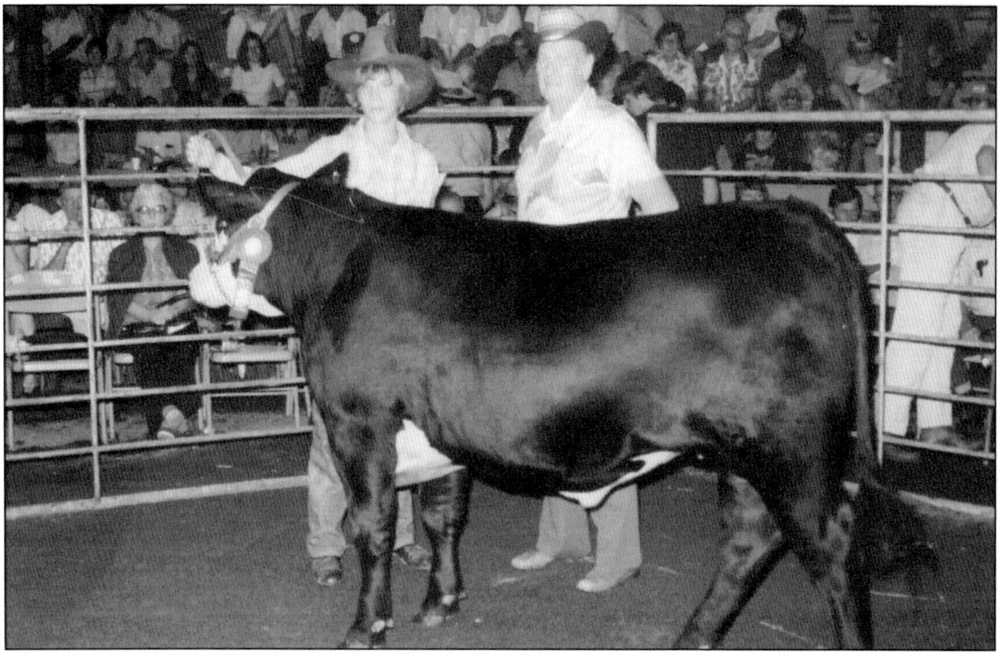

This boy is presenting his prize-winning Simmental steer at the livestock sale. Often, buyers will take a photograph with the youth and his or her animal, especially those that buy champions. Both the youth and the buyer have the photographs to display. Many business owners that buy at auction put their images on display. (Courtesy of Sykes Hall Archives.)

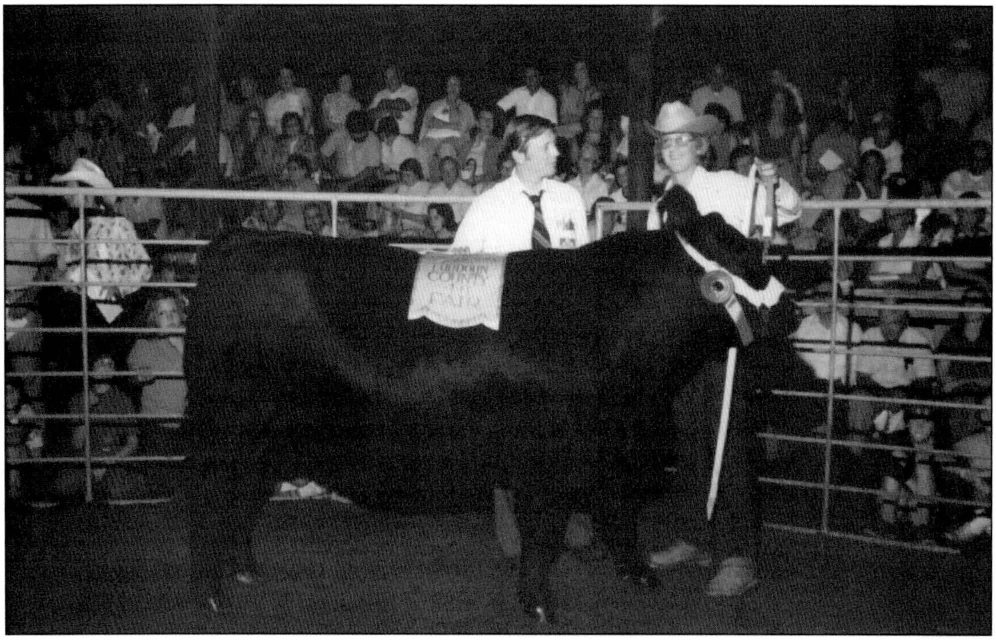

James Johnson presents his prize-winning steer at the fair livestock sale; the steer in the sale usually bring a good profit for the 4-H'er. Many of the youth use the money they earn from their sale animal to purchase an animal for the next fair and help pay for their college educations. (Courtesy of Sykes Hall Archives.)

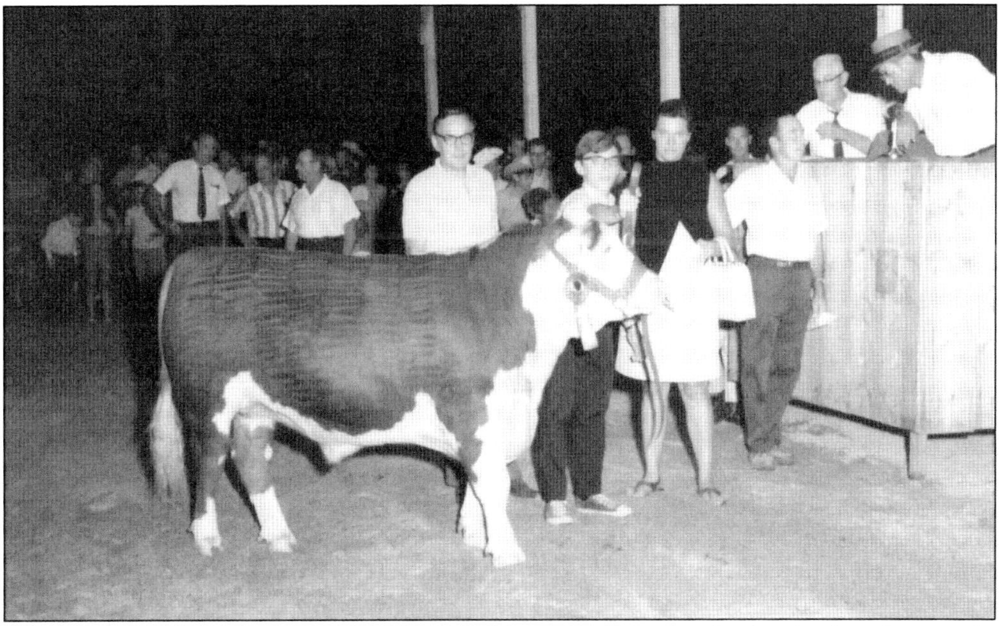

The livestock auction is a highlight of many of the 4-H'ers' time at the fair. In this photograph, Robbie Thompson of Hillsboro is selling his Hereford steer. In the auctioneers' stand on the left is Billy Donaldson and to the right is Leonard Bowman (auctioneer). (Courtesy of Sykes Hall Archives.)

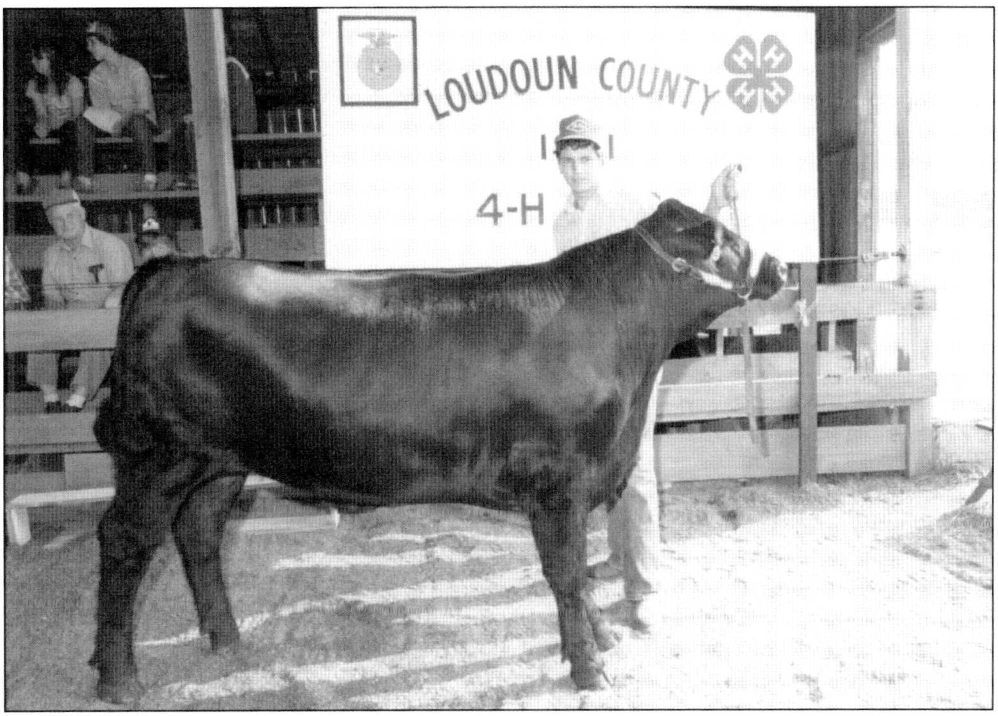

Tommy Payne shows off his prized steer in the show pavilion on the fairgrounds in Leesburg. An area of the show pavilion has been and continues to be set up for photographs of the 4-H'er and his or her animal. Each sign has the year of the fair. (Courtesy of Tommy Payne.)

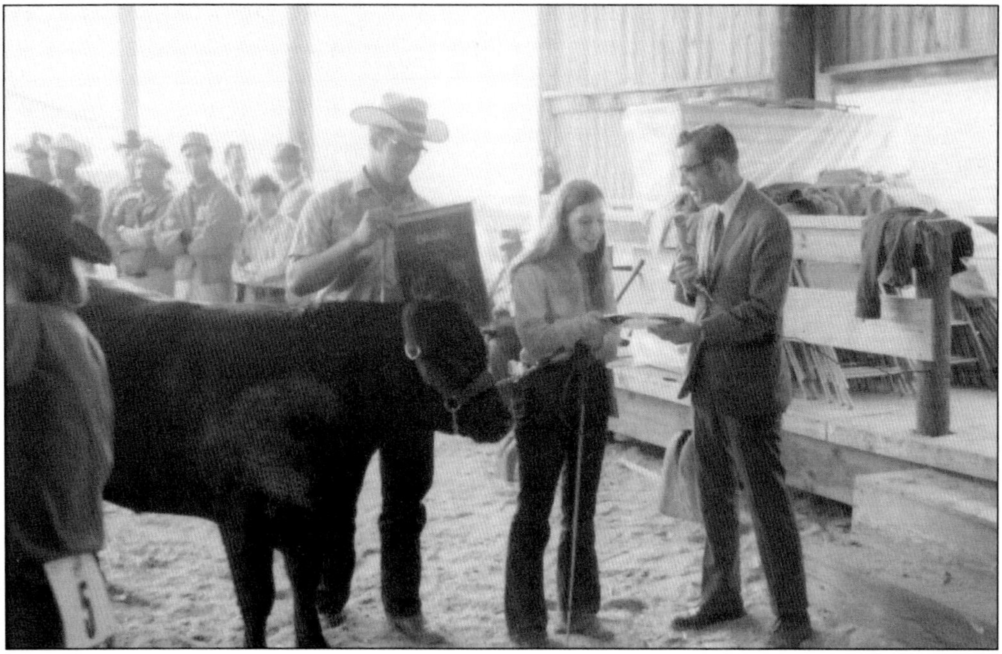

Holding the microphone is Bill Spencer of WAGE radio in Loudoun County. He is presenting Teresa Hoff with an award for her steer, and Steve Gulick is presenting the winning banner. Many award-winning cattle have been shown in the show pavilion on the fairgrounds since it was built in 1958. (Courtesy of William Harrison.)

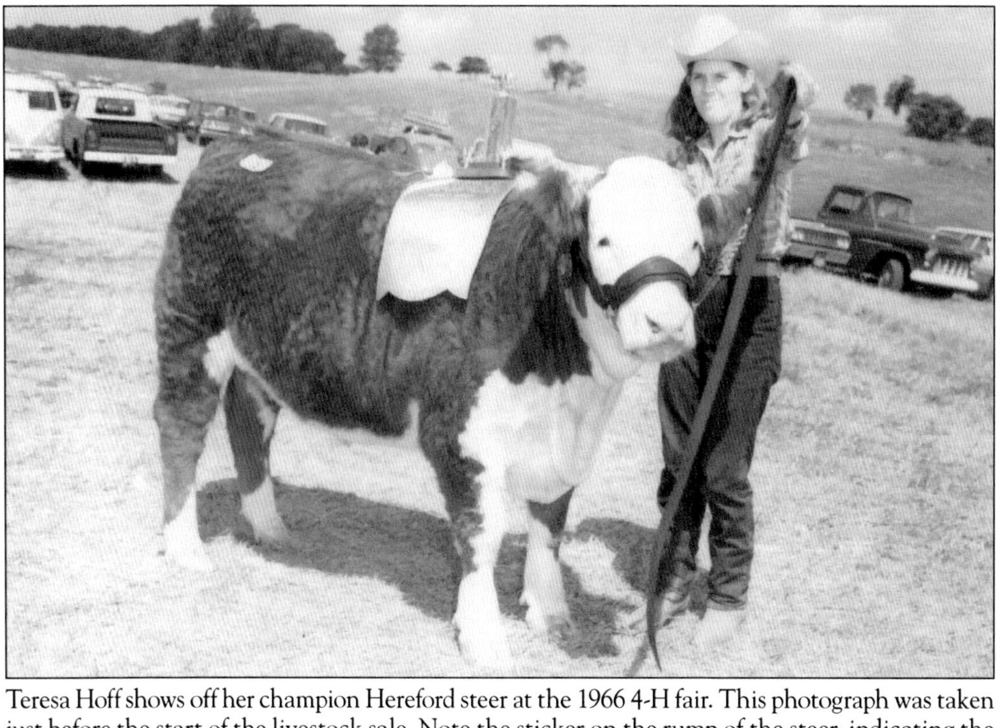

Teresa Hoff shows off her champion Hereford steer at the 1966 4-H fair. This photograph was taken just before the start of the livestock sale. Note the sticker on the rump of the steer, indicating the order of the auction. Hoff was second in the lineup. (Courtesy of Carol Stowers McComb.)

Morning Program

All Exhibits must be in place by 9 A. M.

4-H BOYS' CLASSES

Baby Beef Classes
Dairy Heifer Classes
Fat Swine Classes
Purebred Swine Classes
Poultry Classes
Potato Classes
Garden Classes
Hobby Classes
Handicraft
Project Notebook Classes

4-H GIRLS' CLASSES

Canning Classes
Food Classes
Bread Classes
Flower Classes
Housekeeping Classes
Care of Clothing Classes
Record Book Classes
Garden Classes
Clothing Classes
Hobby Classes
Handicraft
Room Improvement Classes

OPEN CLASSES

Best six stalks of Hybrid Corn, cut at ground level.
Best six stalks of Open Pollinated Corn, cut at ground level.
Tallest Corn Stalk, cut at ground level.
Best peck of Wheat.
Best peck of Barley.
Best peck of Orchard Grass.
Largest field Pumpkin by circumference.
Best dozen Tomatoes.
Best peck White Potatoes.
Best 10 ears Yellow Hybrid Corn.
Best Collection of Garden Vegetables (At least 2 leafy, 2 root, 2 fruit.)
Best sample of Alfalfa Hay (Minimum 6 inches in diameter)
Best dozen White Eggs.
Best dozen Brown Eggs.

Open classes are for children and adults—anyone in the community can enter an open class to show at the fair. The categories generally are the same each year, with some variation. The open classes in the 1947 fair were mostly field crops, with the addition of vegetables and eggs. Open classes in more recent years include scrapbooks, photography, art projects, and project books. Note that the classes for girls and boys are different, each with their own specialty. Girls' classes were more domestic in nature, while the boys were more agrarian. Hobby, handicrafts, and garden classes were for both boys and girls but separated into classes by gender. (Courtesy of Virginia Cooperative Extension, Loudoun County Office.)

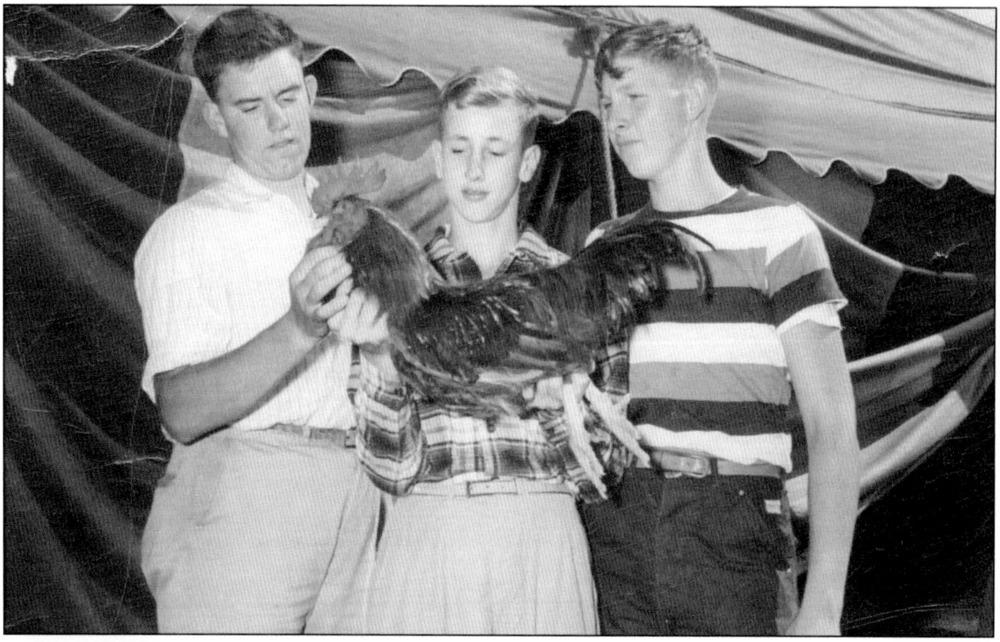

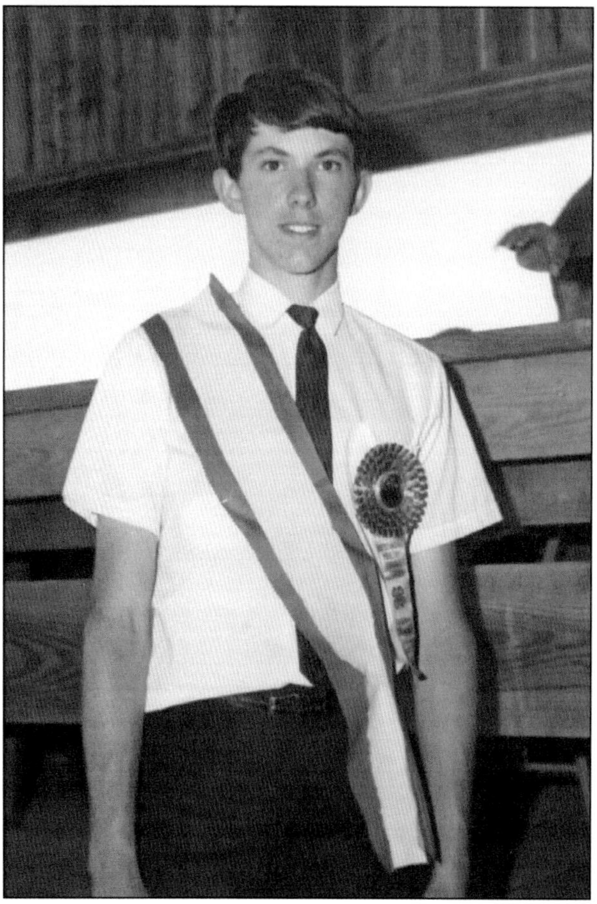

Showing in the 1949 poultry division are, from left to right, Robert Ellis, Charles Poland, and Phil Marshall. The boys were part of the Loudoun 4-H judging team and won the state judging contest at VPI. The rooster in this photograph was the blue-ribbon winner at the Loudoun County 4-H Fair and best in show at the Atlantic Rural Exposition Fair in Richmond. (Courtesy of the William H. Cockerill family.)

While much of what was exhibited at the Loudoun County 4-H Fair were steers and dairy cattle, there were a good number of other animals as well. Steve Brown, son of W. Jack Brown, extension unit chairman, and Helen Brown, showed in the poultry division. Here, Steve is showing off his ribbons won for his champion poultry entry. (Courtesy of Carol Stowers McComb.)

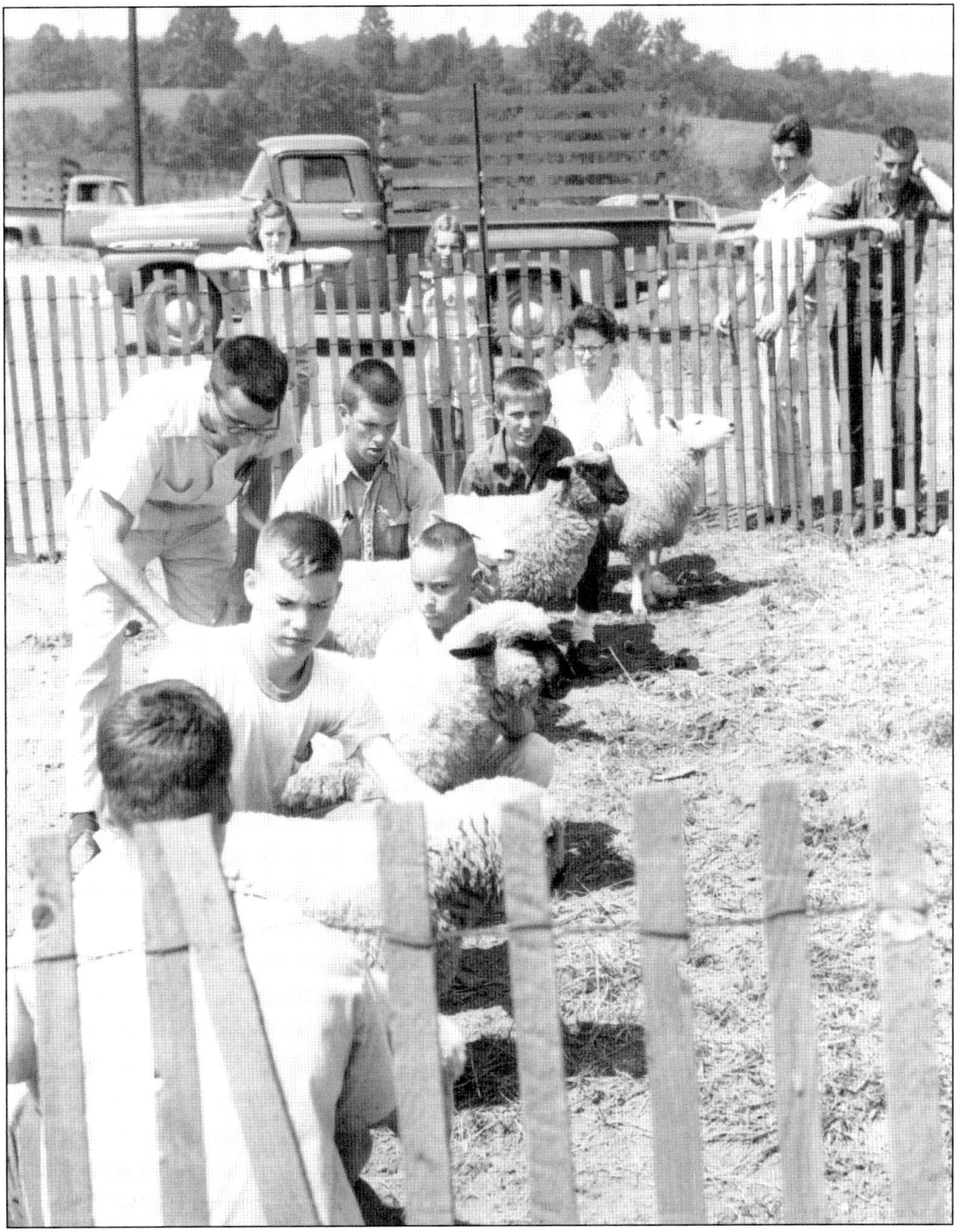

Sheep classes in the 1960s ranged from individual and pens of fat wethers or ewes, any breed, breeding ewes, and a selection of outstanding sheep exhibit. Prizes for the classes were $5 for first place, $4 for second place, $3 for third place, $2 for fourth place, and fifth place received a ribbon. In this photograph, sheep are being shown in front of the judge (far left). The 4-H youth from front to back are Bill Tory, unidentified, Hank McCall, Bobby Virts, and Jane Virts. The Virts family continues to have youth showing sheep at the fair to this day. (Courtesy of the William H. Cockerill family.)

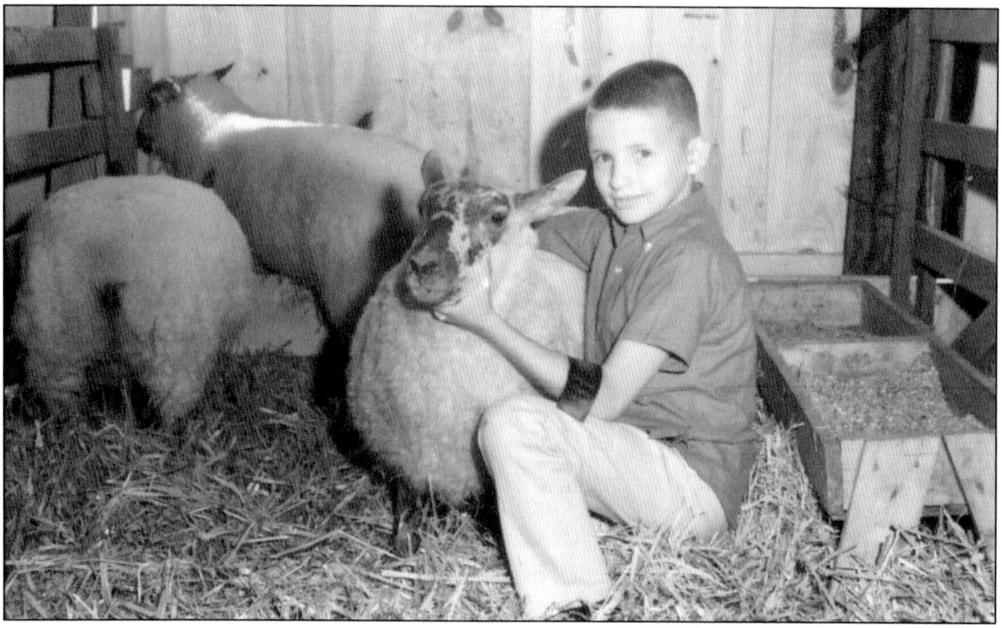

An unidentified boy is posing with his plump sheep at the 1966 fair. For a 4-H'er, learning about showing sheep involves becoming familiar with the management, selection, and health of the animal. The youth will need to know how to identify the major breeds and the parts of the sheep as well as how to halter train the animal for showing. (Courtesy of Carol Stowers McComb.)

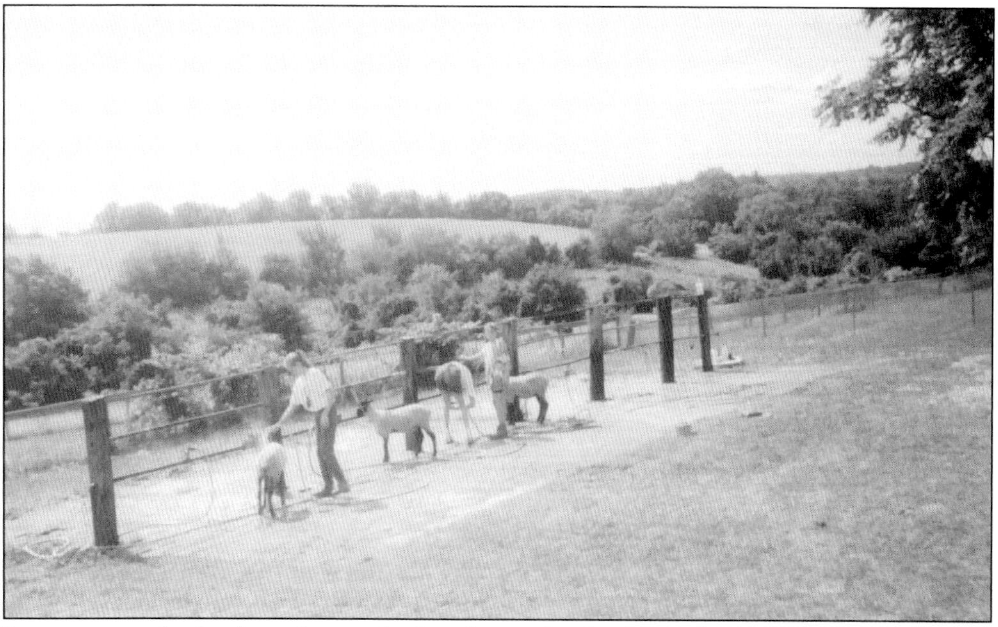

In preparation for the sheep show at the fair, the youth take them to the wash stand for cleaning. Since this photograph was taken, a new wash stand has been built in place of what is shown here and is used regularly throughout the week of the fair. (Courtesy of Sykes Hall Archives.)

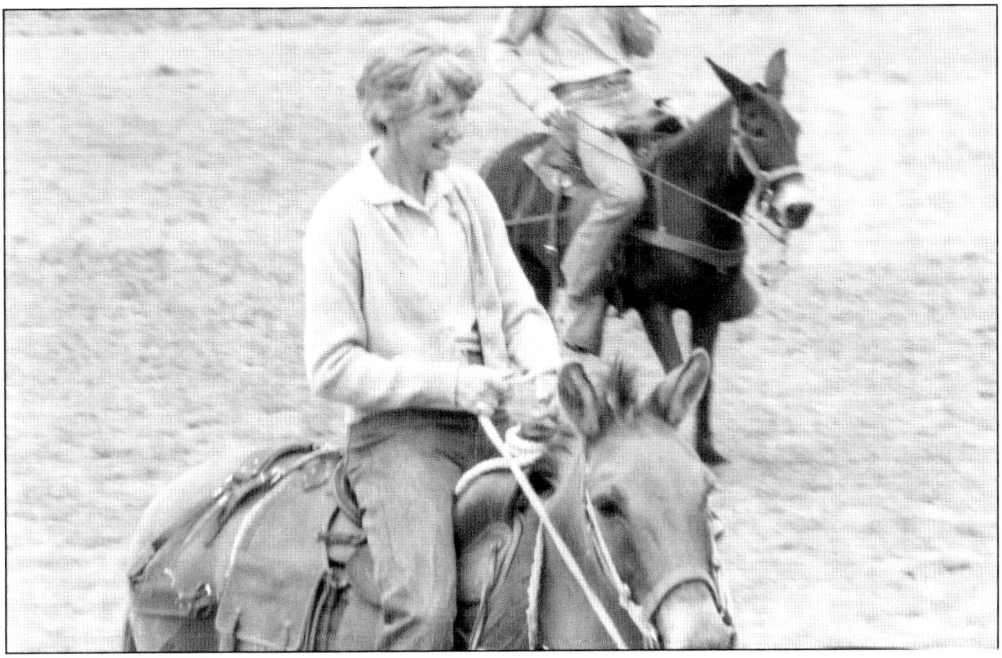

Nancy Dillon rides a mule in the horse show ring with an unidentified rider on a donkey in the background. Nancy is a well-known and well-respected equestrian in Loudoun County and beyond. She has taught lessons to children since the 1960s on Chimney Hill Farm, property she shares with her husband. (Courtesy of Sykes Hall Archives.)

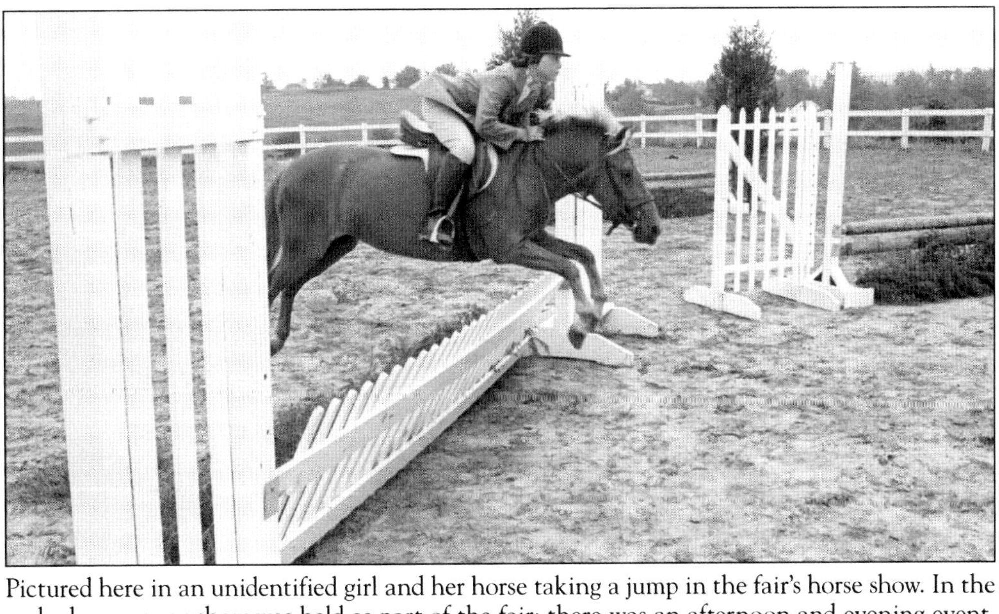

Pictured here in an unidentified girl and her horse taking a jump in the fair's horse show. In the early days, a pony show was held as part of the fair; there was an afternoon and evening event. Peggy Anne Benedum was the superintendent of the pony show in the 1940s. (Courtesy of Sykes Hall Archives.)

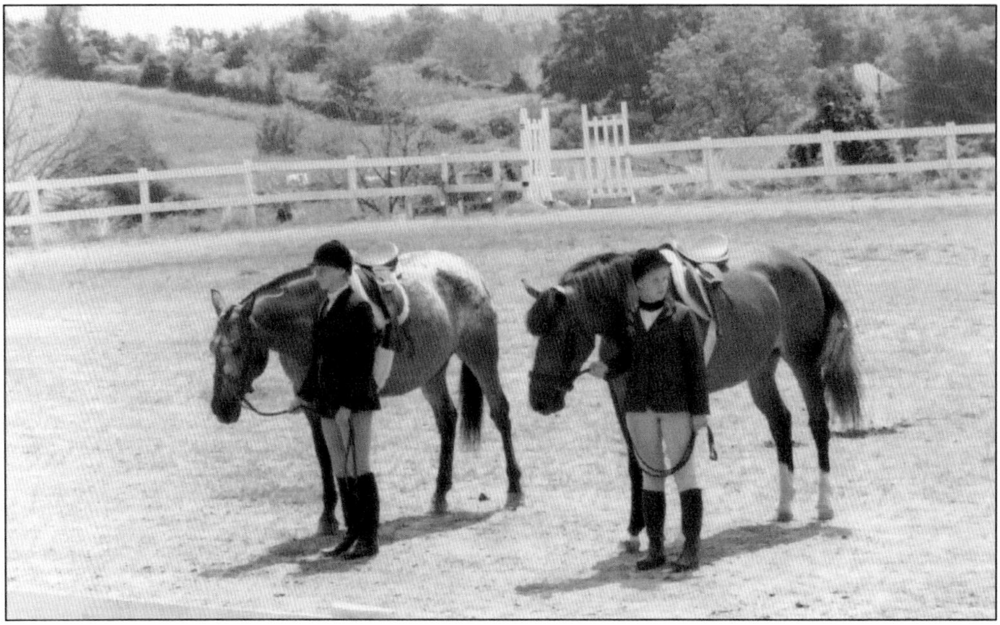

In the above photograph, two girls are dressed in formal show clothes at the horse and pony show at the fair. In the image below, girls are in the ready ring preparing to go into the show ring. Since the fair has been at the Leesburg location, the horse ring has changed size and shape. In the 1960s, it was a small octagonal ring. It was in the 1970s when the ring was excavated and made larger, including a ready-ring area at one end. The ring now holds events such as the demolition derby, the rodeo, opening ceremonies, the Super Farmer contest, and the Kiss-a-Pig contest, among others. (Both, courtesy of Sykes Hall Archives.)

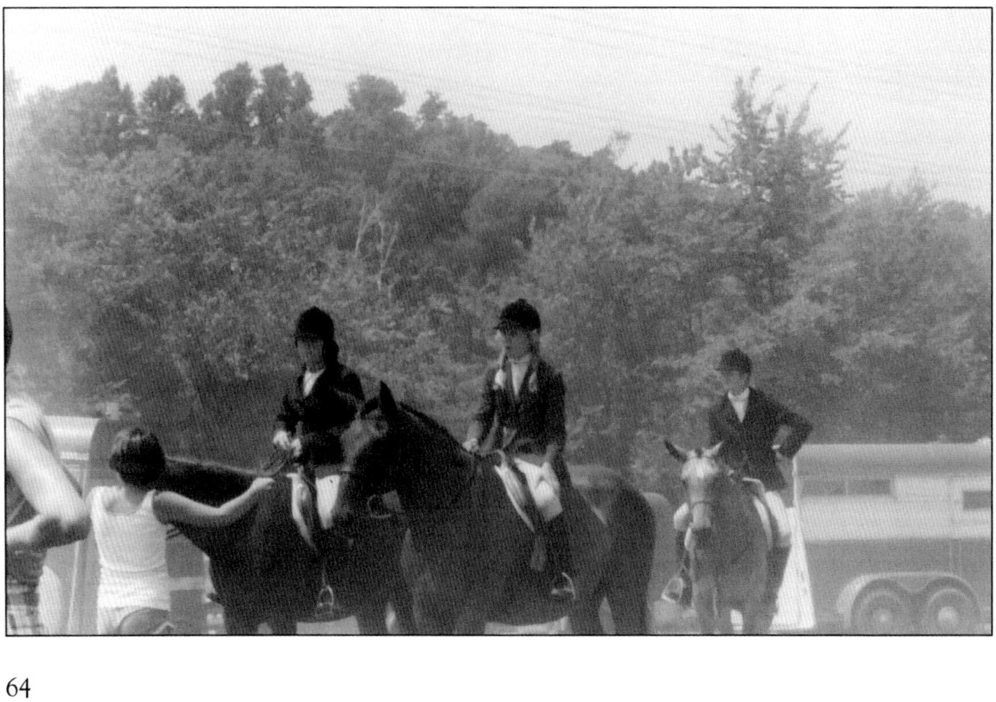

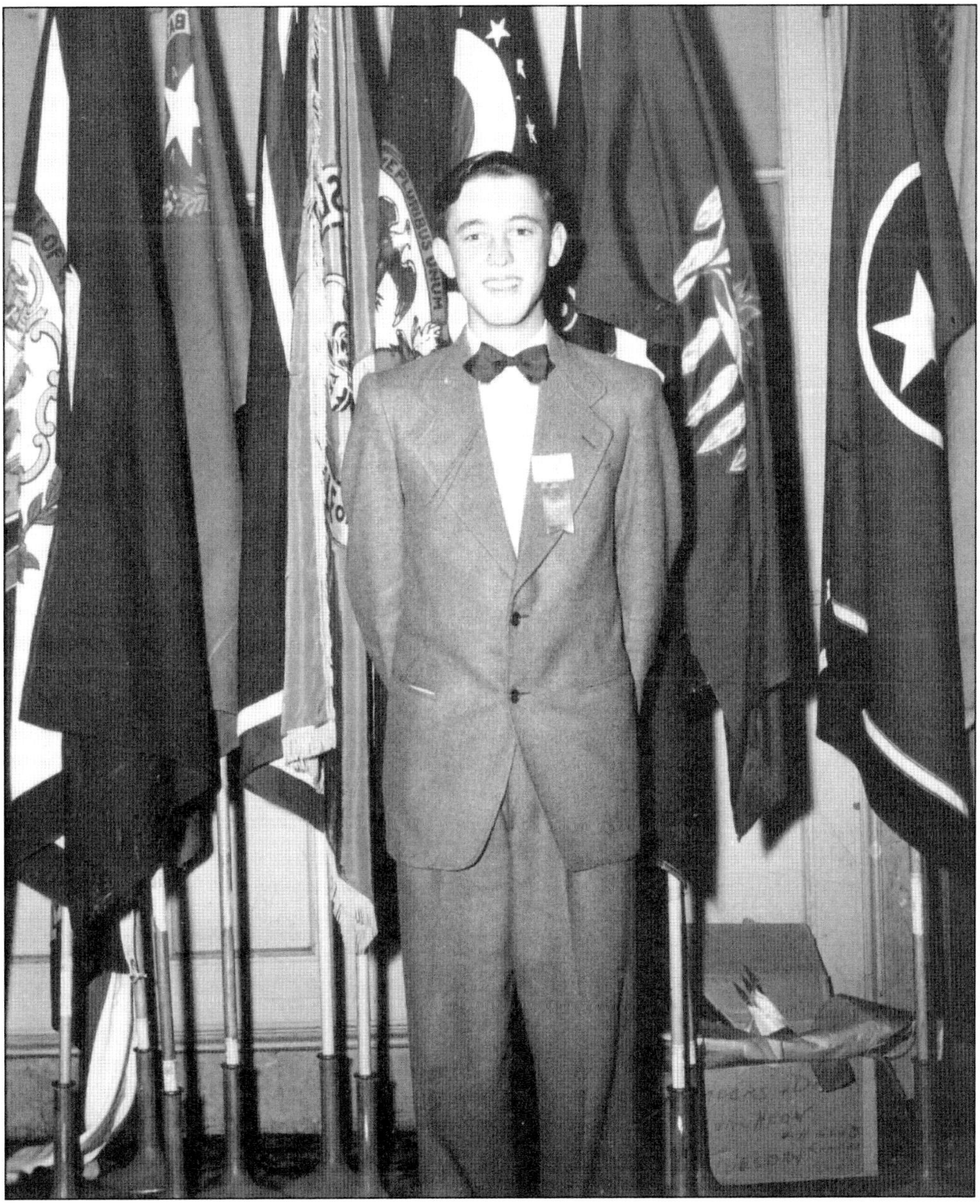

Frank Keesling is shown here in 1947 at the National Livestock judging contest in Chicago. He represented Virginia, along with Edwin and Jack Arnold, Tom Fleming, and extension agent William Cockerill. Keesling was the high points individual in the nation in swine judging, and the team missed being in first place by a mere one point. He began showing at the fair as a young boy as part of the Hillsboro 4-H Club, and in high school he began participating with the Lovettsville Senior Club. As part of the fair, Keesling showed beef, swine, and field crops and helped build parade floats for his club. Keesling served as an IFYE (International 4-H Youth Exchange) in Scotland and was a Virginia 4-H All Star. He was a 4-H member in Loudoun for 11 years. In later years, Keesling served as a 4-H leader, assistant superintendent and superintendent of agricultural exhibits and livestock, assistant superintendent of the fair, and many other roles. In 1984, the fair was dedicated to Frank Keesling and his family. (Courtesy of the William H. Cockerill family.)

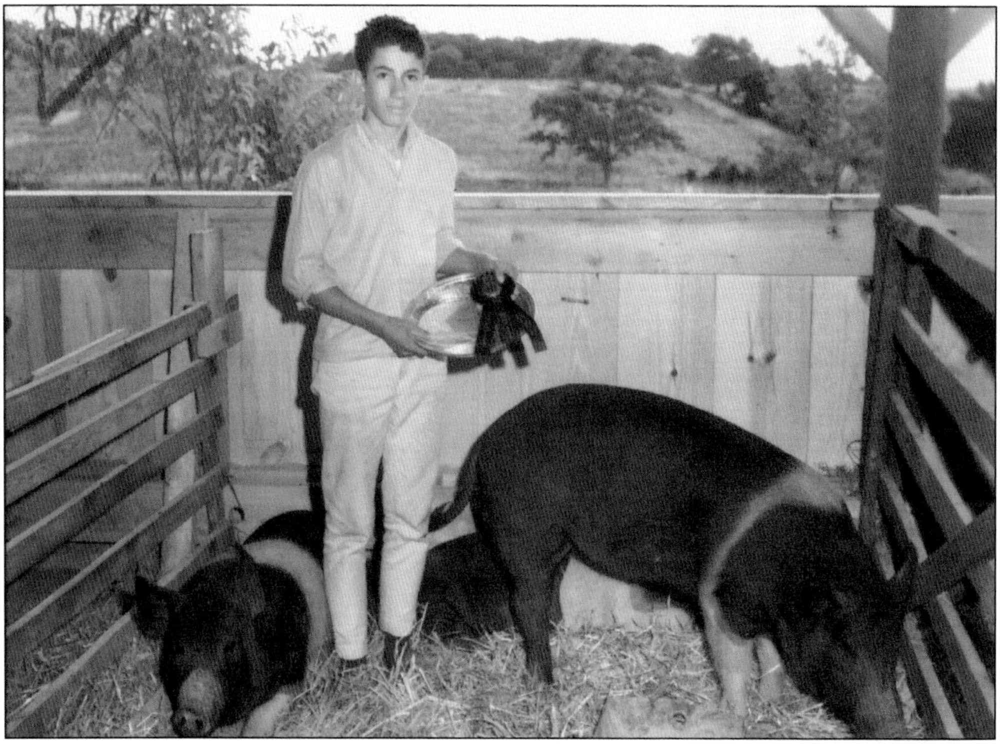

An unidentified boy poses with his Hampshire hogs at the 1966 fair. The plate he is holding is for the Sweepstakes Award; he was given points for various aspects of showing his project animals. The silver plate, a great honor, was sponsored by the Feeder Pig Association. (Courtesy of Carol Stowers McComb.)

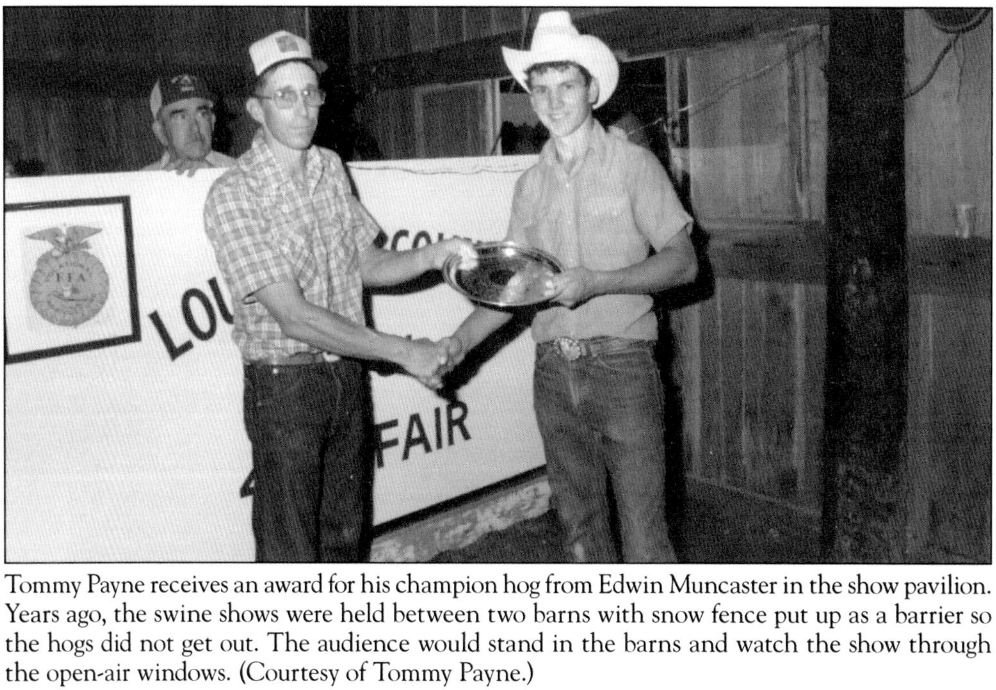

Tommy Payne receives an award for his champion hog from Edwin Muncaster in the show pavilion. Years ago, the swine shows were held between two barns with snow fence put up as a barrier so the hogs did not get out. The audience would stand in the barns and watch the show through the open-air windows. (Courtesy of Tommy Payne.)

Five

Fun at the Fair

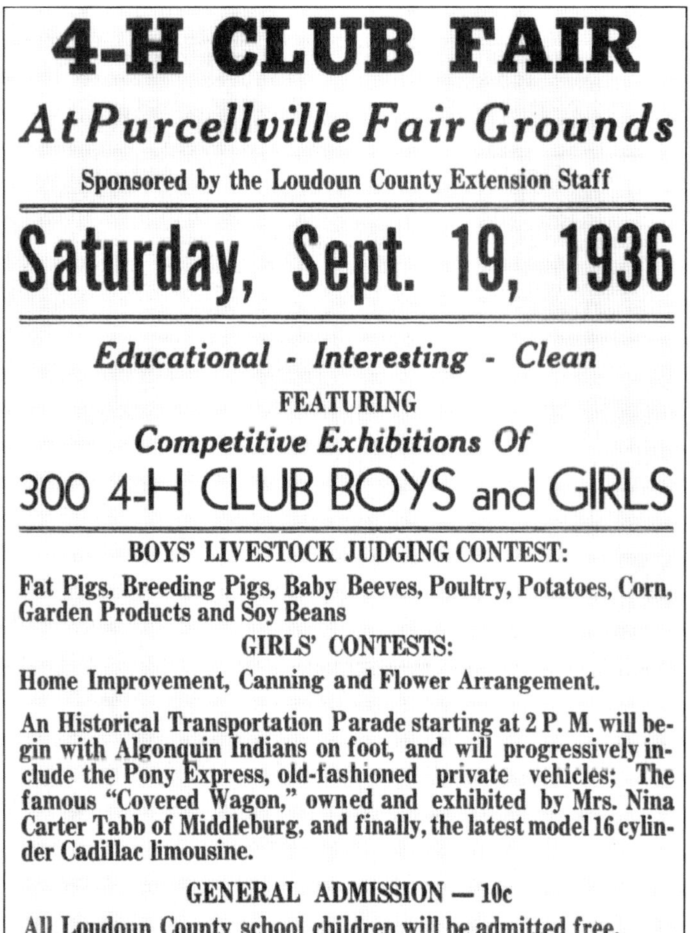

4-H CLUB FAIR

At Purcellville Fair Grounds

Sponsored by the Loudoun County Extension Staff

Saturday, Sept. 19, 1936

Educational - Interesting - Clean

FEATURING

Competitive Exhibitions Of

300 4-H CLUB BOYS and GIRLS

BOYS' LIVESTOCK JUDGING CONTEST:

Fat Pigs, Breeding Pigs, Baby Beeves, Poultry, Potatoes, Corn, Garden Products and Soy Beans

GIRLS' CONTESTS:

Home Improvement, Canning and Flower Arrangement.

An Historical Transportation Parade starting at 2 P. M. will begin with Algonquin Indians on foot, and will progressively include the Pony Express, old-fashioned private vehicles; The famous "Covered Wagon," owned and exhibited by Mrs. Nina Carter Tabb of Middleburg, and finally, the latest model 16 cylinder Cadillac limousine.

GENERAL ADMISSION — 10c

All Loudoun County school children will be admitted free.

This is an advertisement for the very first 4-H fair in Loudoun County, Virginia. Prior to the 4-H fair there had been a Loudoun County Fair that included some 4-H'ers. Events in this fair were divided into boys' classes and girls' classes. J.R. Lintner, home demonstration agent Karle Bundy, and assistant county agent William H. Cockerill worked to make the first 4-H fair a reality. (Courtesy of Carol Stowers McComb.)

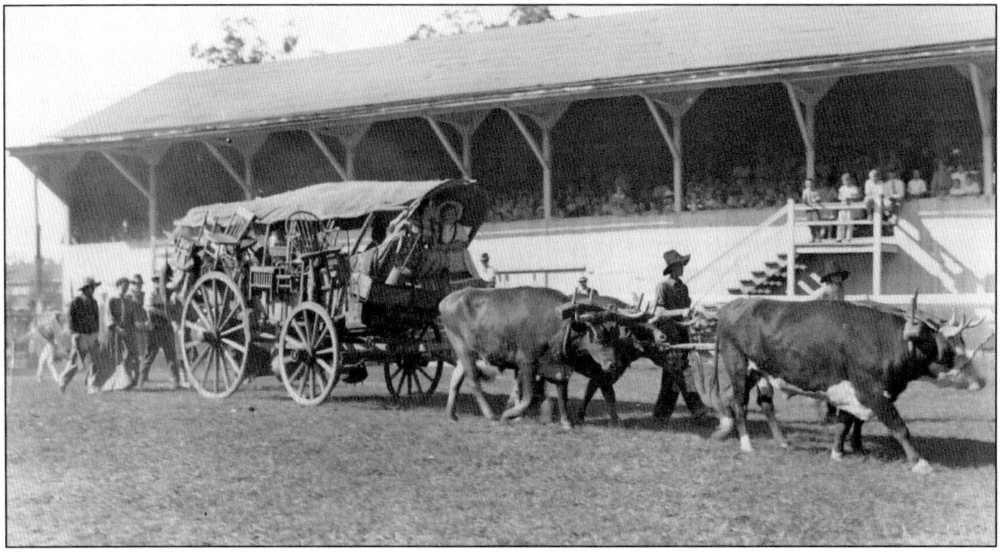

As part of the first fair, a historical transportation parade was held in the afternoon. Beginning with Algonquin Indians on foot, the parade progressed through the years of transportation with the Pony Express on horseback, early motorized vehicles, and a 1936 Cadillac limousine. Pictured here is a covered wagon that was exhibited by Nina Carter Tabb of Middleburg. The objects in the wagon represent household items that would have been packed for the move heading West. Note the oxen that are pulling the wagon instead of horses. In the background are the grandstands, which used to be where the bleachers are now at Fireman's Field in Purcellville. (Above, courtesy of the William H. Cockerill family; below, courtesy of Carol Stowers McComb.)

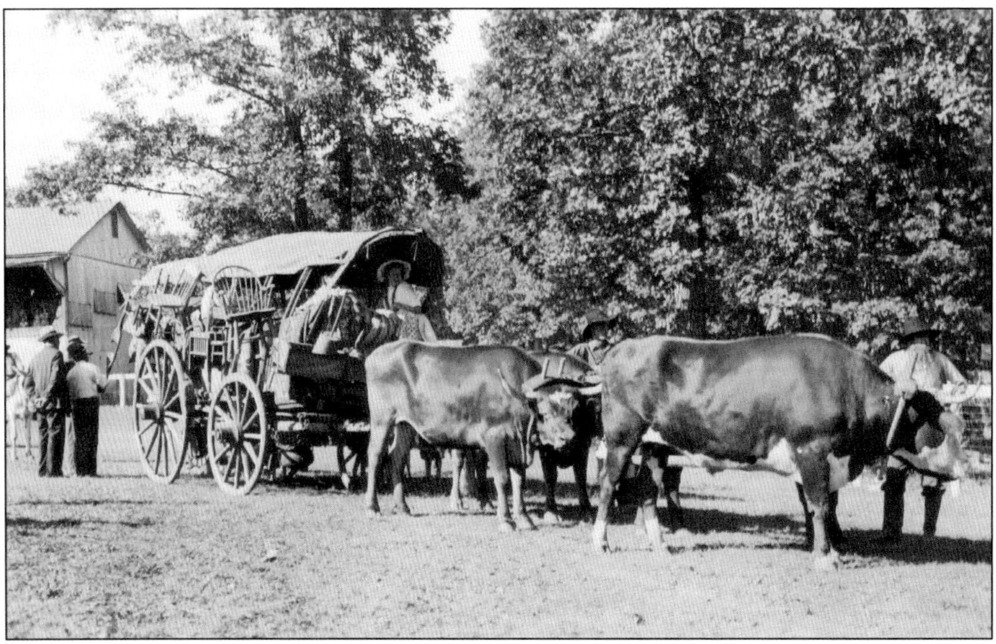

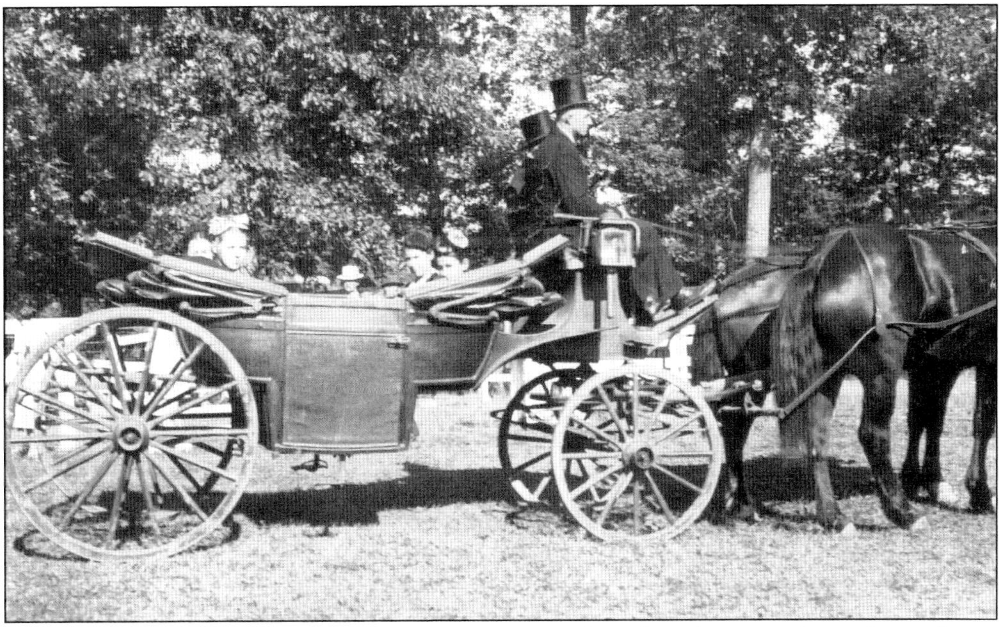

Another photograph from the 1936 transportation parade is this of young girls in a horse-drawn carriage. Note the men in the top hats. These hats were typically worn by those in the upper class. This carriage is a replica of what one mode of transportation would have been like many years ago. (Courtesy of the William H. Cockerill family.)

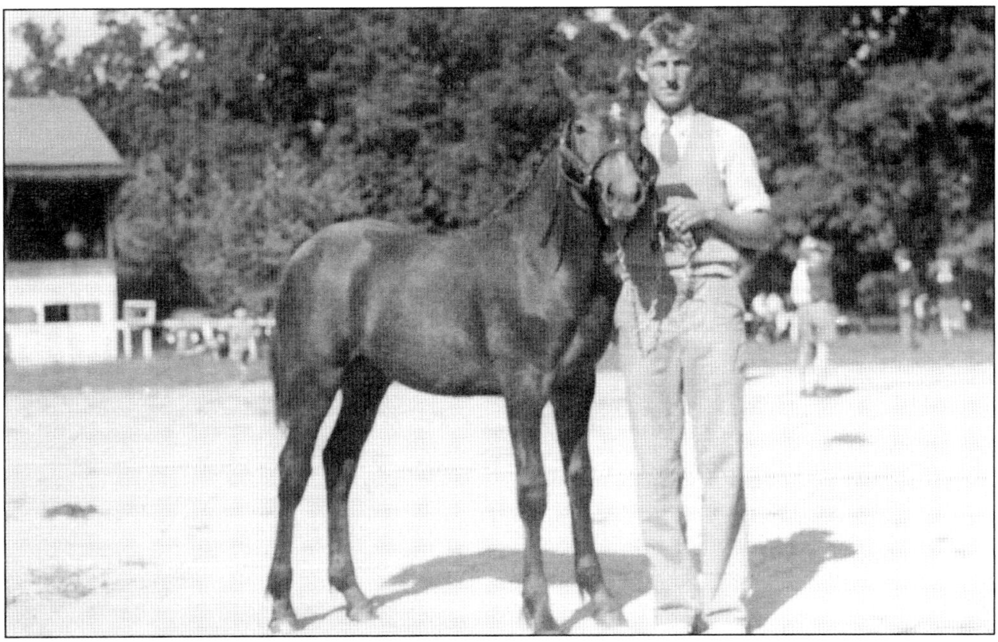

This unidentified man stands at the halter of his foal. This photograph was taken within the first years of the fair being held in Purcellville in the 1930s, and in the background are the grandstands where fairgoers would view the events. The grandstands are no longer on the grounds in Purcellville, having been gone for many years. (Courtesy of the William H. Cockerill family.)

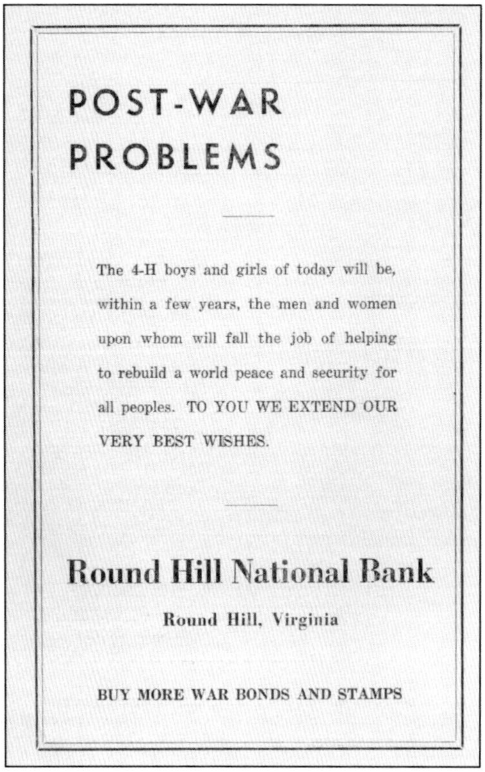

Businesses have always been an important part of the success of the fair. This page shows advertisements placed in the fair catalog from local businesses. The money from the advertisements went toward printing the catalog, which included a schedule of events and classes, as well as funds to run the fair and upkeep of the grounds. Of particular interest is the mention of the war and time of recovery. In the photograph at left, an advertisement for the Round Hill National Bank encourages people to buy war bonds and stamps in 1943. War bonds were sold to help finance the war and control inflation. Many of the businesses in the image below from 1949 are no longer in operation. (Both, courtesy of Virginia Cooperative Extension, Loudoun County Office.)

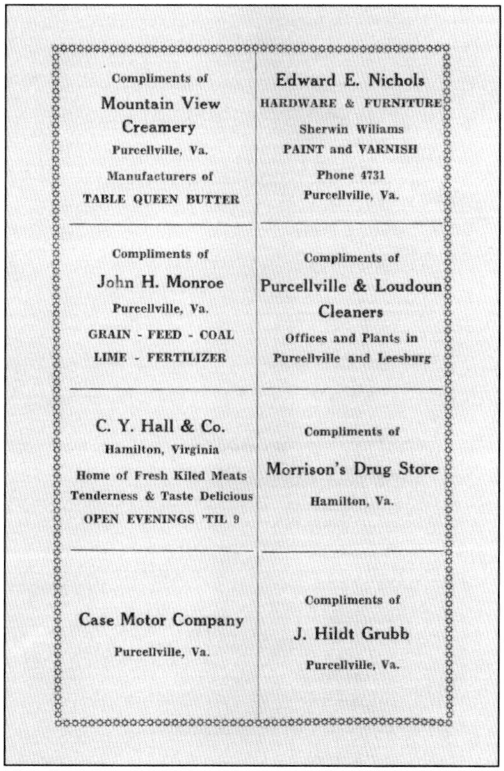

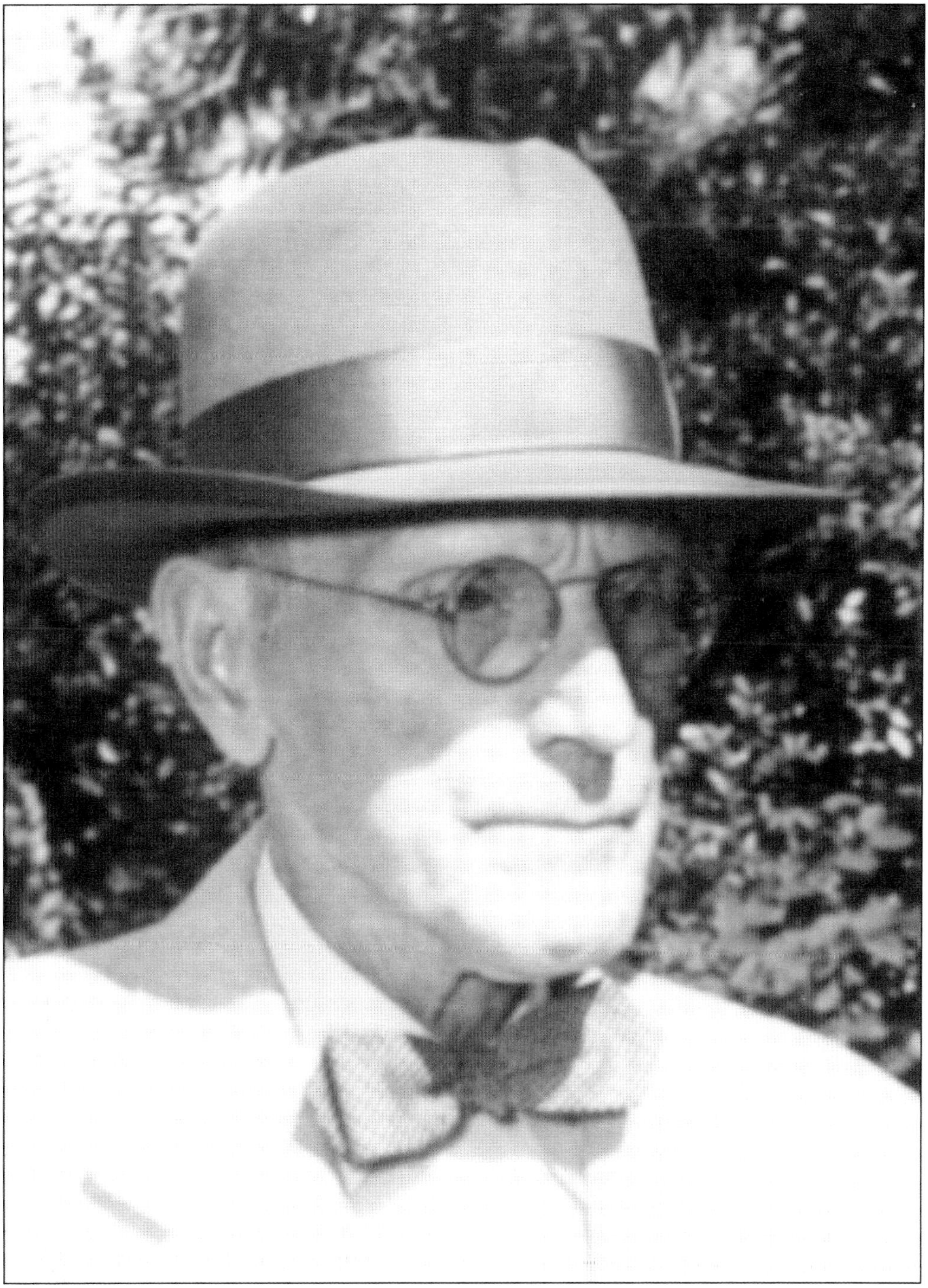

J.R. Lintner, county extension agent, was responsible for the initiation and development of many improvements to Loudoun's agriculture and the Loudoun County 4-H Fair. Lintner worked with the Loudoun County Fair before it dissolved. In 1936, he decided it was time for the 4-H youth to have a fair of their own. (Courtesy of Carol Stowers McComb.)

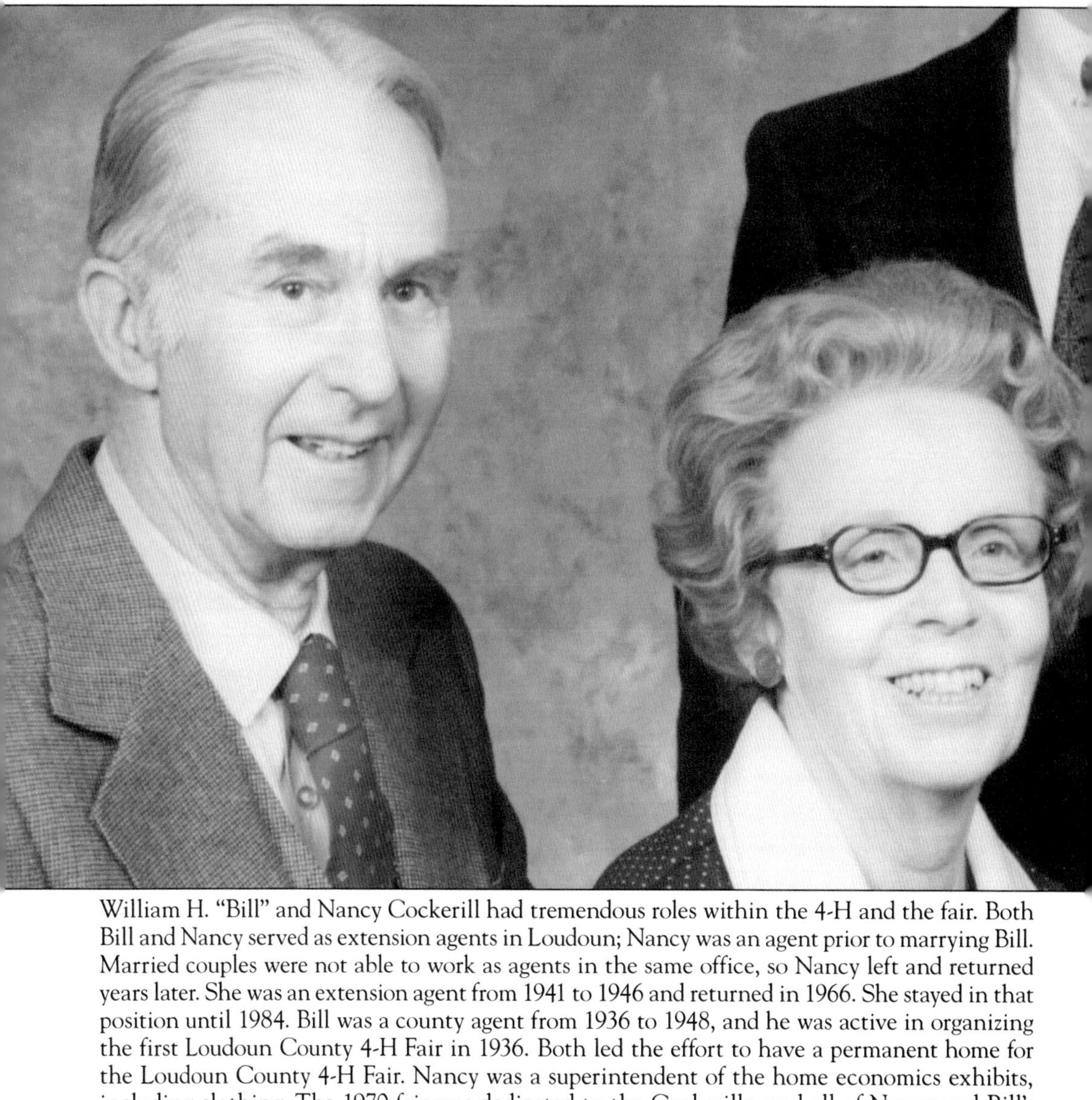

William H. "Bill" and Nancy Cockerill had tremendous roles within the 4-H and the fair. Both Bill and Nancy served as extension agents in Loudoun; Nancy was an agent prior to marrying Bill. Married couples were not able to work as agents in the same office, so Nancy left and returned years later. She was an extension agent from 1941 to 1946 and returned in 1966. She stayed in that position until 1984. Bill was a county agent from 1936 to 1948, and he was active in organizing the first Loudoun County 4-H Fair in 1936. Both led the effort to have a permanent home for the Loudoun County 4-H Fair. Nancy was a superintendent of the home economics exhibits, including clothing. The 1970 fair was dedicated to the Cockerills, and all of Nancy and Bill's children were active in the 4-H and fair, as well as many of their grandchildren. (Courtesy of the William H. Cockerill family.)

The pony show was a part of the early days of the fair, and this image shows a program in the 1949 catalog. Examples of the classes in the show were walk, trot, and canter, open jumping, hunter hack, and a championship class. A consolation class was offered for those that had not won a first- or second-place ribbon at that show. (Courtesy of Virginia Cooperative Extension, Loudoun County Office.)

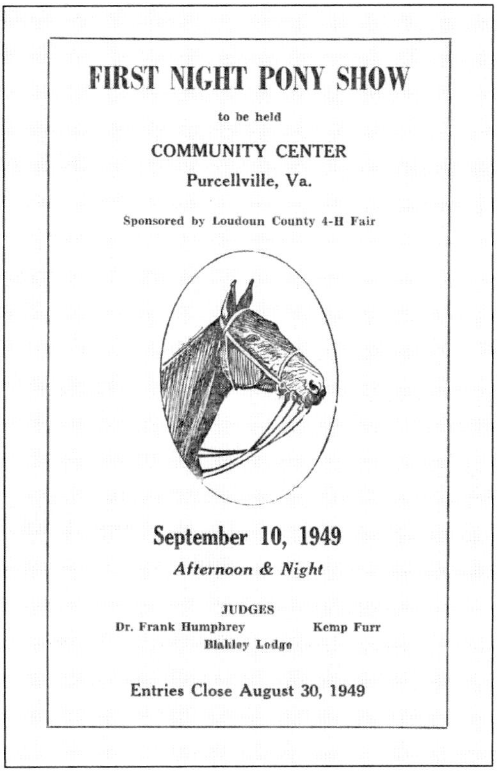

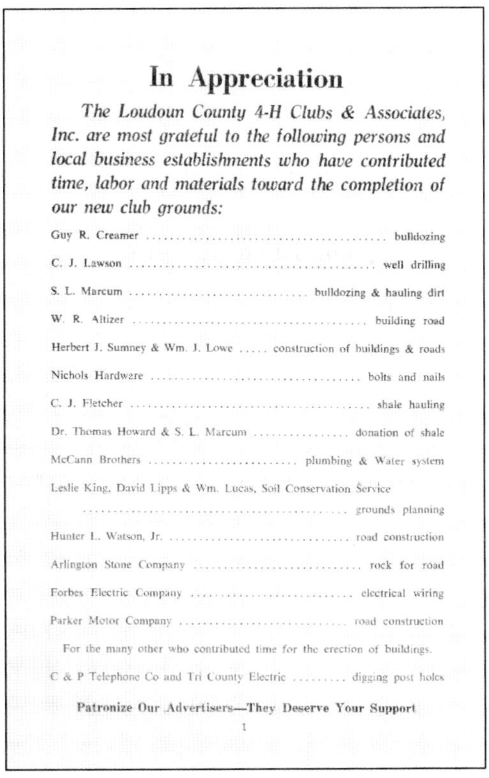

In Appreciation

The Loudoun County 4-H Clubs & Associates, Inc. are most grateful to the following persons and local business establishments who have contributed time, labor and materials toward the completion of our new club grounds:

Guy R. Creamer .... bulldozing

C. J. Lawson .... well drilling

S. L. Marcum .... bulldozing & hauling dirt

W. R. Altizer .... building road

Herbert J. Sumney & Wm. J. Lowe ..... construction of buildings & roads

Nichols Hardware .... bolts and nails

C. J. Fletcher .... shale hauling

Dr. Thomas Howard & S. L. Marcum .... donation of shale

McCann Brothers .... plumbing & Water system

Leslie King, David Lipps & Wm. Lucas, Soil Conservation Service .... grounds planning

Hunter L. Watson, Jr. .... road construction

Arlington Stone Company .... rock for road

Forbes Electric Company .... electrical wiring

Parker Motor Company .... road construction

For the many other who contributed time for the erection of buildings.

C & P Telephone Co and Tri County Electric .... digging post holes

Patronize Our Advertisers—They Deserve Your Support

1

Without volunteers and donations from the community, the Loudoun County 4-H Fair would not have become a reality. This image is from the 1957 catalog and provides an example of the types of donations that were given to the fair. Many improvements needed to be made to the land in order to hold the first fair on the new grounds that year. (Courtesy of Virginia Cooperative Extension, Loudoun County Office.)

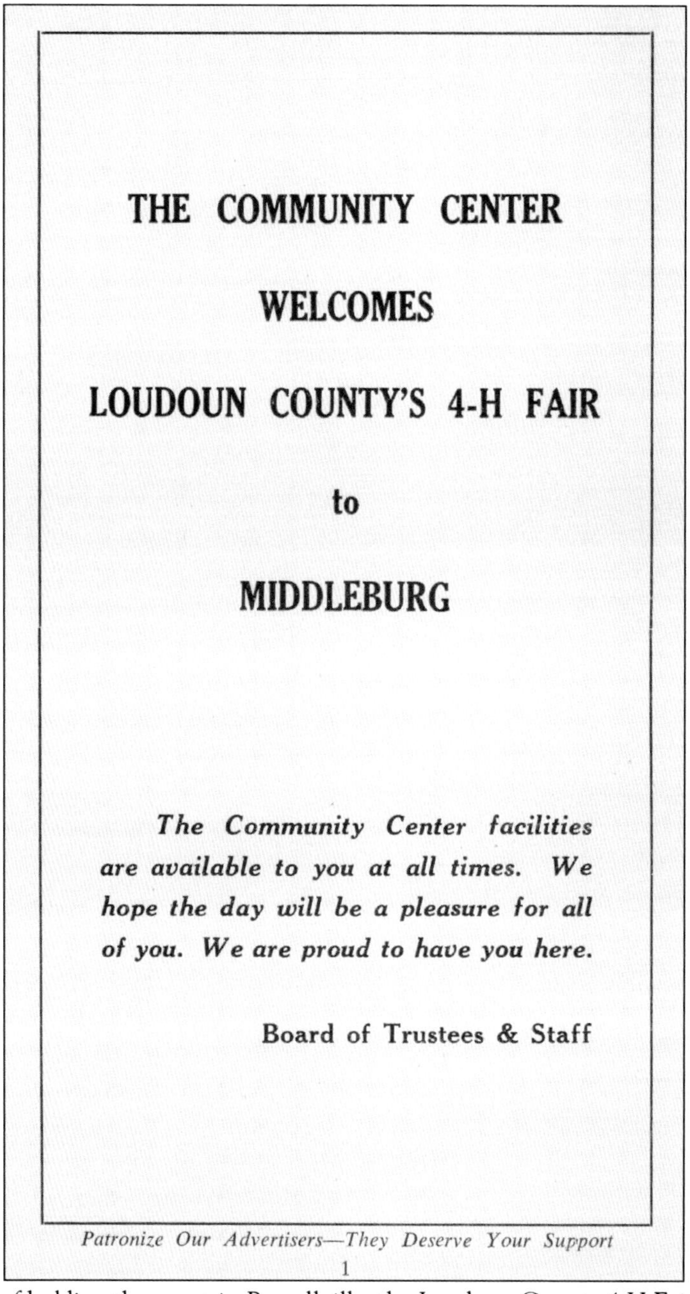

After 16 years of holding the event in Purcellville, the Loudoun County 4-H Fair moved to the community center in Middleburg. The image on this page is an advertisement from the first page of the 1953 fair catalog. The community center was happy to share their facility with the 4-H youth and exhibitors. During the early days of the fair, the event was only one day. Admission to attend the fair during this year was free. The day began at 8:30 a.m. and ended after the completion of the special entertainment, which began at 2:30 p.m. The community center housed the field crops, garden exhibits, food, clothing, and flower arranging. Behind the community center was a grassy area that was able to accommodate the livestock as well as the grand parade. At the time of the move to Middleburg, Jack Brown was the county agent. (Courtesy of Frank Keesling.)

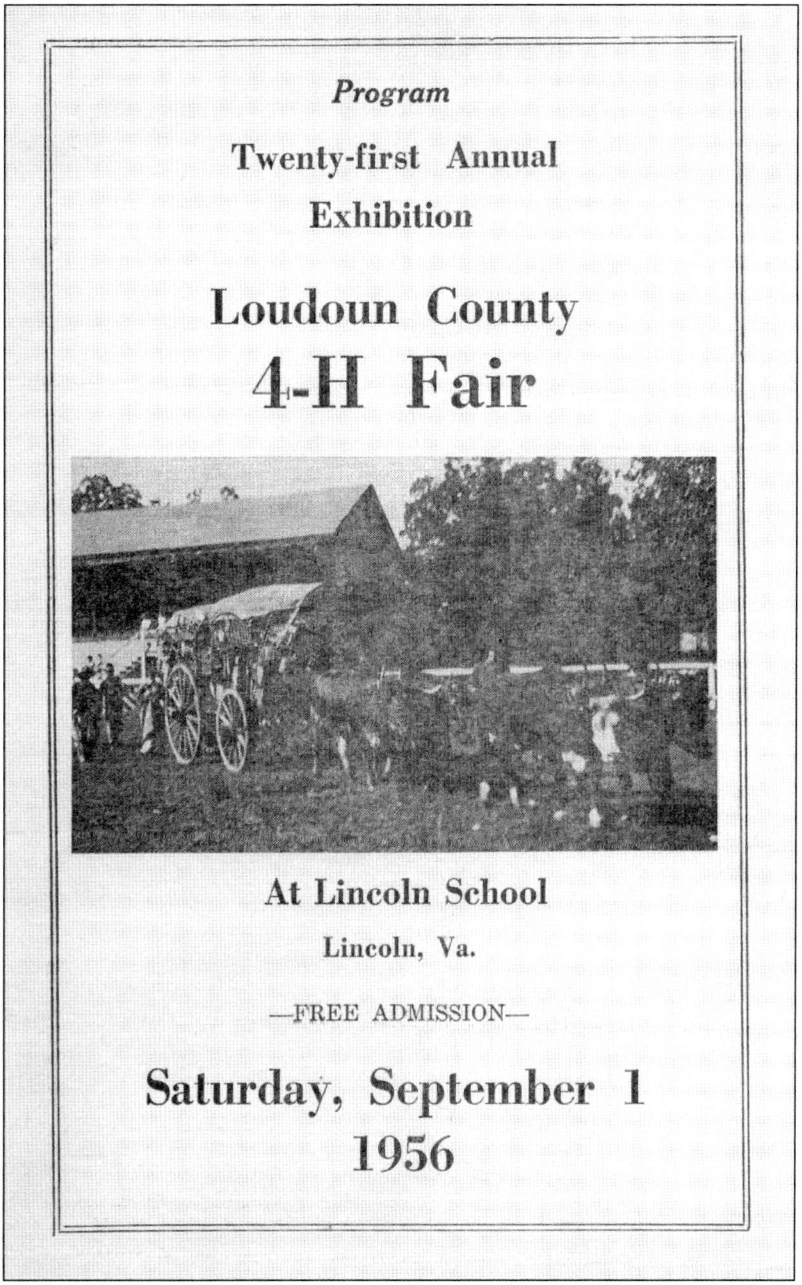
Program

Twenty-first Annual

Exhibition

Loudoun County

4-H Fair

At Lincoln School

Lincoln, Va.

—FREE ADMISSION—

Saturday, September 1

1956

After only three years in Middleburg, the fair moved to the Lincoln School in Lincoln, Virginia. Lincoln hosted the 21st Loudoun County Fair. On Saturday, September 1, 1956, the Lincoln fair began at 9:00 a.m. and ended at 3:30 p.m. This was also a one day fair that included livestock exhibits, poultry, eggs and rabbits, garden exhibits, field crops, clothing, and food exhibits. Volunteers for this fair included some that had donated their time for multiple years: Owen Thomas III, Henry Stowers, Allen McKay, A.L. Hutton, Nancy Cockerill, and Randy Rust. Jack Brown continued as an agent and facilitated the move from Middleburg to Lincoln. The Lincoln School has been a school for all grade levels over the years. Currently, it is an elementary school serving kindergarten through grade five. (Courtesy of Frank Keesling.)

THE LOUDOUN COUNTY 4-H FAIR

AND ASSOCIATES

are most grateful

and sincerely appreciate

MR. C. R. AHALT'S

generous gift

of a land site

for our permanent

FAIR GROUNDS

Patronize Our Advertisers—They Deserve Your Support

2

In 1956, efforts were made by William H. Harrison and Eugene Sykes, among others, to acquire property for a permanent 4-H and fair location. Clarence R. and Tillie A. Ahalt sold land to the Loudoun 4-H Clubs and Associates, Inc., for $10. The 13.63 acres was located on the east side of the Washington & Old Dominion Railroad about two miles west of Leesburg. This is the current property where the fair is held today. One condition tied to the donation of this land was that if the land was not used for the purposes for which it was given—4-H events and the fair—for two consecutive years, it would be forfeited to the Loudoun County Board of Supervisors. If this occurred, the board would have full authority to devote it to the youth of Loudoun for recreational, social, and educational purposes in the field of agriculture, home economics, livestock breeding and raising, and related functions. The deed was signed on December 28, 1956. (Courtesy of Virginia Cooperative Extension, Loudoun County Office.)

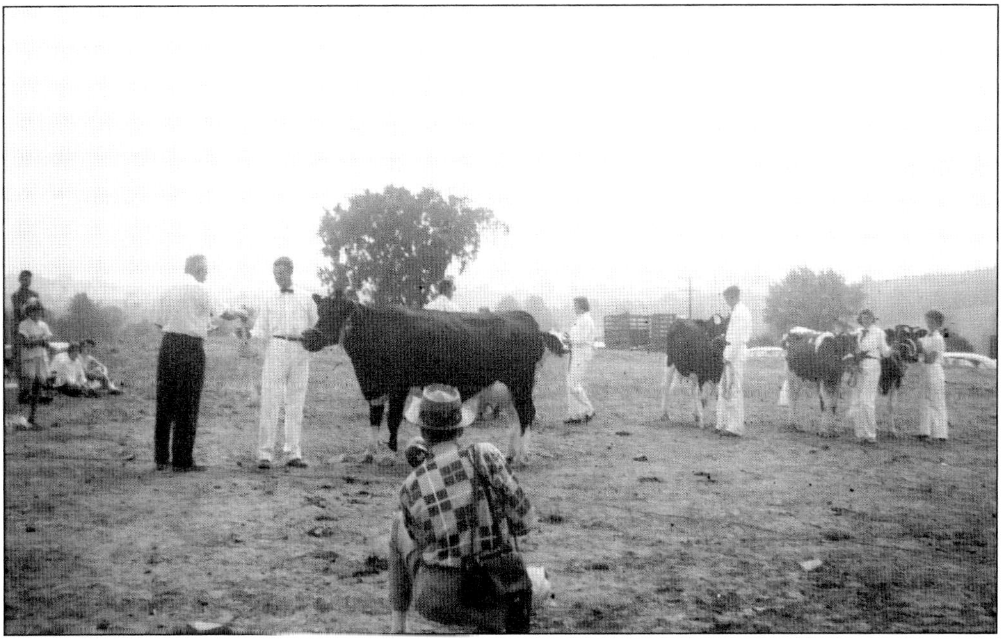

The first Loudoun County 4-H Fair was held at its Leesburg location near Clarke's Gap on Saturday, August 31, 1957. In the above image, Clarence Ahalt presents an award to Bill Cole of Purcellville. In the center of the image is Peggy Anne Benedum with her dairy cow. The three youth on the right are unidentified. At the time of the fair, two livestock barns had been erected on the grounds, with many to come in the few years following. At right, Clarence Ahalt presents Bill Brown with a trophy for his prize-winning Guernsey cow. (Both, courtesy of the William H. Cockerill family.)

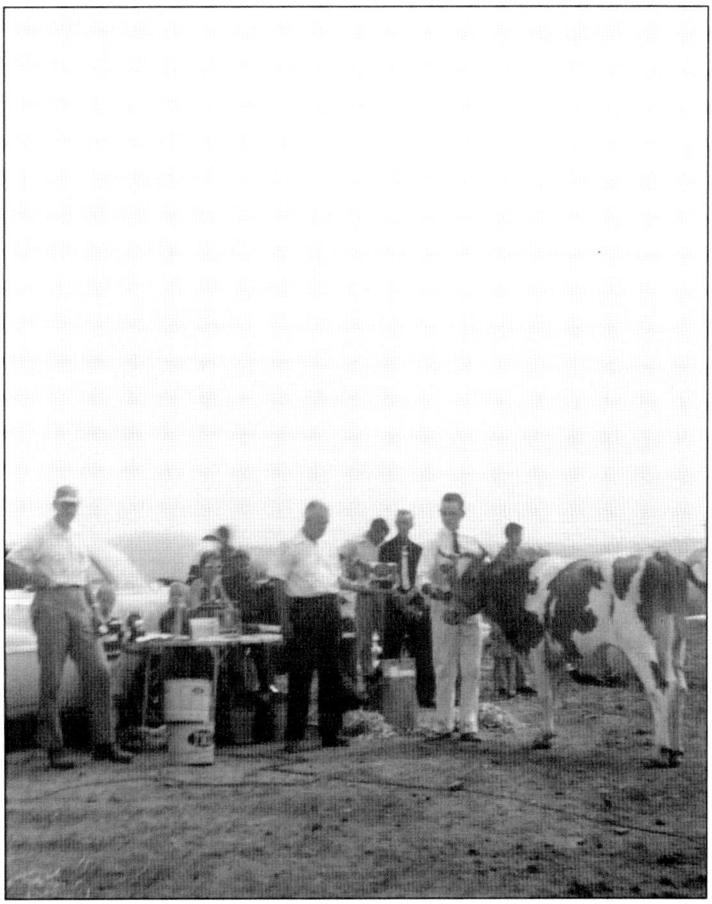

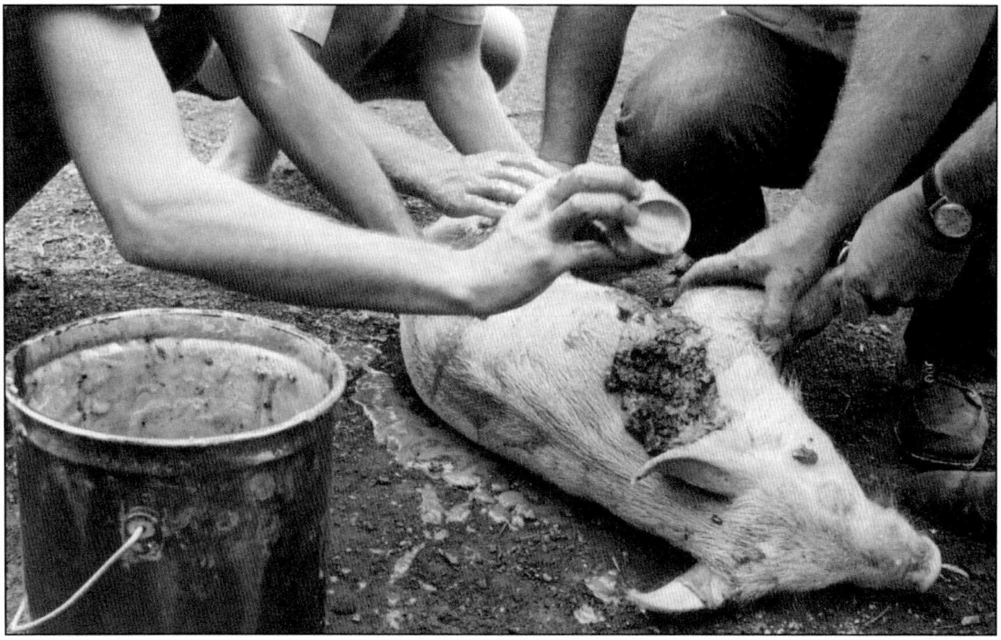

The greased-pig contest was an event that many of the youth looked forward to each year. The pig would be let go in an open field on the grounds, and the children would chase it. The child who was lucky enough to hang on was the winner of the pig. Junior 4-H boys and girls and senior 4-H boys were able to participate. According to various fair catalogs, some years, only juniors were allowed to enter the contest. In the above image, the youth are greasing the pig, preparing it for the contest. The photograph below was taken just after the contest; Holmes Welch, in the center, was the winner of this event in 1958. (Above, courtesy of Courtesy of Loudoun County Fair and Associates Collection, Rust Archive, Thomas Balch Library; below, courtesy of Carol Stowers McComb.)

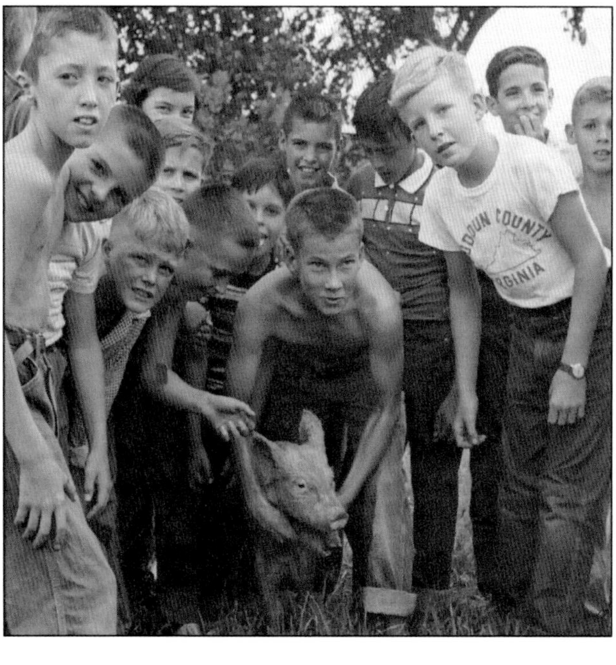

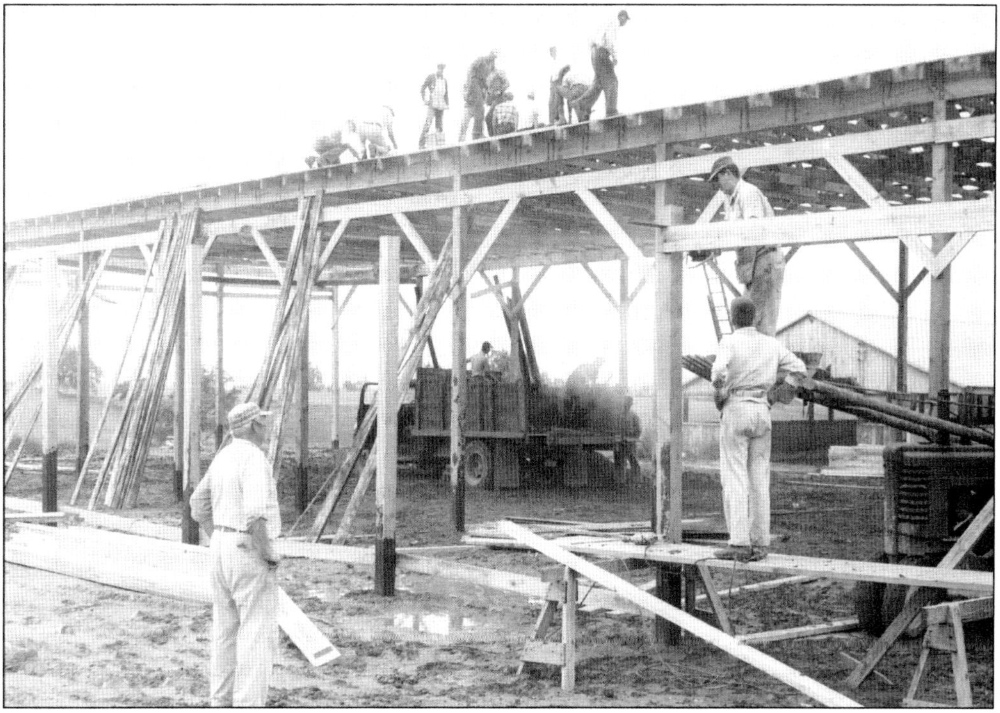

Shown here are volunteers building the show pavilion in 1958. To the left of the photograph is Roy Frambaugh; everyone called him "Boss Carpenter." He oversaw the construction of this building as well as others on the grounds. Frank Keesling remembers that he, George Washington, and others would go down at night and put together the trusses for the barn. (Courtesy of Carol Stowers McComb.)

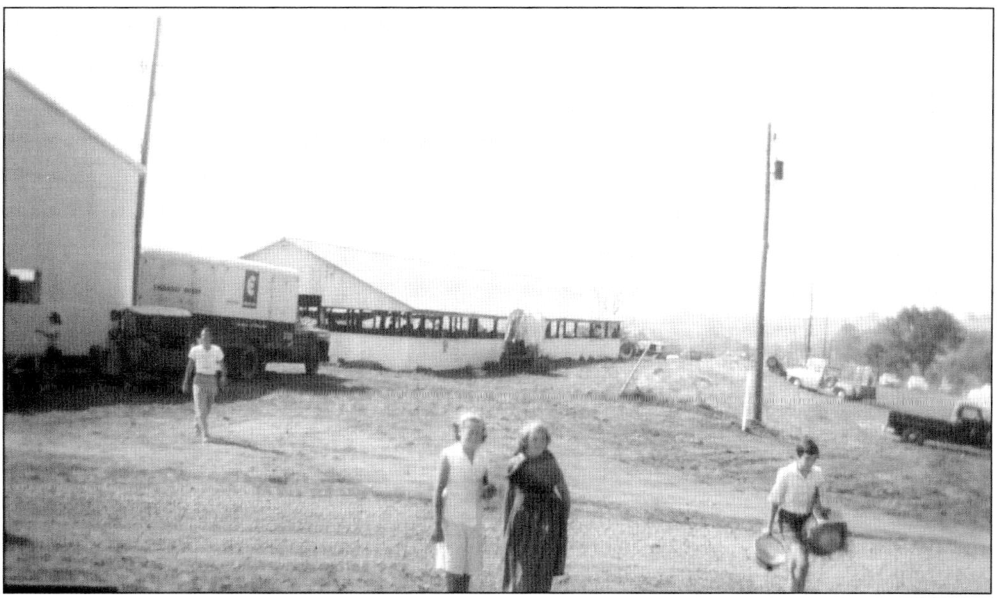

This photograph captures the view from the hill looking toward the barns in 1960. The building in the center is the beef barn, and to the left of the image is the show pavilion. Standing at center are Dianne Dye Horton (left) and Maureen Lawson (right). (Courtesy of Mary Virginia Keesling.)

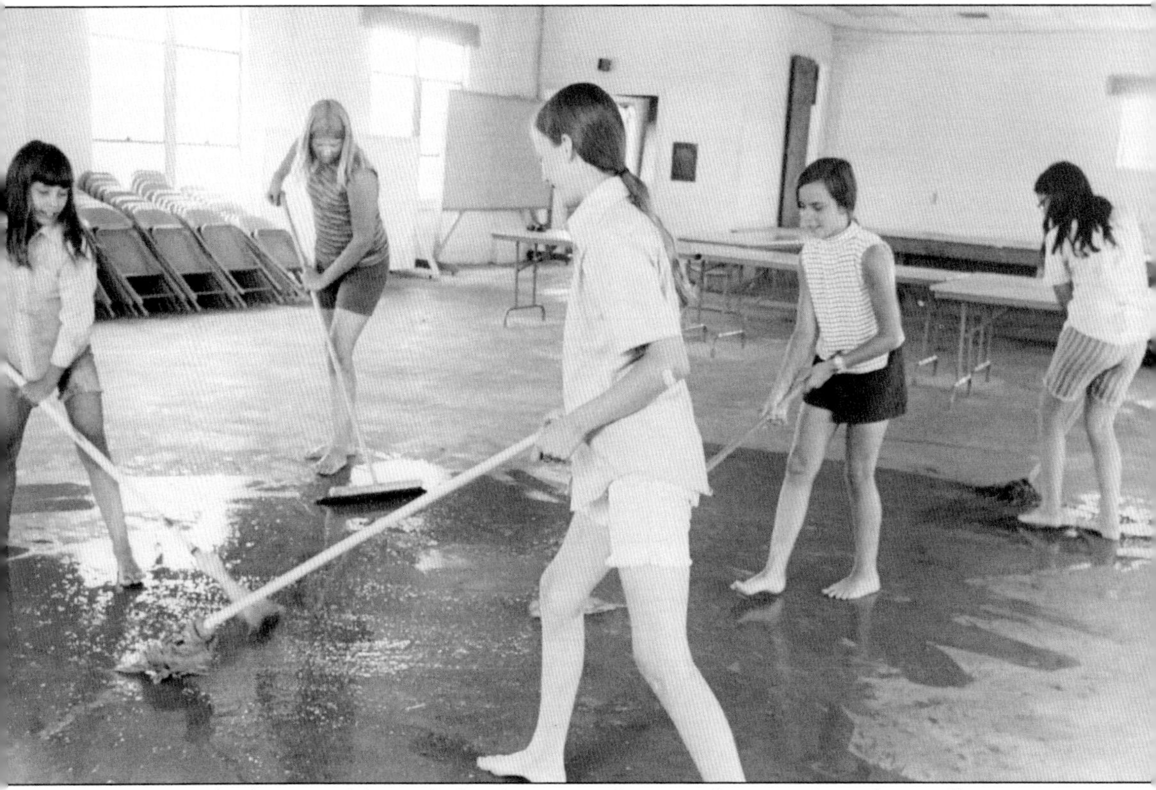

Preparing for the annual fair includes cleaning and getting the animals ready as well as preparing the grounds for the big event. The grass has to be mowed, the barns cleaned, the fences painted, and gravel hauled in for the roads, among a long list of other items. Parent volunteers, community members, and 4-H'ers all lend a hand to complete tasks from the list. The girls in this photograph are cleaning Sykes Hall in preparation for the fair. In Sykes Hall, the floors needed to be scrubbed, the bathrooms cleaned, and the kitchen prepared. At the time of this photograph, the tile floor had not been laid in Sykes Hall. The cinder-block walls were still exposed, and the windows were original to the building. Since this time, the hall has undergone numerous renovations. (Courtesy of Carol Stowers McComb.)

The Story of The

RURAL YOUTH CENTER

OF LOUDOUN COUNTY

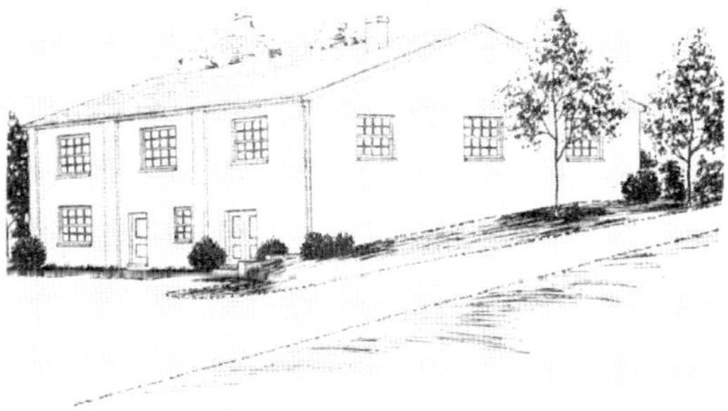

Architect's Sketch

NOW BEING DEVELOPED BY THE

LOUDOUN 4-H CLUBS
&
ASSOCIATES INC.

The cover to a pamphlet promoting the construction of a new building for the grounds includes an architect's sketch. Blueprints for the building were prepared at no cost to the Loudoun 4-H Clubs and Associates, Inc., by Albert Leuders. The Loudoun 4-H Clubs and Associates, Inc., wanted to build an auditorium to hold meetings for the 4-H, home demonstration, and farmers' groups. With this building, the educational work of the extension agents with the farm groups would be made more effective. The plans for the auditorium included a kitchen and dining facilities, and the fundraising goal for the center was $30,000. The money was also going to go toward completing the road and parking area, as well as the extension of the existing pipeline and electrical lines. The 4-H members had also planned to develop a picnic area on the grounds, which would be available for use by the public as well. (Courtesy of the William H. Cockerill family.)

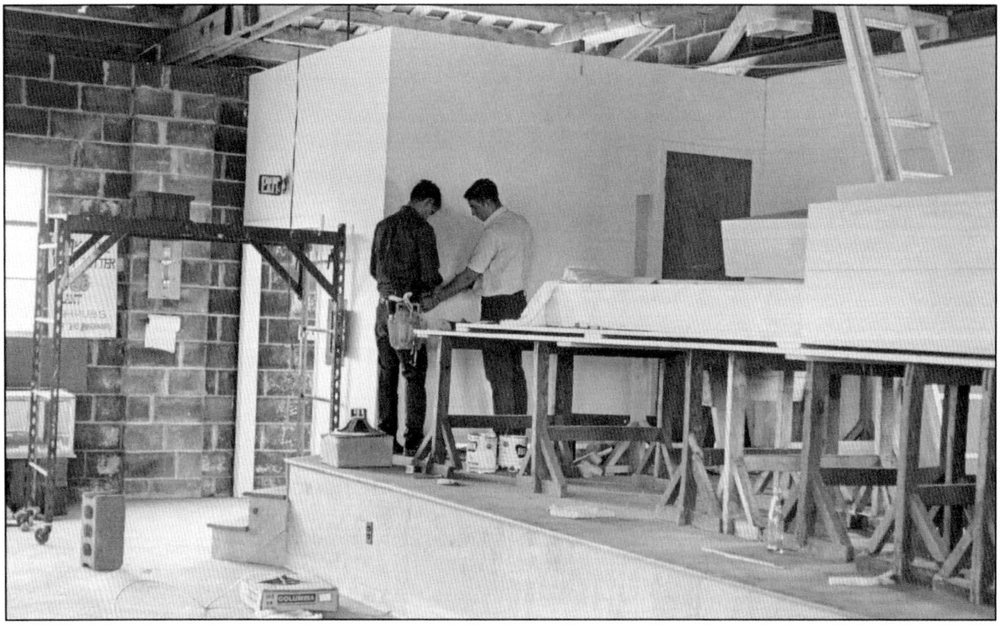

In the image above, electrical work is being done on the new auditorium's second floor. The 50-foot-by-50-foot two-story building was made of cinder-block construction, which can be seen here, with a ground level entrance on both floors. The hilly land was a benefit to giving outdoor access to both levels. The photograph below is looking toward what is now known as Sykes Hall, not long after it was constructed. When it was first constructed, the outside of the building was not painted. The show pavilion is on the right. Since this time, an addition with larger restroom facilities and a picnic pavilion have been added onto Sykes Hall. (Both, courtesy of the William H. Cockerill family.)

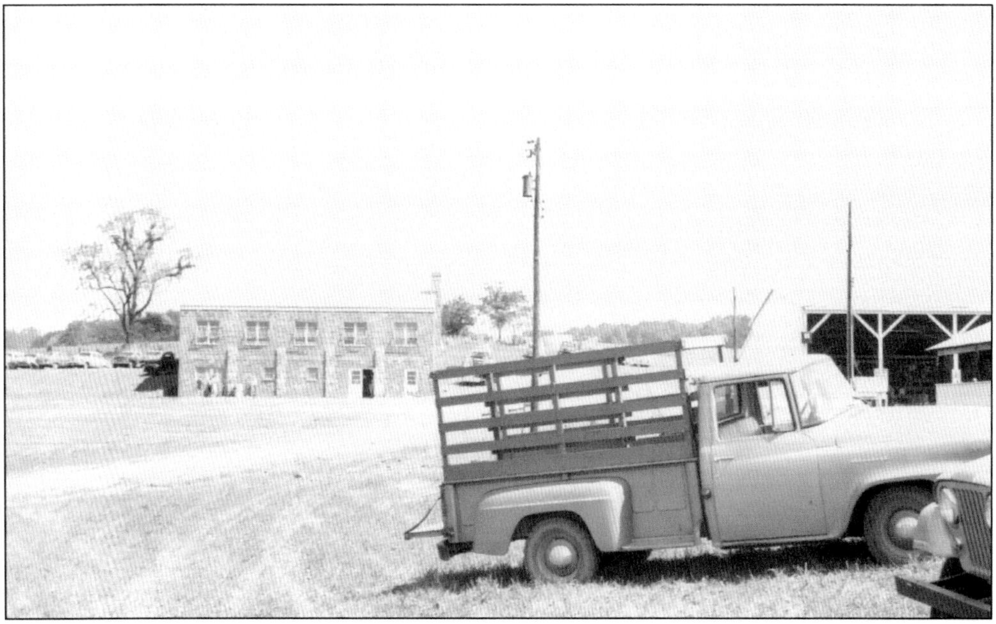

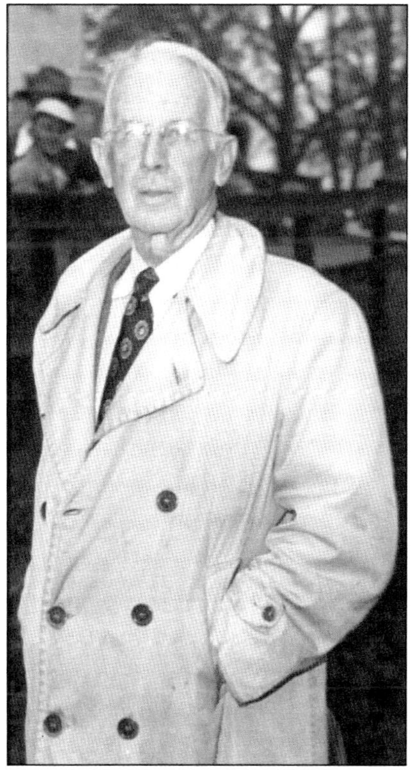

Prior to the dedication of the new auditorium, it was called the Loudoun 4-H Clubs and Associates' Agricultural Center. During the 25th annual fair, a ceremony was held dedicating the building to Eugene E. Sykes. Sykes was a well-known name around the fair since before it was located in Leesburg. He helped acquire the permanent grounds, was treasurer of the fair for 18 years, and spent countless hours working for the 4-H youth. In the image below, Thomas Slater accepts a $1,500 donation for the 4-H fairgrounds from 4-H treasurer Eugene Sykes at the 1959 fair. (Both, courtesy of Carol Stowers McComb.)

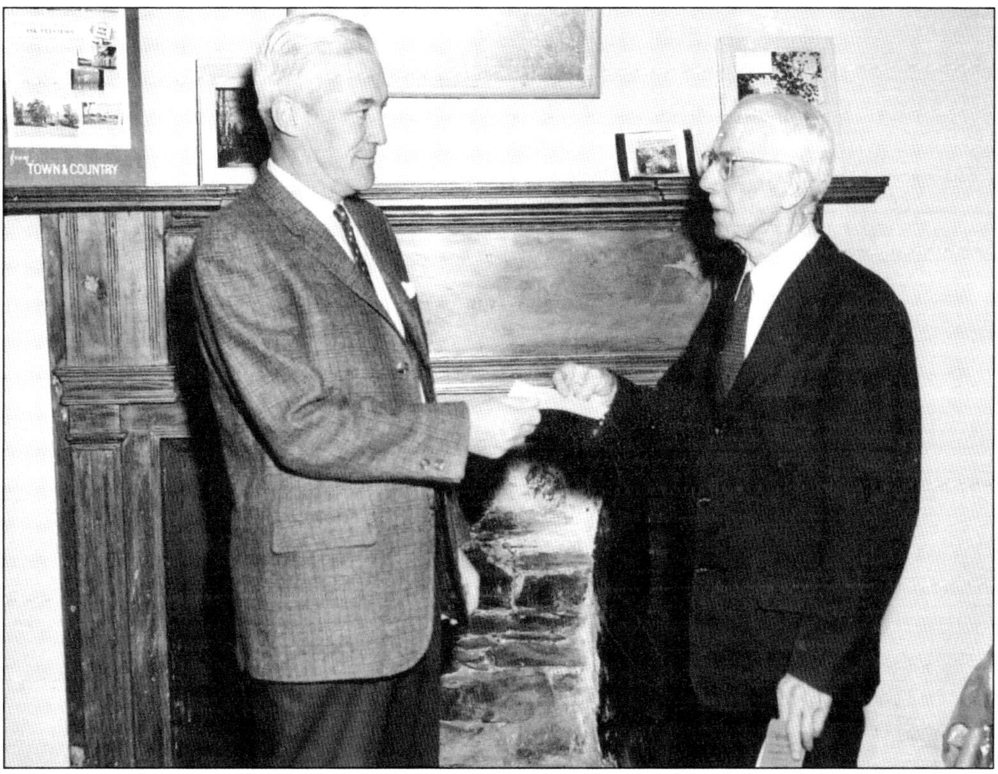

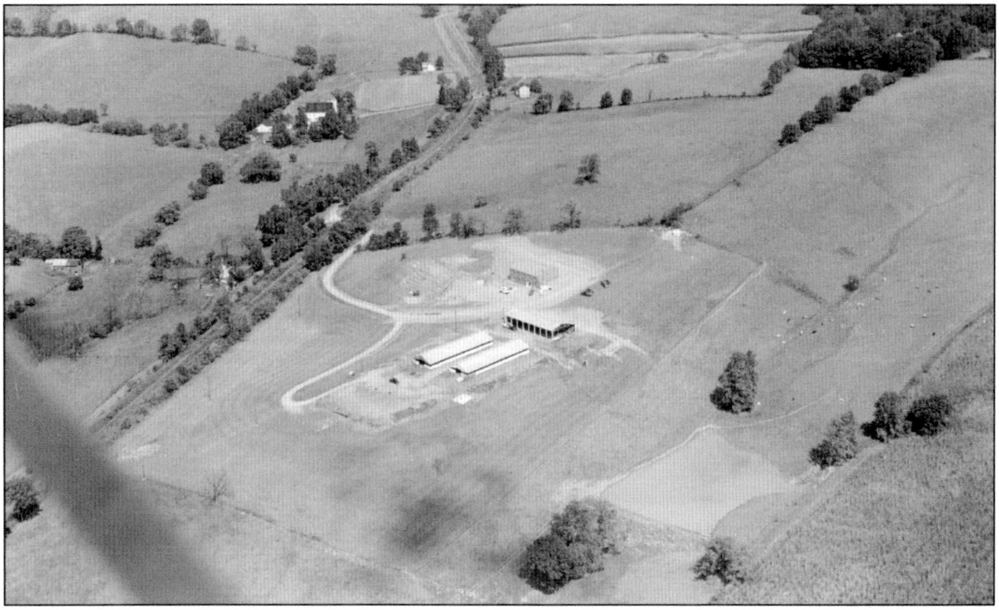

Since at least 1960, Sam Legard has taken aerial photographs of the fairgrounds. In the above image, from 1960, there are only four buildings on the grounds: two livestock barns, the show pavilion, and the most recent addition, Sykes Hall. From the dirt showing around Sykes Hall, this photograph was likely taken just after construction was completed. The tree line to the left of the buildings is next to the Washington & Old Dominion Railroad. In the 1964 photograph below, an additional pole-type building had been added, and Sykes Hall was painted white. In this image, the hills surrounding the ground are visible. (Courtesy of Carol Stowers McComb.)

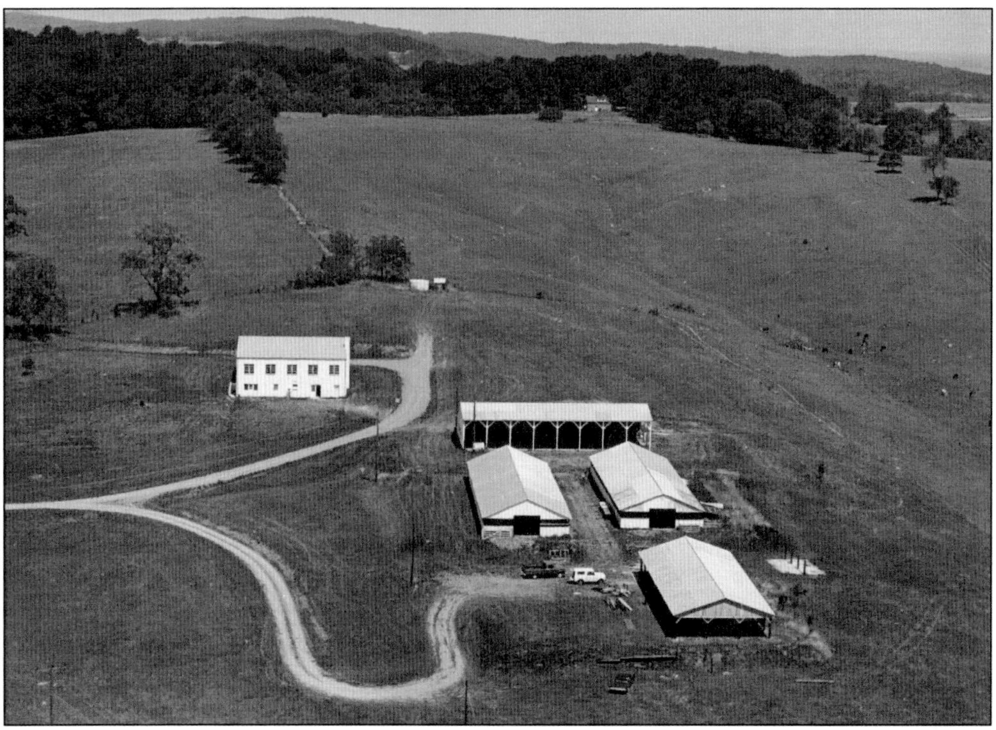

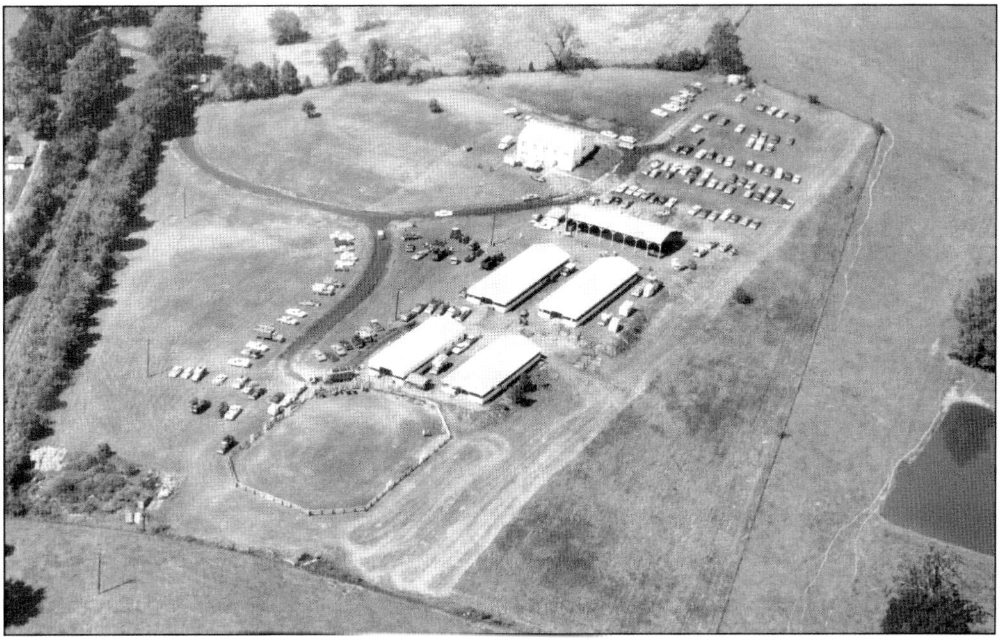

By 1968, an additional livestock barn had been added, as well as a horse ring (above). The enclosed area of the new barn to the left was used for poultry and rabbits. A closer view of the W&OD Railroad is on the left side of the photograph. Trains used this track until the year this image was captured. The trail for recreational purposes was not completed in the western part of Loudoun until the late 1980s. The photograph below, from 1996, shows the land being excavated and graded. This landscaping was undertaken to add more usable space to the property. The horse ring had also been expanded. Since this image was taken, two horse barns, a grandstand, a fair office, and a livestock shed have been built. (Above, courtesy of Carol Stowers McComb below, courtesy of VCE, Loudoun County Office.)

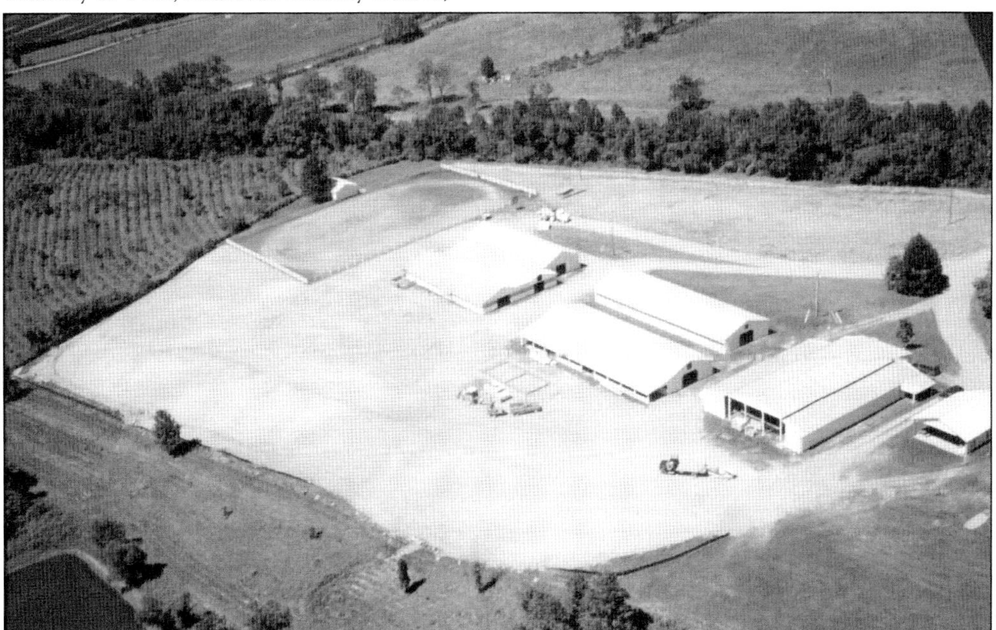

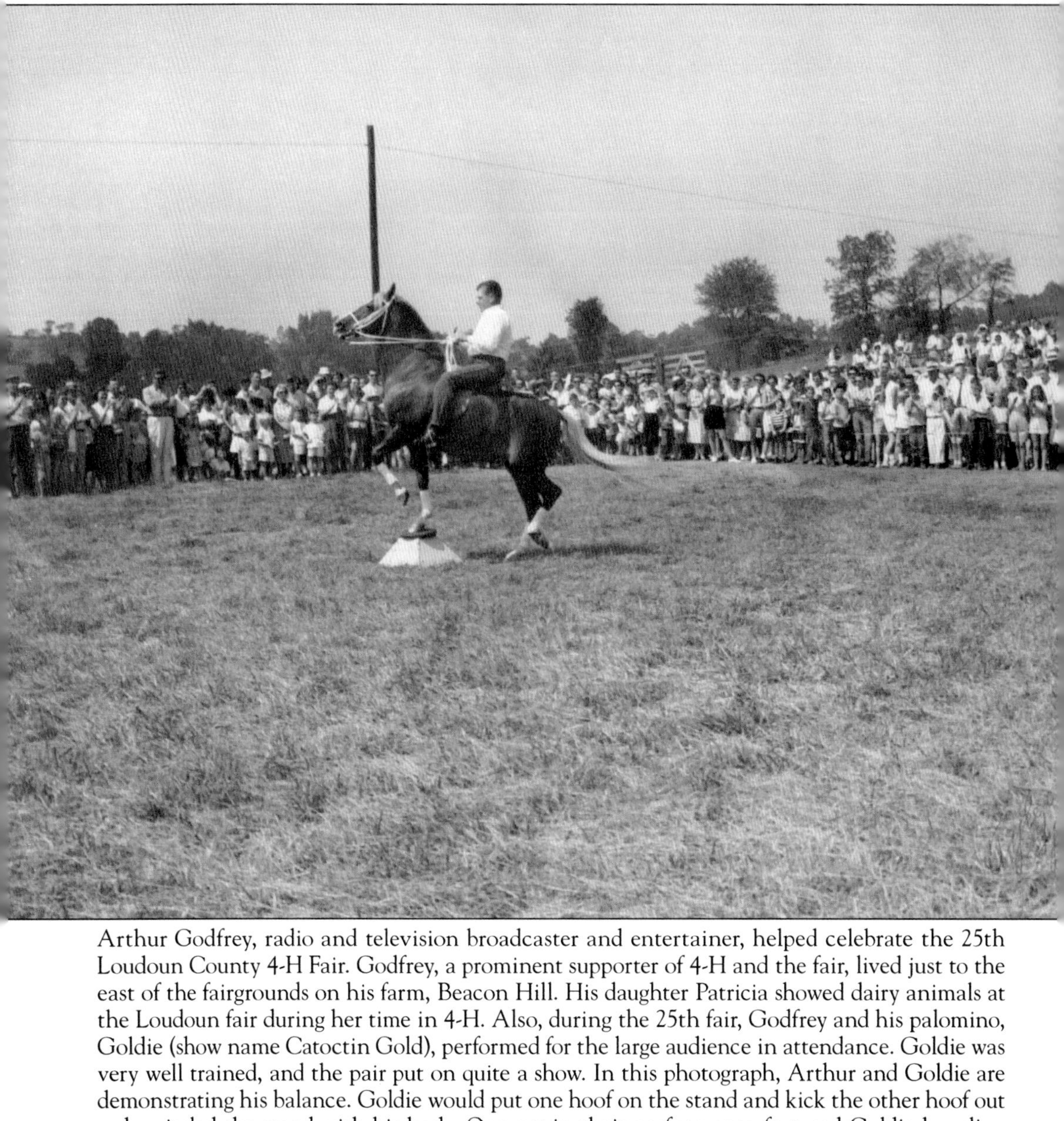

Arthur Godfrey, radio and television broadcaster and entertainer, helped celebrate the 25th Loudoun County 4-H Fair. Godfrey, a prominent supporter of 4-H and the fair, lived just to the east of the fairgrounds on his farm, Beacon Hill. His daughter Patricia showed dairy animals at the Loudoun fair during her time in 4-H. Also, during the 25th fair, Godfrey and his palomino, Goldie (show name Catoctin Gold), performed for the large audience in attendance. Goldie was very well trained, and the pair put on quite a show. In this photograph, Arthur and Goldie are demonstrating his balance. Goldie would put one hoof on the stand and kick the other hoof out as he circled the stand with his body. One act in their performance featured Goldie kneeling down saying his prayers. Godfrey affectionately called Goldie the "smartest horse in the world." (Courtesy of the William H. Cockerill family.)

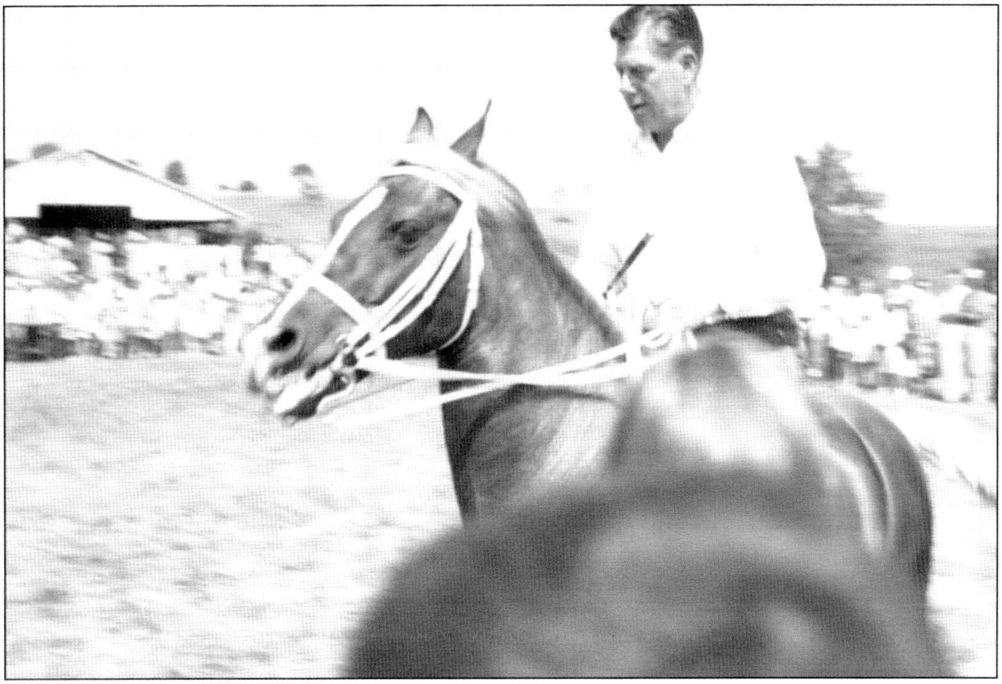

A closer image of Arthur Godfrey and Goldie shows the complex bridle and double reins used to help guide the animal with commands from Godfrey. Goldie would make the light dance steps associated with dressage. At one point during their performance at the fair, Godfrey and Goldie galloped around, delighting the audience. (Courtesy of the William H. Cockerill family.)

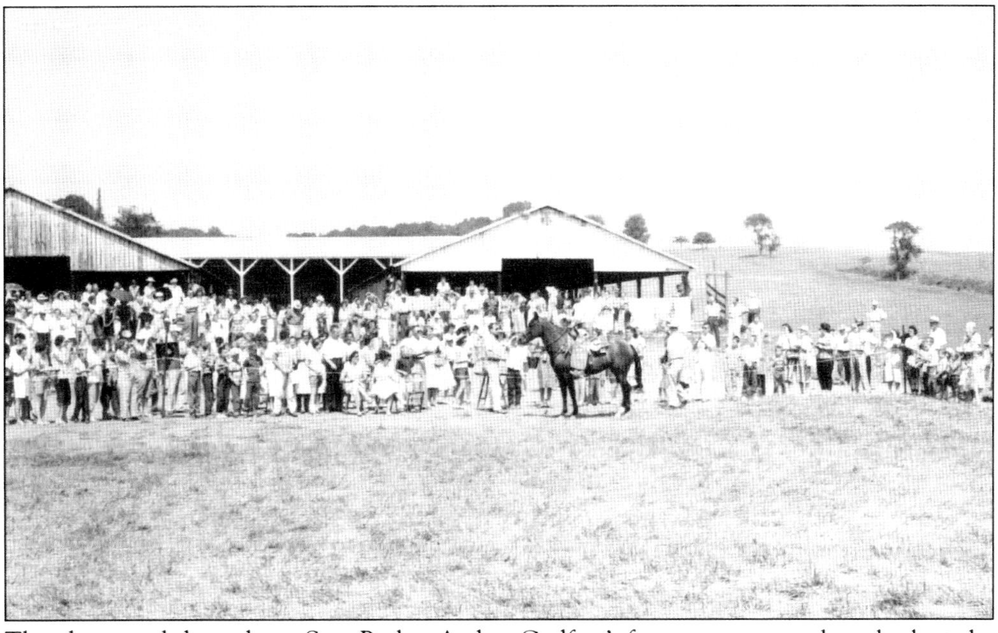

The photograph here shows Sam Paylor, Arthur Godfrey's farm manager, on horseback at the 25th fair. Paylor took a great interest in the youth of Loudoun County, and his own children showed horse and beef animals. Paylor was very active with the 4-H horse club. (Courtesy of the William H. Cockerill family.)

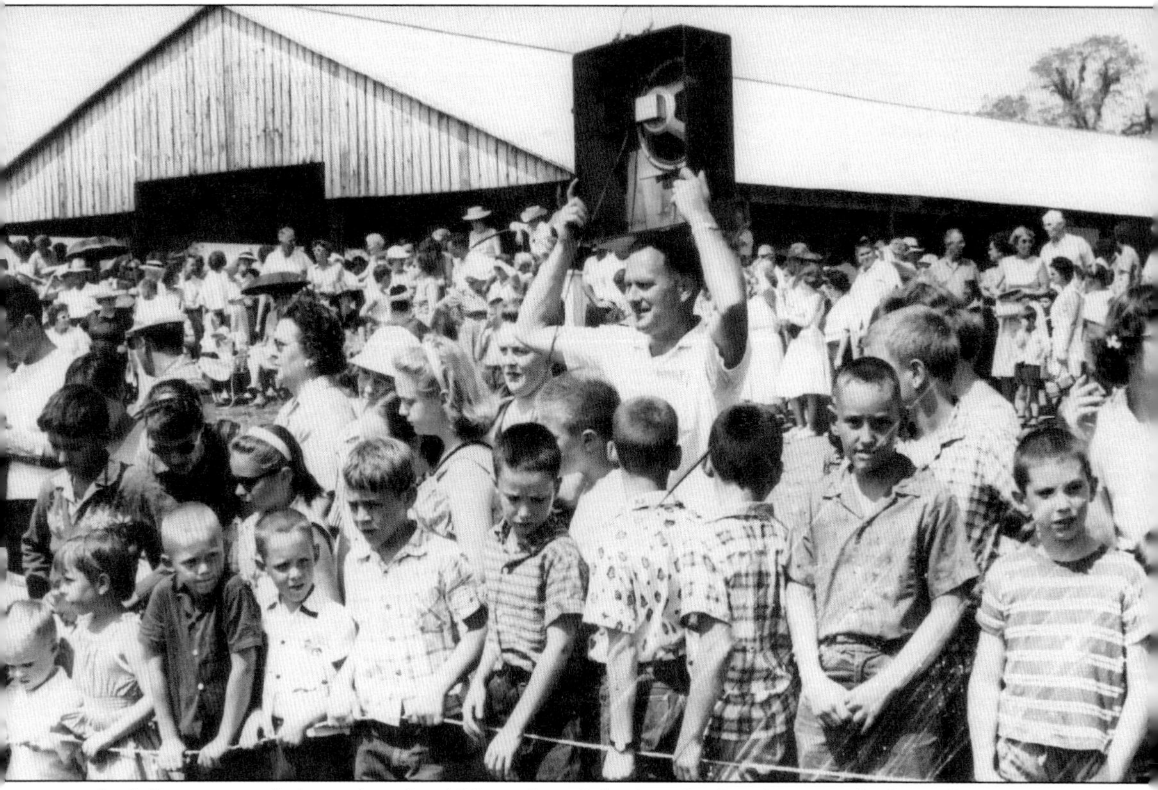

Jack Brown was dedicated to the 4-H youth and the fair. In the photograph above, Brown is seen holding a speaker on his head so the large audience could hear Arthur Godfrey's explanation of his and Goldie's movements during the 25th annual fair. This was classic Jack. There was not a job he would not do—nothing was beneath him. As stated in a fair catalog, Brown was everywhere: dishing out breakfast to the 4-H'ers, giving a word of encouragement to one who did not place well, congratulating those who did, checking with officials during judging and weigh-in, sweeping the bleachers, helping cut watermelon for the watermelon contest, guiding, and explaining to a parent about a particular class placing. He was there to lead and guide. (Courtesy of the William H. Cockerill family.)

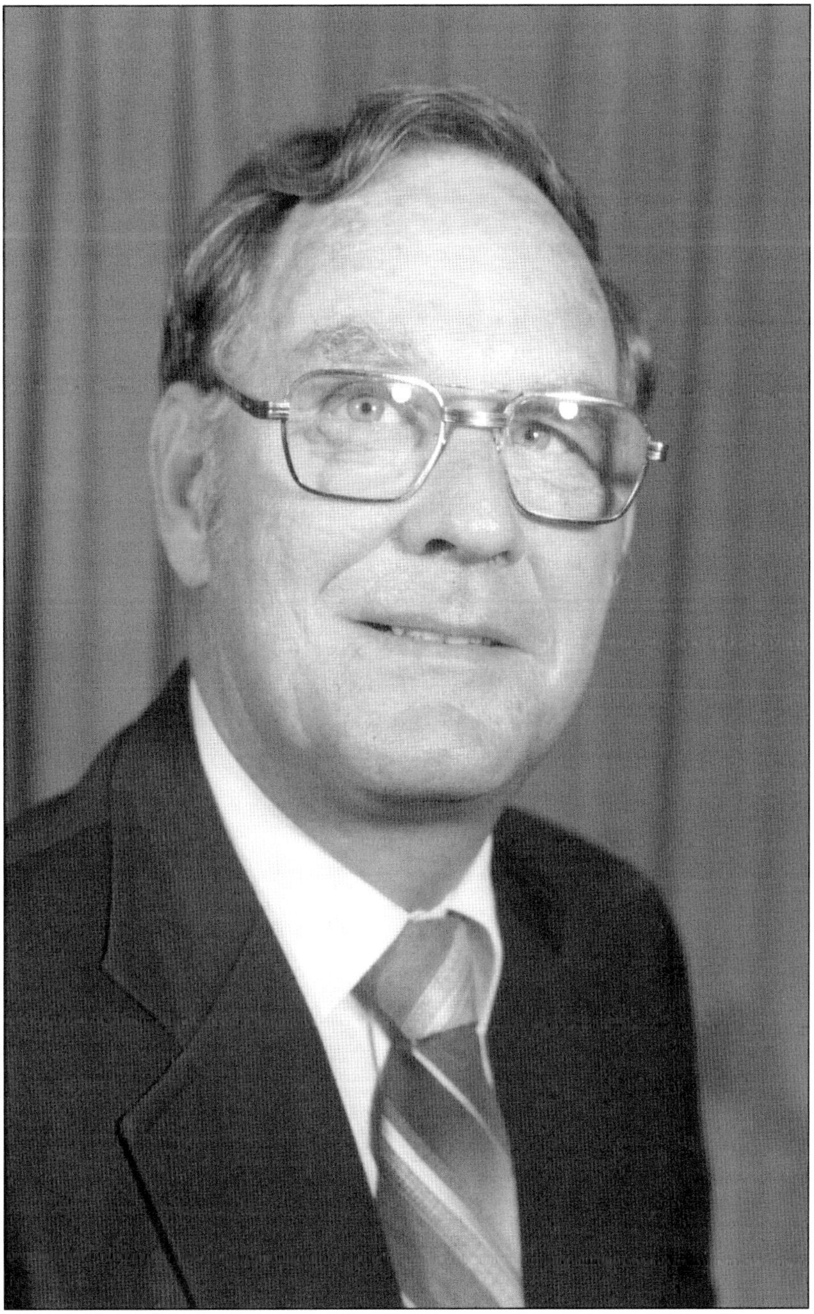

Jack Brown served as an extension agent in Loudoun County from 1953 to 1981. When interviewed for the *Times-Mirror Citizen* for recognition in 1972, he stated that during his 20-year tenure as an extension agent in Loudoun, the activity of which he was most proud was his part in the development of the Loudoun County 4-H fairgrounds. Brown felt the fair was not just a job commitment; it was one that involved the heart. At the time, under his guidance, the fair became one of the largest in Virginia. In 1982, a multipurpose shelter was built and named the Jack Brown Pavilion in honor of his dedication to the fair. The 38th county fair was also dedicated to him, and this photograph of Brown is on display in Sykes Hall. (Courtesy of Sykes Hall Archives.)

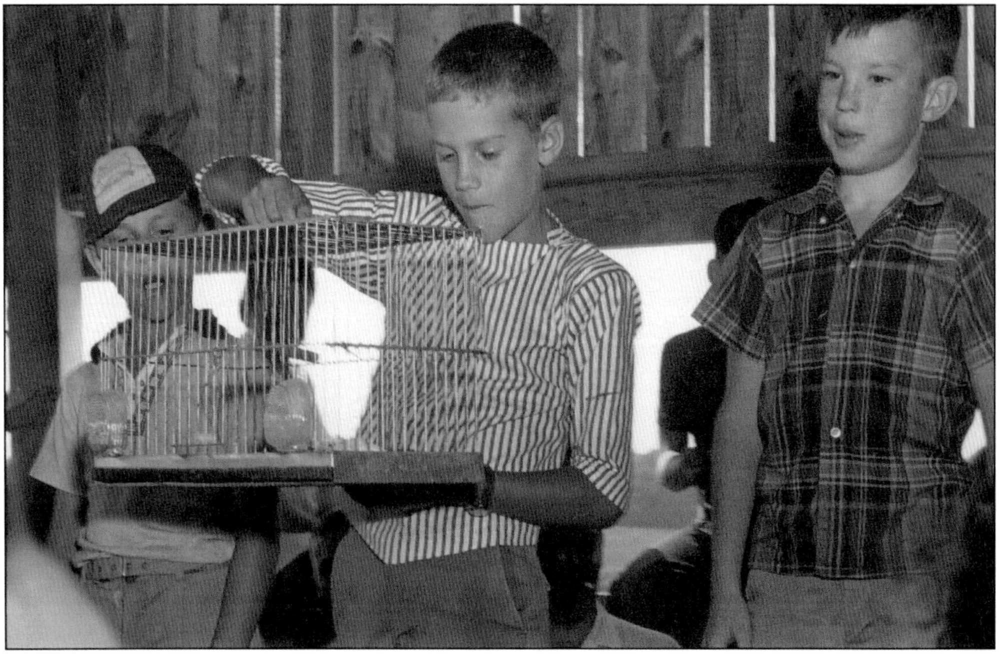

Three unidentified boys participate in the bubble gum blowing contest. Over the years there have been many types of contests at the fair in addition to bubble gum blowing. Watermelon eating, corn eating, pie eating, milk chugging, and egg toss are just a few. In the photograph above, the boys get their wads of gum ready while examining what is thought to be the prize for winning the contest. Below, the boys begin to blow while hoping the bubble does not burst. One observer of the bubble gum blowing contest remembers contestants with gum all over their faces and in their hair. (Both, courtesy of Carol Stowers McComb.)

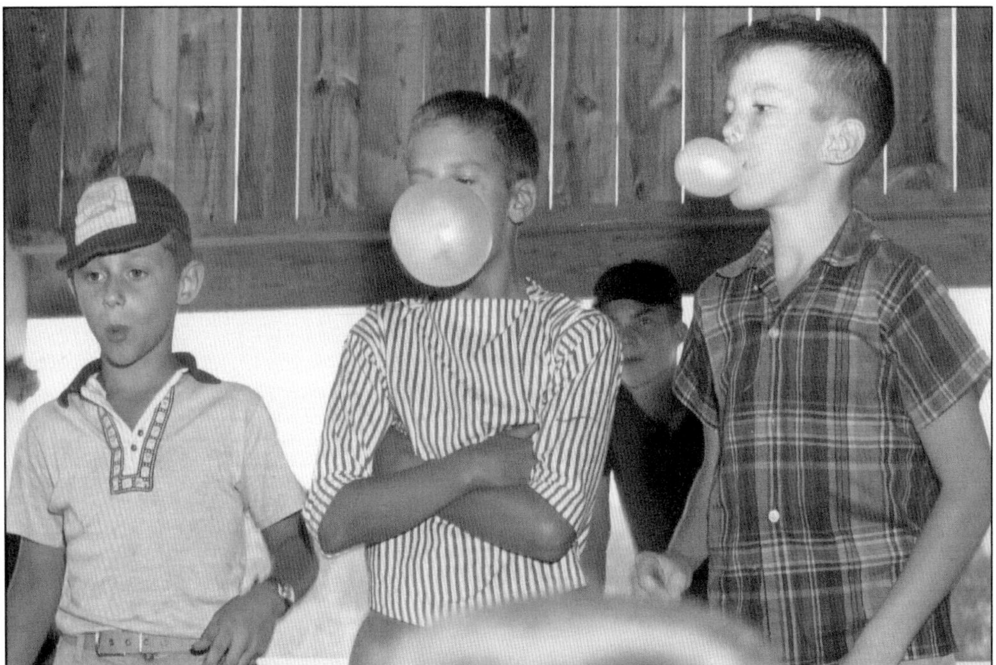

As the last event of the fair each year, a parade of champions was held. In this 1960s parade, the champion livestock animals were led around the grounds by their owners. Animals that could be led around on halters were in the parade, though Jane Virts McCall remembers the only time she participated in the parade was with her chicken. (Courtesy of Mary Virginia Keesling.)

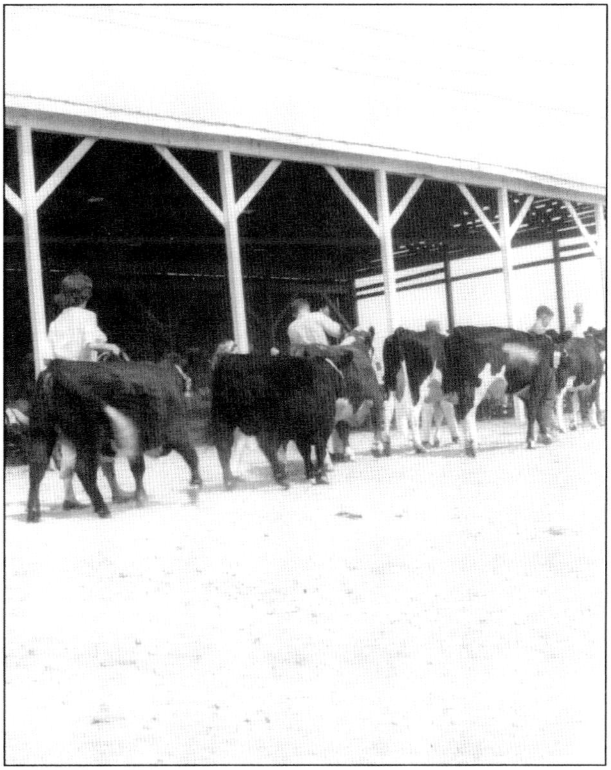

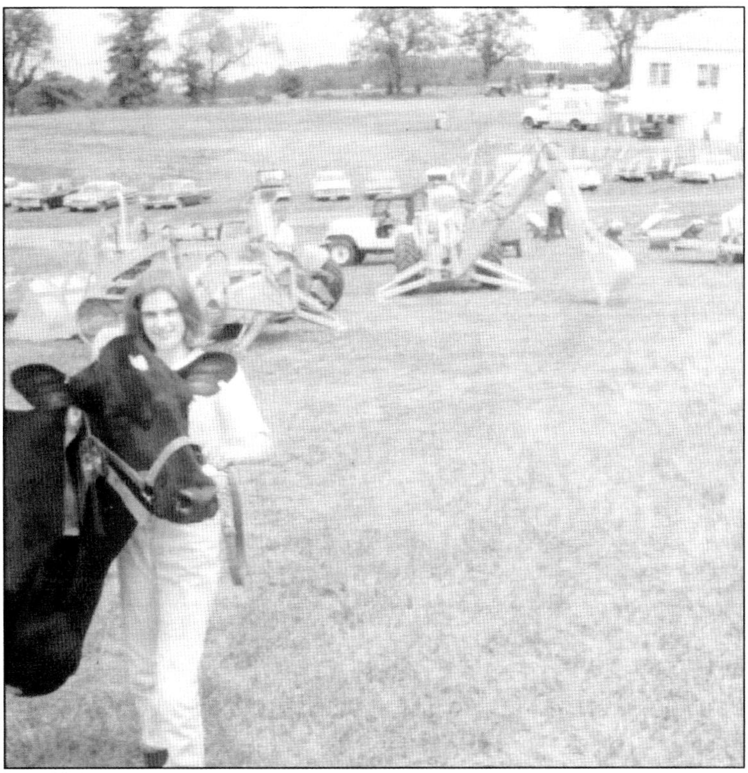

Catherine "Kitty" Brown stands with her cow Gladys at the fair in 1964. As part of the fair, there was a display of tractors for the fairgoers to view. Tractors have been displayed during the fair for many years and continue to be something the younger children flock to see. In the background is Sykes Hall. (Courtesy of the William H. Cockerill family.)

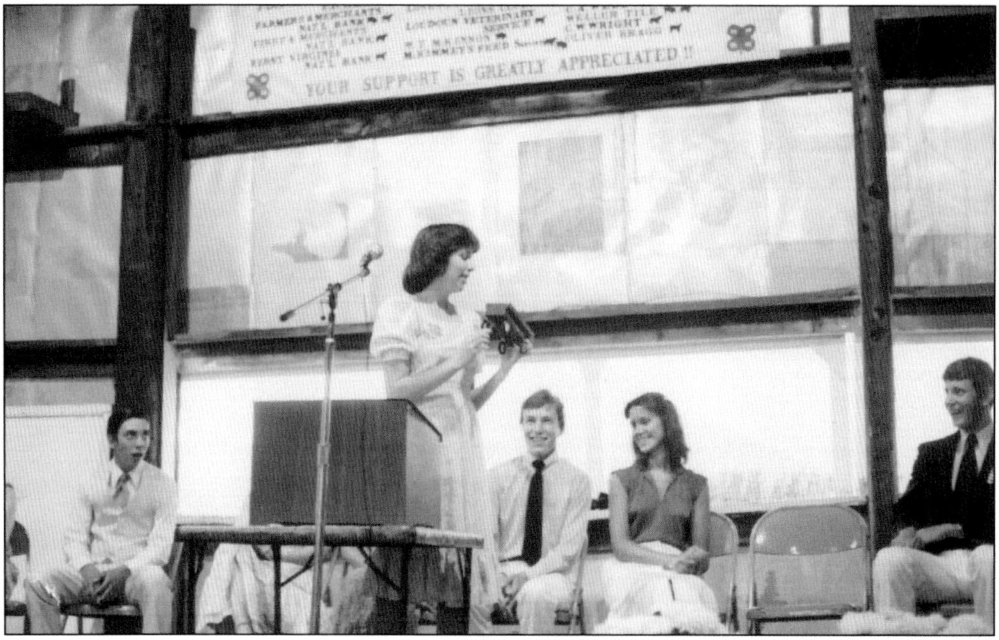

The stage of the show pavilion has been the setting for numerous events since it was built: the Miss Loudoun Fair Pageant, the Womanless Beauty Pageant, bands, and awards ceremonies, just to name a few. In the photograph above, the stage is the setting for this presentation. The youth on the stage are, from left to right, Keith Frye, unidentified, O.T. Trumbo, and two unidentified individuals. (Courtesy of the William H. Cockerill family.)

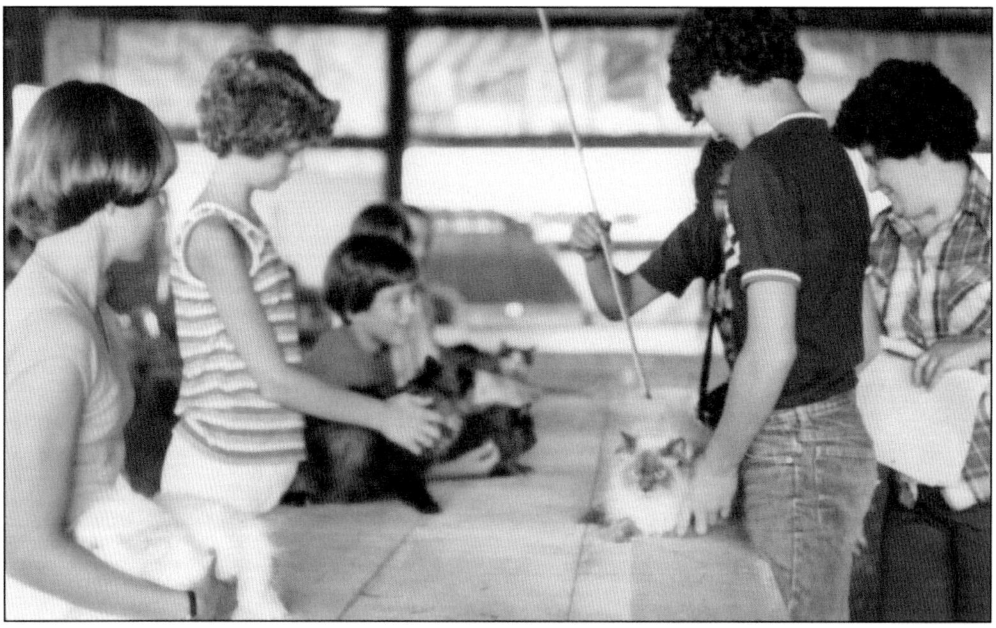

The pet show was one of the fun events held at the fair. There were classes for the 4-H youth and open classes for anyone else that wanted to participate. Animals that could be brought in a carrier or on a leash were welcome. This group is showing their pet cats. On the far right is Geraldine Gardner from the Loudoun Board of Supervisors. (Courtesy of Sykes Hall Archives.)

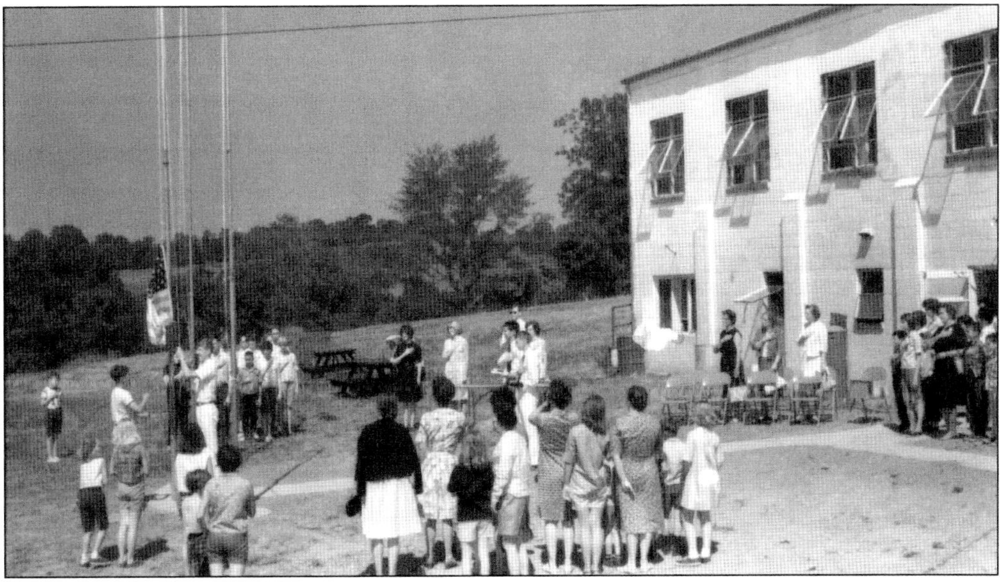

The flag raising was part of the opening ceremony, held in front of Sykes Hall. For the 1966 fair, the photograph above shows the group standing with their hands over their hearts as the flag is raised. Activities were held in and around Sykes Hall throughout the fair days. In the background, one can see the picnic tables that the 4-H planned when the building was under construction. At the ceremony in the image below are, from left to right, (first row) Tommy Herndon, Carol Stowers, Anne Cockerill, and Barbara Fletcher; (second row) Bentz Rhoades, Allen Rollins, Jimmy Cole, and Tommy Fletcher. (Above, courtesy of Carol Stowers McComb; below, courtesy of the William H. Cockerill family.)

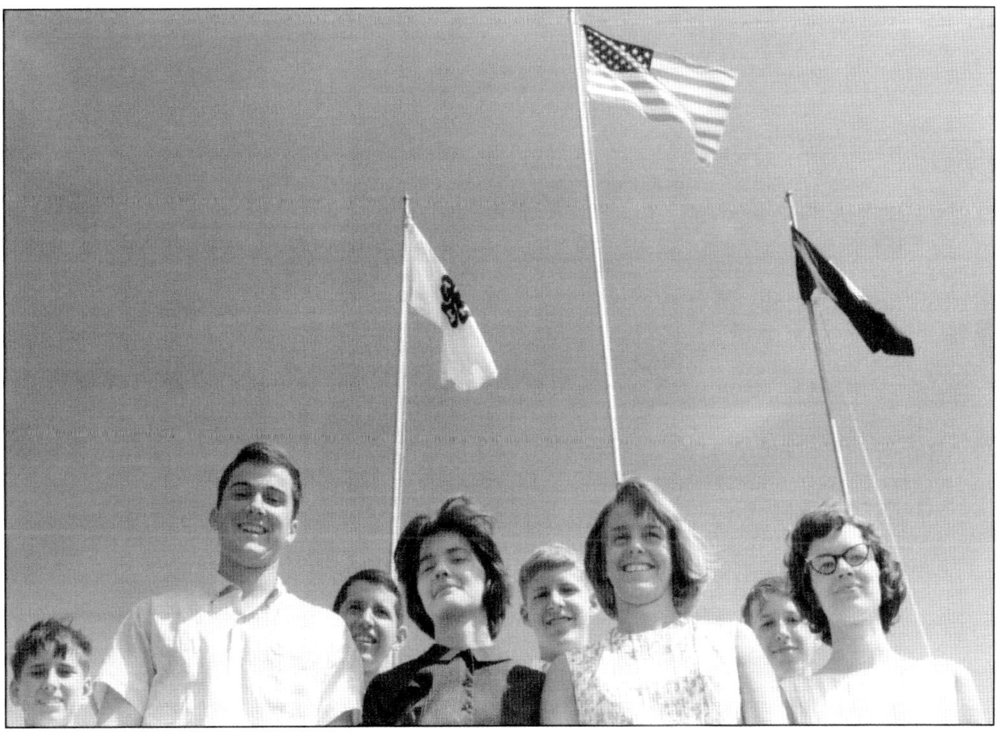

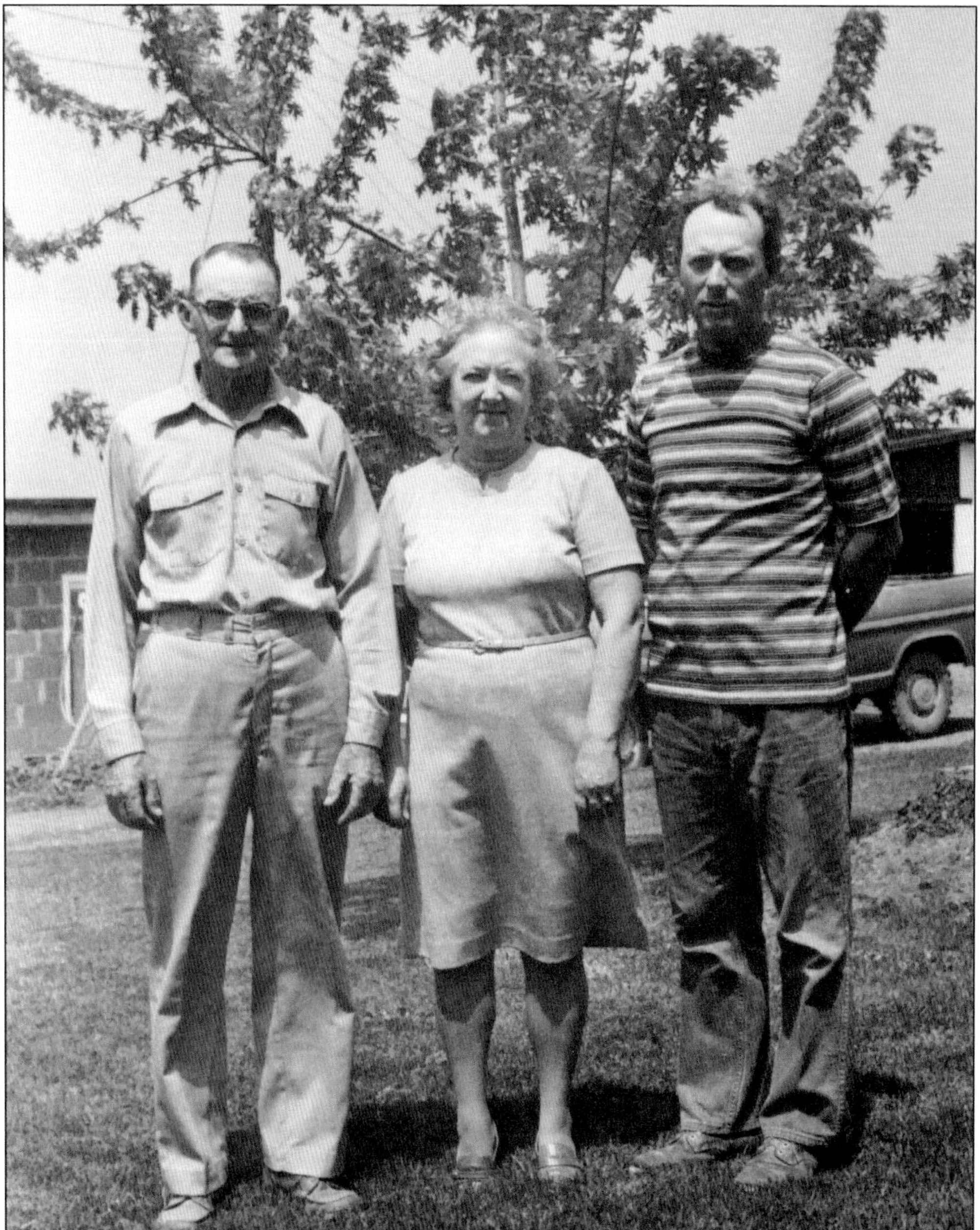

In 1963, the county fair began dedicating the annual event to an individual or family that served the 4-H and the fair in an outstanding way. Some of the earlier dedications were to Eugene E. Sykes, Robert J. McCray, Frank W. McComb, Lawrence H. Taylor, Marvin B. Simpson, William L. Whitmore, J. Lupton Simpson, Lucy Taylor, Ellen "Granny" Stowers, William and Nancy Cockerill, Joe and Cecilia Dillon, and Dorothy Heasley. The fair was dedicated in 1979 to the Peacock family, pictured here, whose farm was not far from the fairgrounds. One of the things they were known for doing was loaning their manure spreader to help clean out the barns after the fair had ended. From left to right are Francis and Virginia Peacock with their son David. (Courtesy of Carol Stowers McComb.)

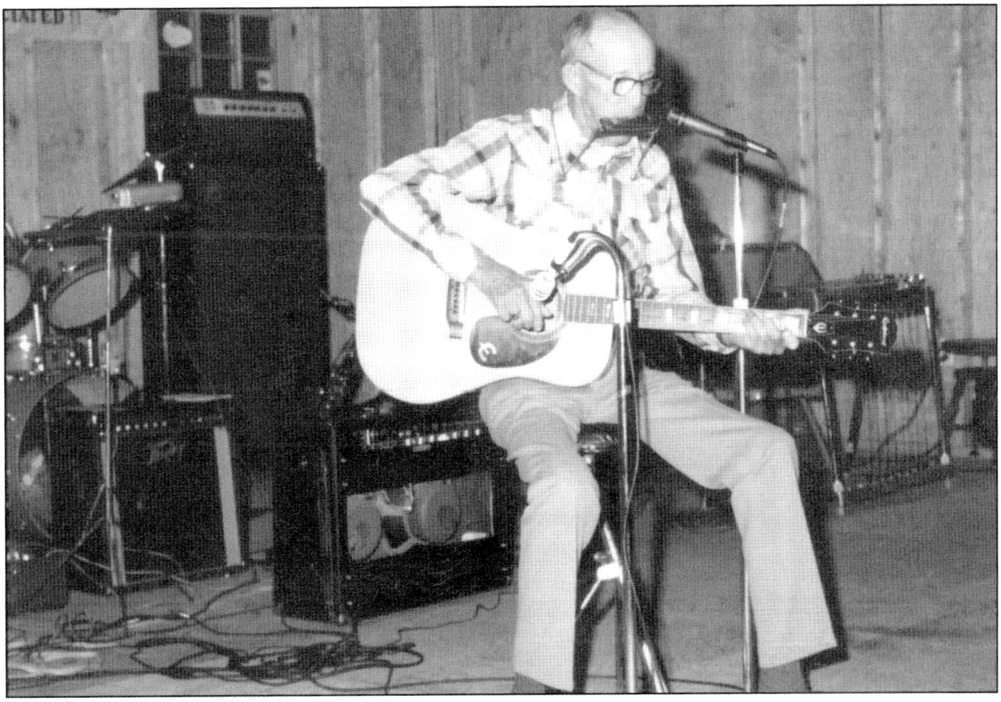

Entertainment acts were used as a way to draw people into the fair and entertain the 4-H clubs and became popular events. One of the favorite entertainment events was the Hootenanny, started by four brothers, Tommy, John, Adin, and Richard Herndon. It was an event that included performances by different people; the Navy band came to play one year. There was a bit of competition between the acts, though purportedly no prizes were awarded. In the above photograph, Jack Hutchison of Aldie plays his guitar for the audience. Below, the gentleman facing toward the camera with the guitar is John Herndon. (Above, courtesy of William Harrison; below, courtesy of Sykes Hall Archives.)

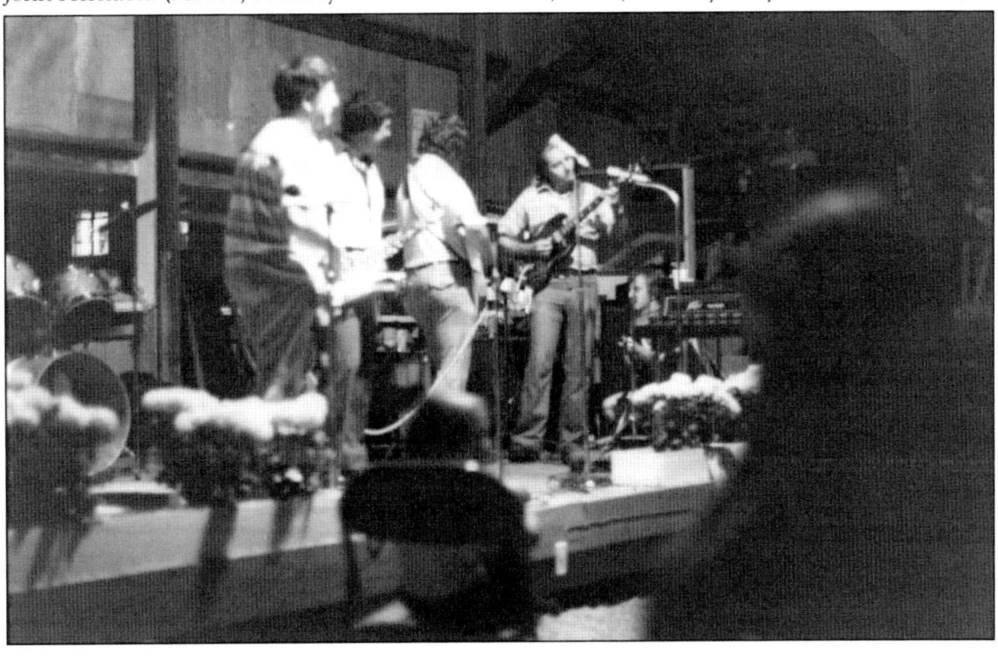

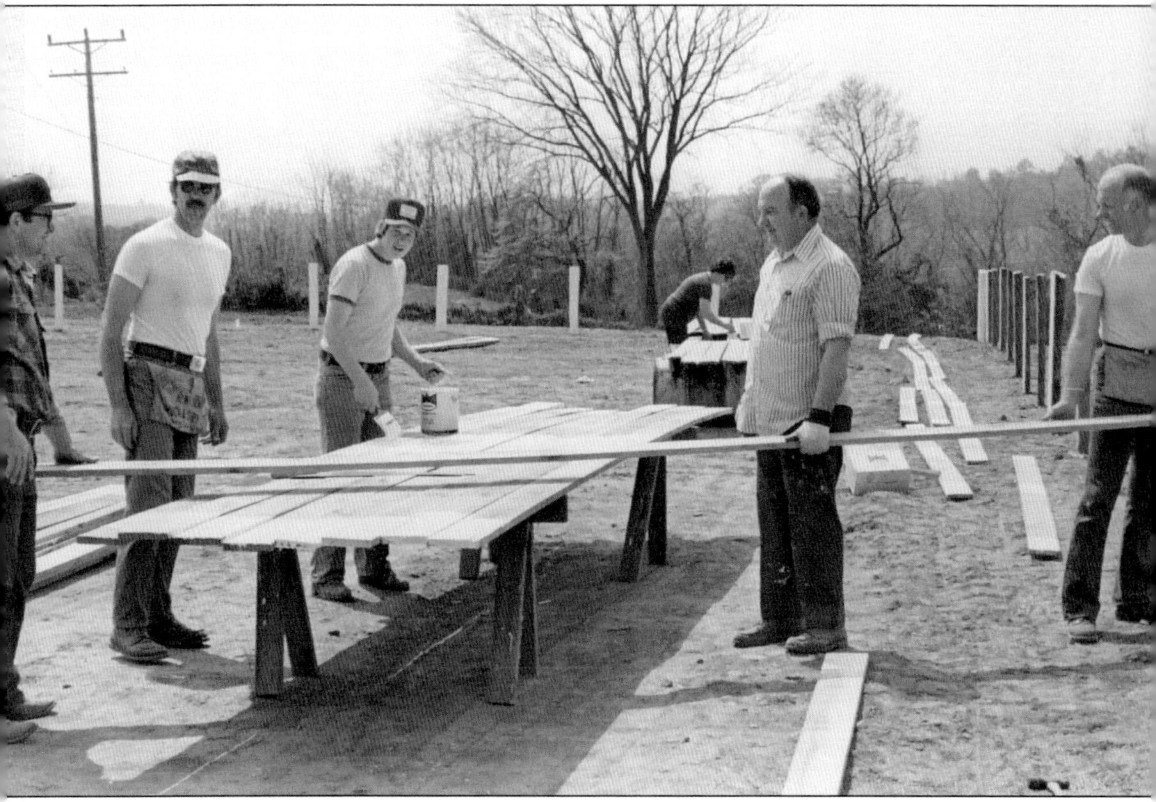

In 1975, the horse ring was rebuilt; when the ring was first constructed on the grounds, it was small and octagonal. The need for a bigger ring was agreed upon, and volunteers worked to enlarge and rebuild. Thomas E. Payne owned an excavating business and was one of the volunteers to work on this project. Holding the board in the center of this photograph is Dan Clemons, an active volunteer with the horse club. Since it was first constructed, the horse ring has held events ranging from Western and English horse shows to pie-eating contests, opening ceremonies, he-man competitions, bike shows, and in later years, the rodeo and demolition derby. It was, and still is, a multipurpose area. (Courtesy of the William H. Cockerill family.)

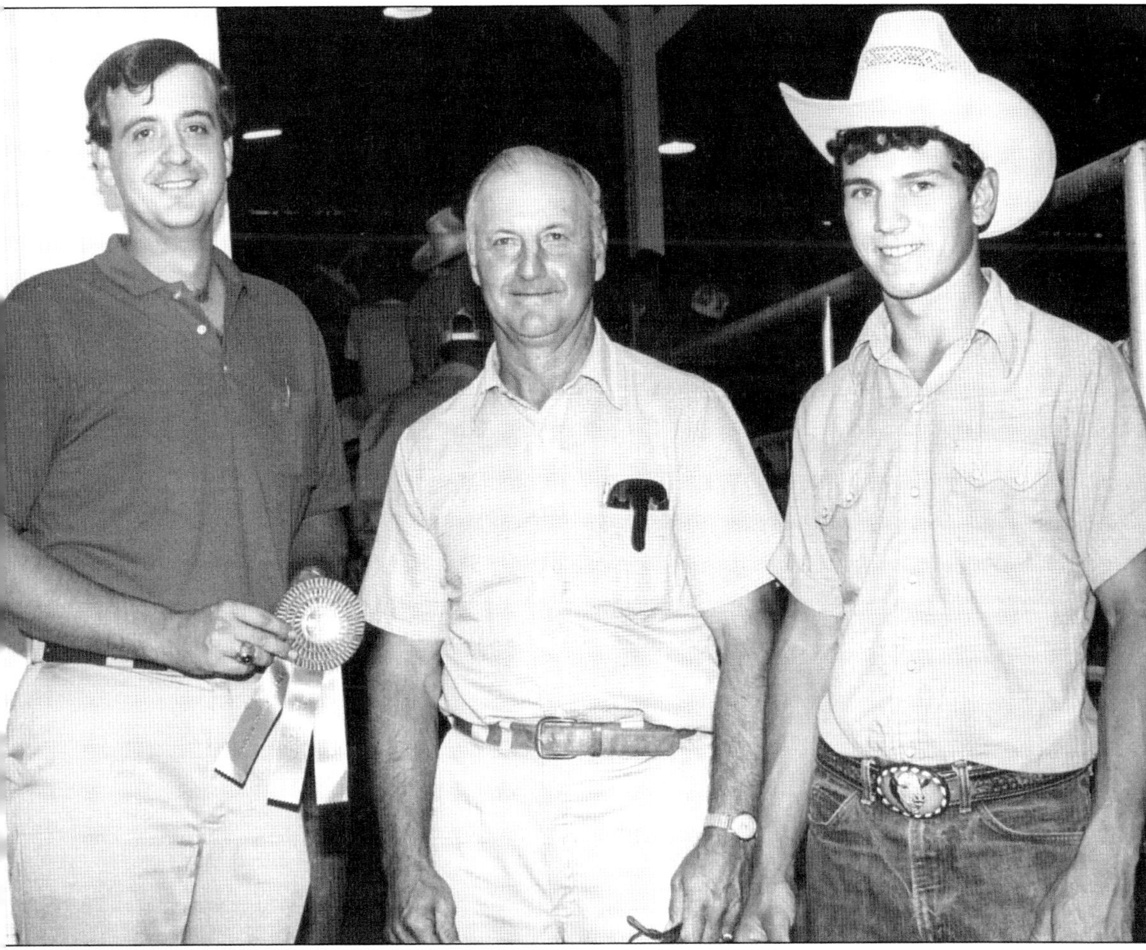

In this photograph, Tommy Payne stands with the buyer of his grand champion hog. Tommy's hog was a Hampshire breed that weighed 228 pounds, and it was purchased by McKimmy Feeds for $2.50 per pound. The 4-H youth work hard to raise an animal they can sell at the livestock auction. When they raise a champion animal, it is an especially proud moment. From left to right are Mel Whitely, James McKimmy, and Tommy Payne. During his years in 4-H, Payne showed swine and cattle. Years later, after aging out of 4-H, he volunteered with the fair. He is credited with leading and assisting in many accomplishments on the grounds, including acquiring a water tank and adding onto Sykes Hall, among others. Without the tireless support of Payne and other volunteers like him, the fair could not continue to grow each year. (Courtesy of Tommy Payne.)

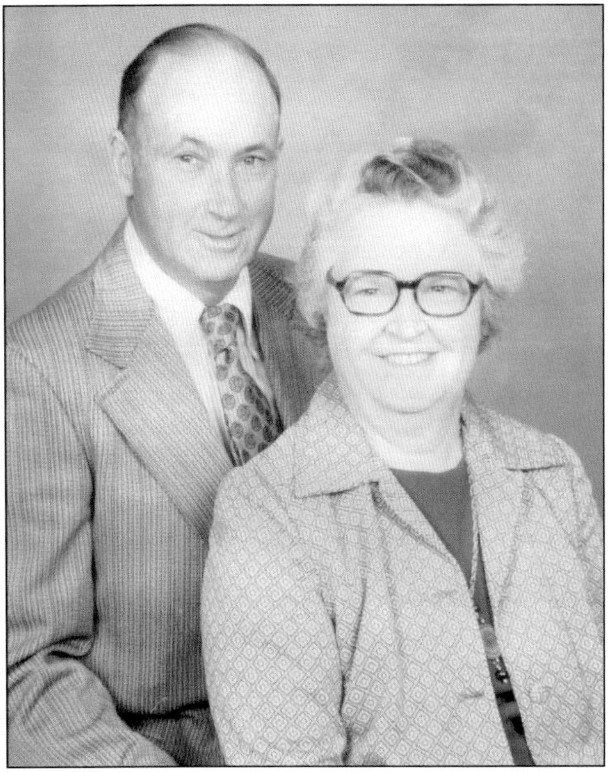

Pictured at left are Nelson and Ethel Ashby; both have dedicated time and energy toward making the Loudoun 4-H youth and the Loudoun County 4-H Fair a success. The fair was dedicated to Nelson in 1978. In 1993, a 4-H scholarship was established to honor the efforts of Nelson Ashby and Ellen "Granny" Stowers. The womanless fashion show was a time for the men to dress up as women and compete against each other. In the photograph below, Nelson Ashby is dressed in his finest dress, holding a dog collar with an invisible dog. The men are, from left to right, unidentified, Nelson Ashby, James "Jim" Colbert, and Francis Peacock. (Both, courtesy of Carol Stowers McComb.)

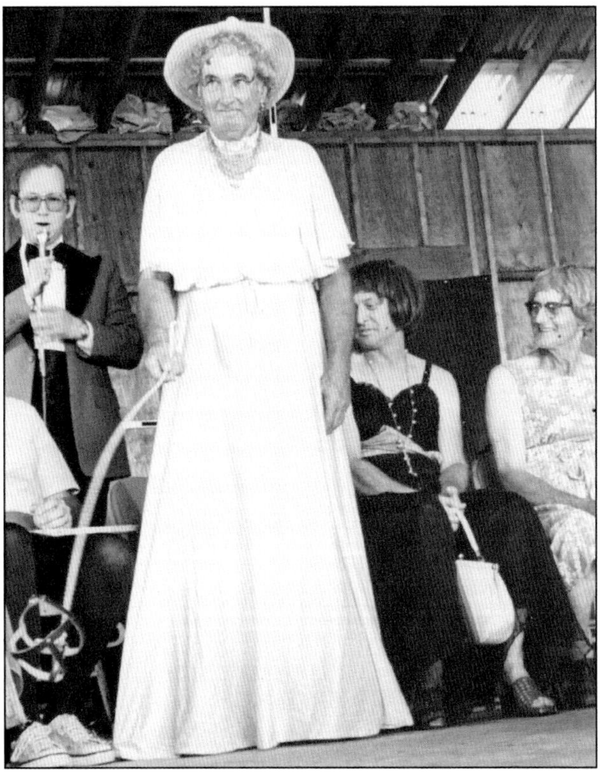

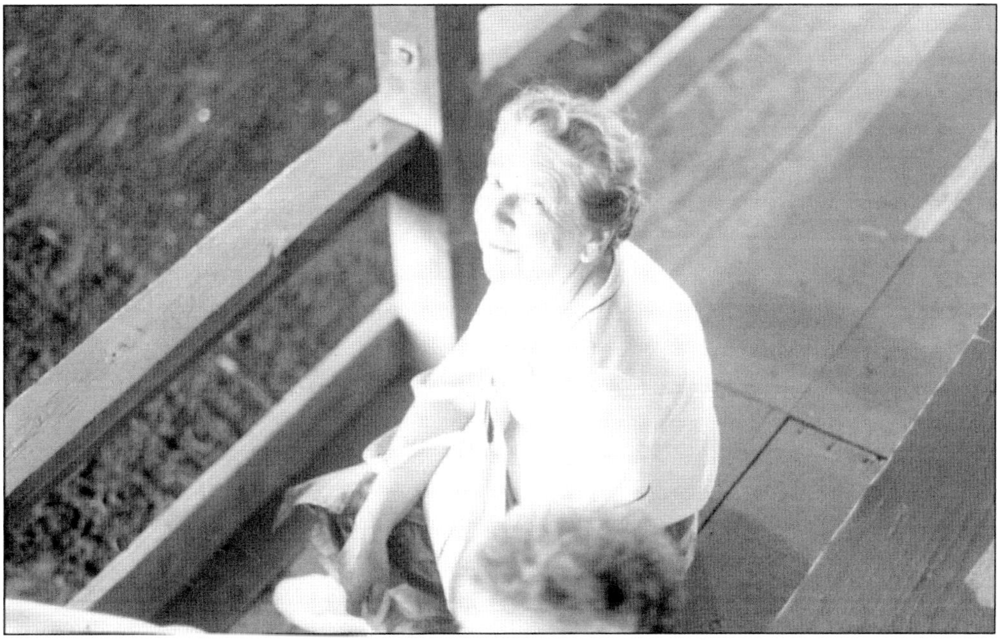

Ellen Stowers takes time from watching an event in the show pavilion to smile for the camera. Known by everyone as Granny, the fair was dedicated to her in 1969 for her tireless work with the 4-H. The Ashby/Stowers Scholarship was established in part to honor Stowers for her dedication as a 4-H leader and supporter. (Courtesy of Sykes Hall Archives.)

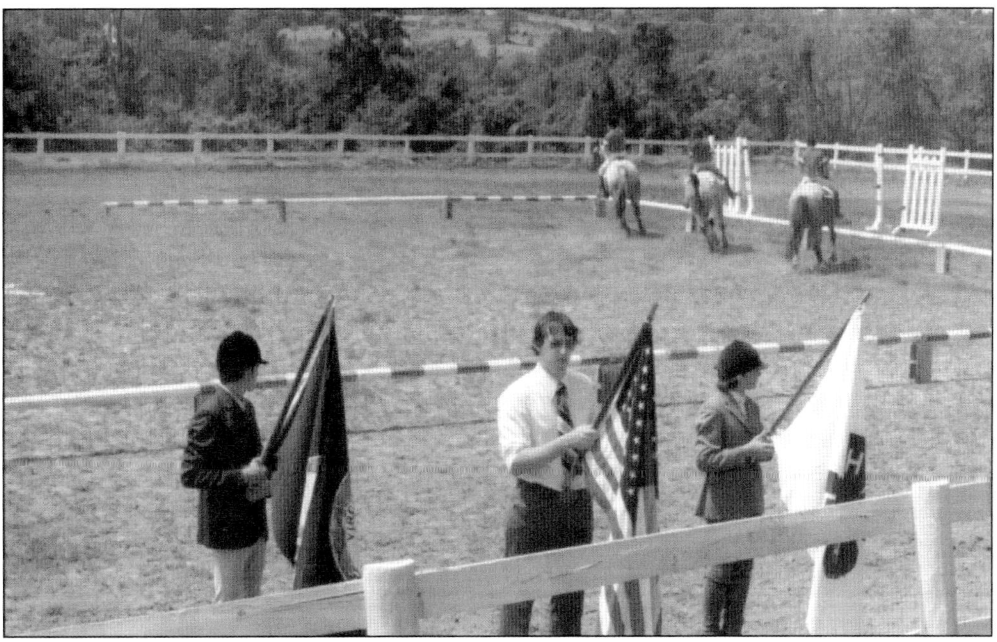

The opening ceremony of the Loudoun County 4-H Fair was a big event during which the volunteers welcomed the public to the fair and volunteers were honored. In this photograph, the horses are a part of the ceremony. The flags shown are the flag of Virginia, the American flag, and the 4-H flag. Holding the American flag is Jimmy Cromer. (Courtesy of Sykes Hall Archives.)

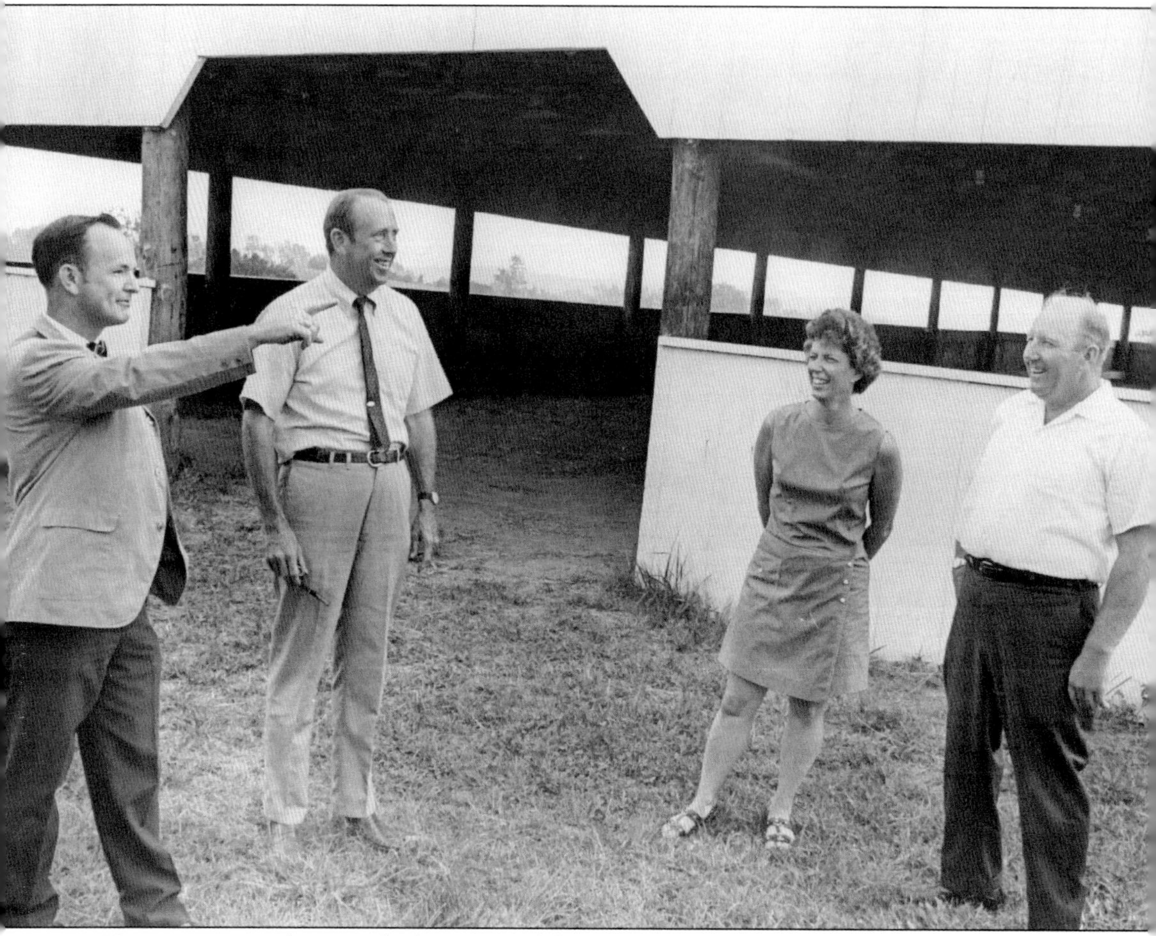

Hours went into planning the big event celebrating the 50th annual fair. An article on the fair's history was written for a catalog by Carol Stowers McComb, images were compiled for the cover of the catalog, and an official 50th logo was designed by Maxine Cole. Events for the celebration included an open horse show, burying a time capsule, and the greased pole contest. The greased pole contest was a fun event for the 4-H'ers. According to Hank McCall, the perfect locust tree had to be found, cut down, and trimmed smooth. The goal was to climb a slick, greased pole to the top and claim the prize of a silver dollar. The boys would cover themselves in mud so they could have more traction to get farther up the pole. The 4-H alumni from left to right are Fred Howard, Jim Tyler, Peggy Anne Benedum, and Edgar Tillett. (Courtesy of Carol Stowers McComb.)

Six

The Grand Parade

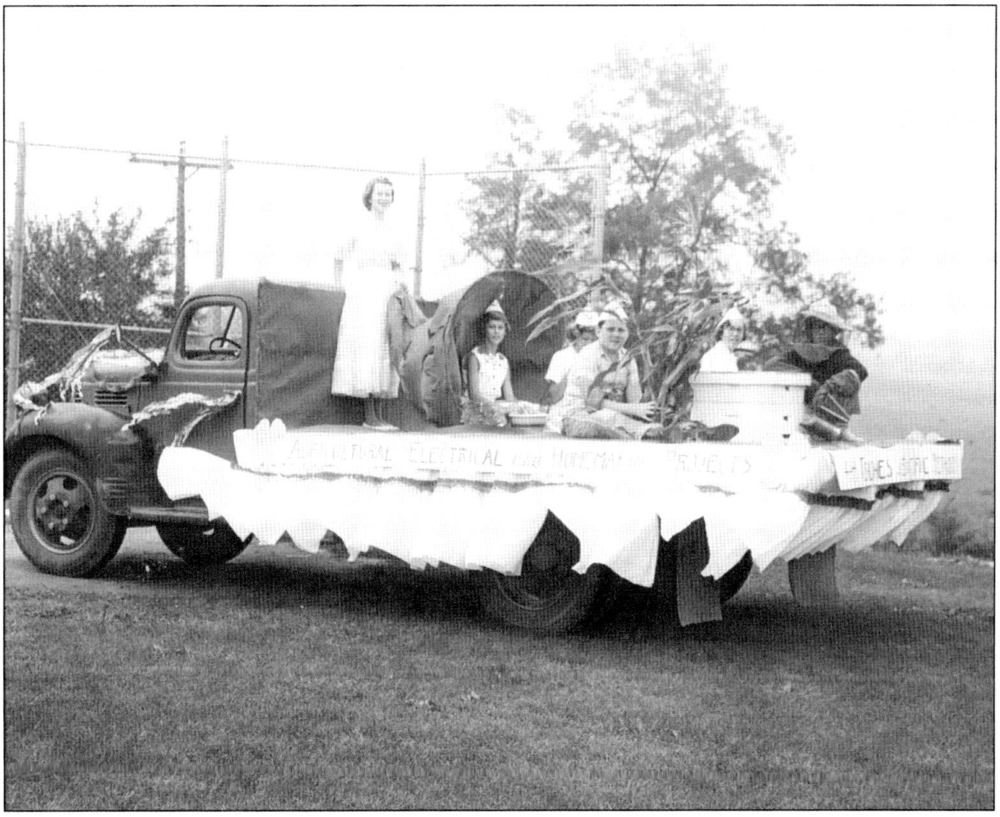

As part of the Parade of Champions (originally known as the Grand Parade of Livestock and Exhibits) at the end of each fair, the 4-H clubs designed, built, and rode on floats representing their organizations. This float features the Leesburg Junior Club at the Purcellville fairgrounds in the 1940s. The banner across the float read, "Agricultural, and Homemaking Projects. 4-H Teaches Scientific Method." (Courtesy of the William H. Cockerill family.)

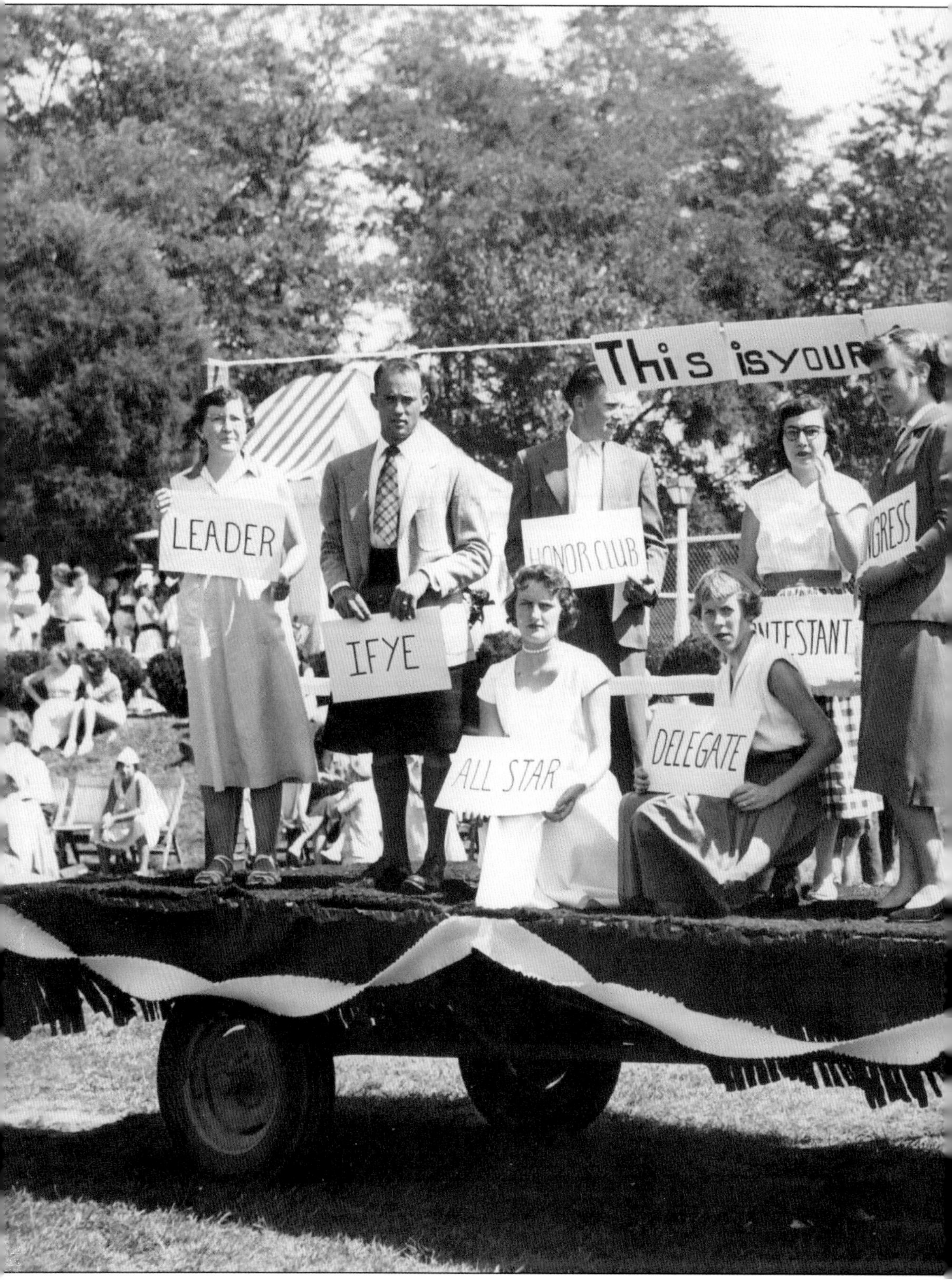
This is your
LEADER
IFYE
HONOR CLUB
ALL STAR
DELEGATE
NTESTANT
NGRESS

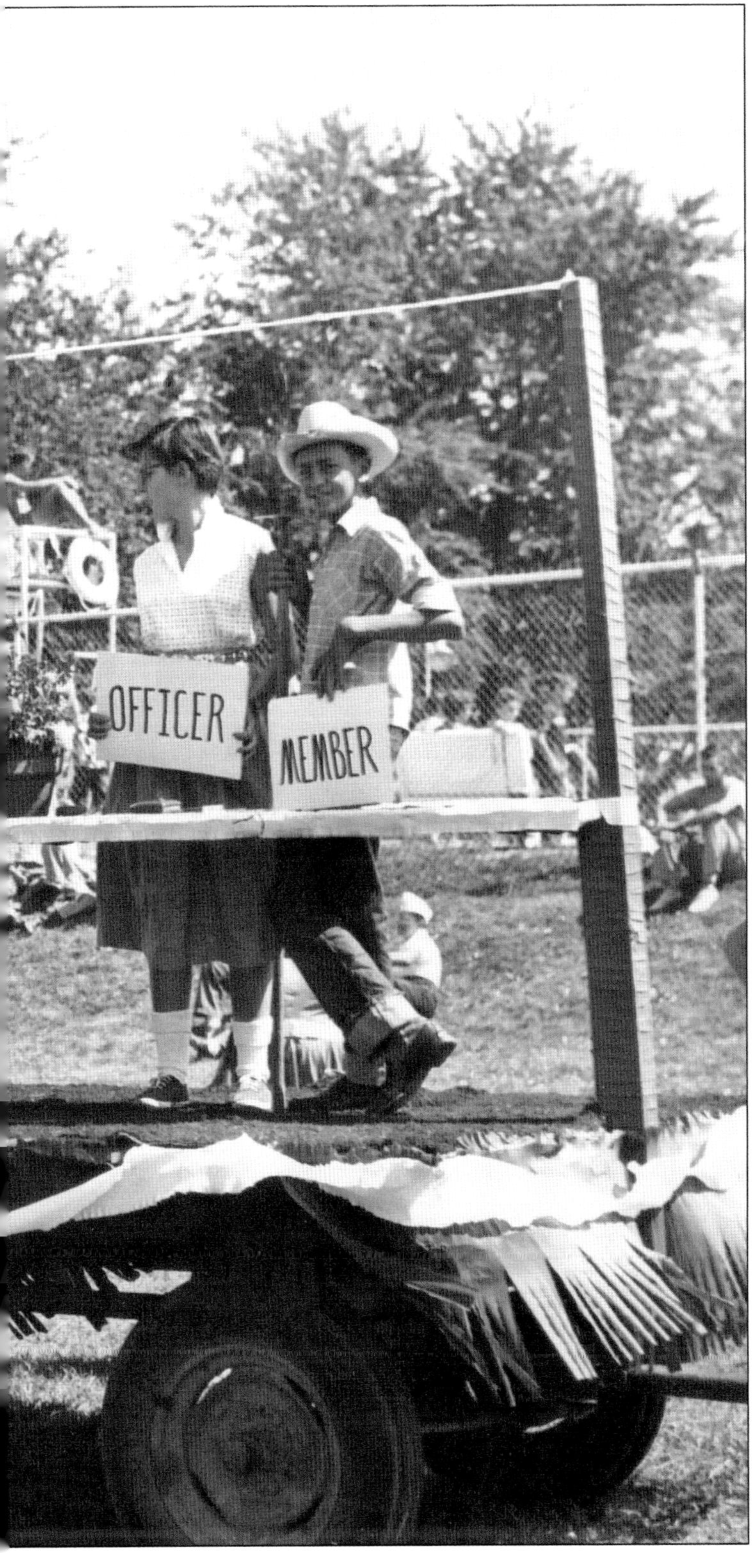

The Lovettsville Senior Club was competitive when it came to building and designing their float. This float from the 1954 parade in Middleburg features high school youth and their leader showing roles or positions they have held in 4-H. Their attire is also a reflection of the roles in 4-H. The banner states, "This is your 4-H'er." Standing on the left is the club leader, Dorothy Rickard, who exhibited at the first 4-H fair in 1936. Beside Rickard is Frank Keesling holding his IFYE sign with pride. The IFYE program was established in 1948 to give young adults an in-depth experience learning about life in other countries. Keesling was an IFYE to Scotland; note the kilt he is wearing to demonstrate his time across the pond. A small number of 4-H'ers become IFYEs. The other youth on the parade float are unidentified. (Courtesy of Carol Stowers McComb.)

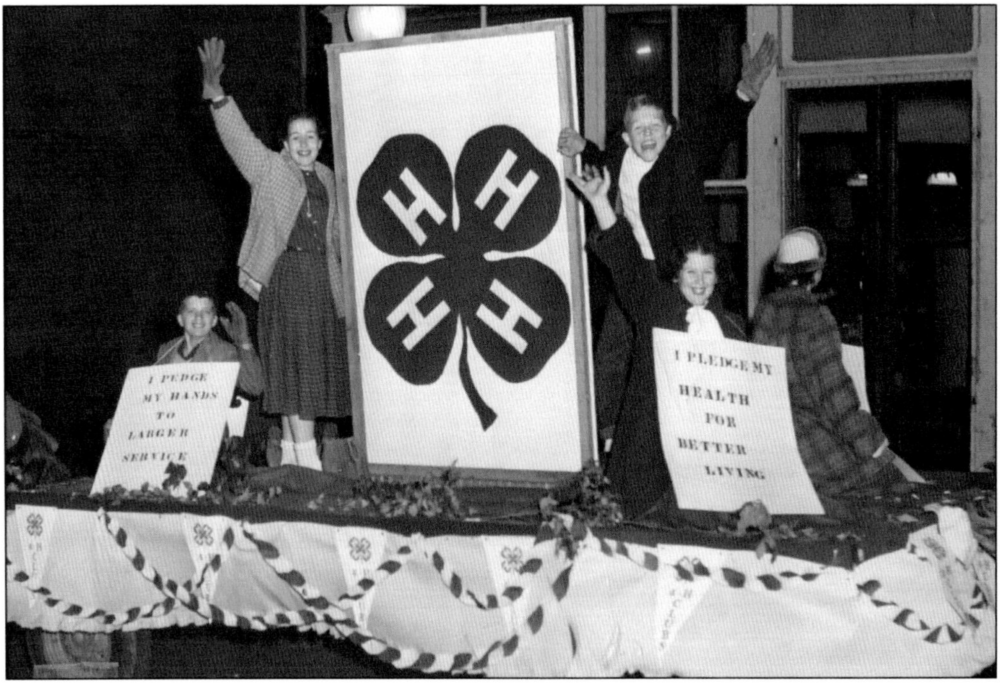

While most of the parade floats were shown in the fair parades, there was the opportunity for the 4-H'ers to display their float in a community parade. This photograph shows a 4-H float in the Leesburg Halloween Parade in 1954. On the float are, from left to right, John Stowers, Ruthie Crosen, Sonny Crosen, and unidentified. (Courtesy of Sykes Hall Archives.)

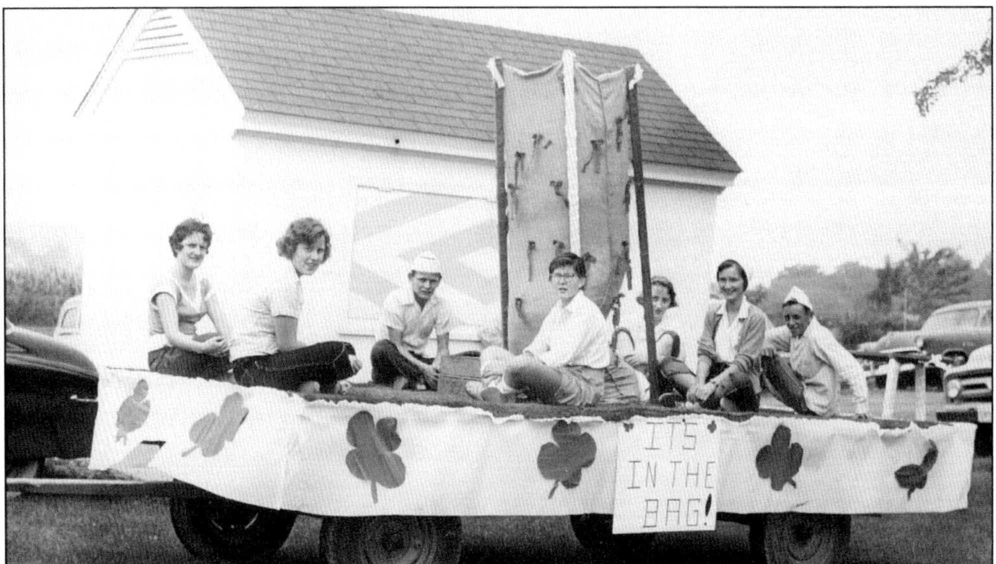

This is the Lovettsville first-place parade float in 1955. In the bag were prize-winning exhibits from that year's fair that the 4-H'ers would pull out as the float progressed. The last item in the bag was 4-Her Edwin Utterback, surprising the audience when he appeared. On the float are, from left to right, unidentified, Betty Jo Utterback, George Washington, Jane Keister, Juanita Love, Ann Hickman, and David Frye. (Courtesy of Carol Stowers McComb.)

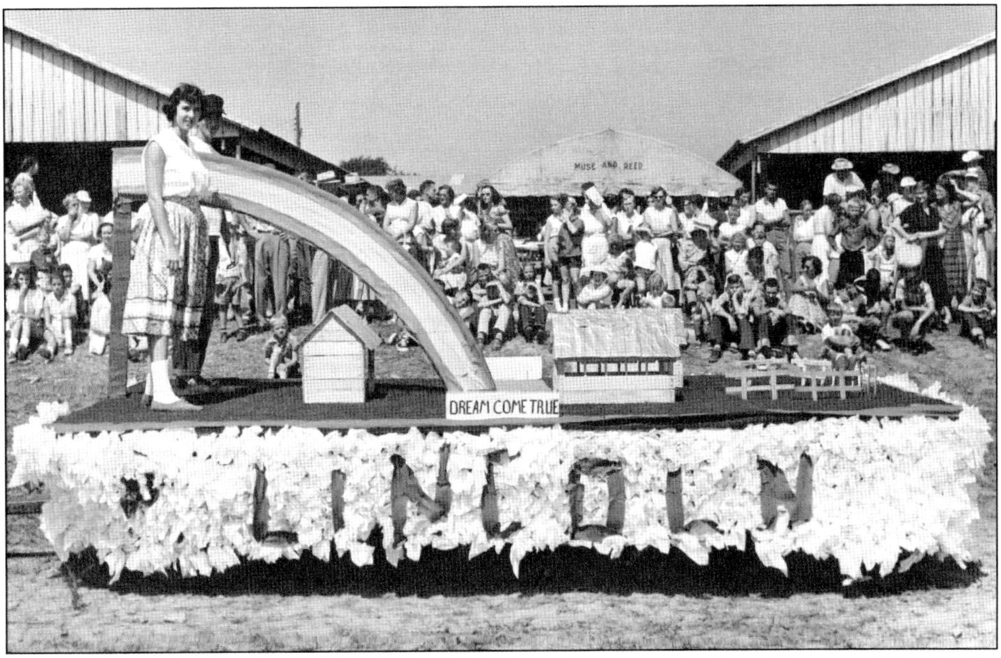

The Lincoln Community parade float from 1958 showed barns and a fenced-in area with animals. The setting at the end of the rainbow is a "Dream Come True." Riding on the float is Mariam Simpson. Underneath the rainbow in the audience watching the parade is Tommy Cockerill. (Courtesy of the William H. Cockerill family.)

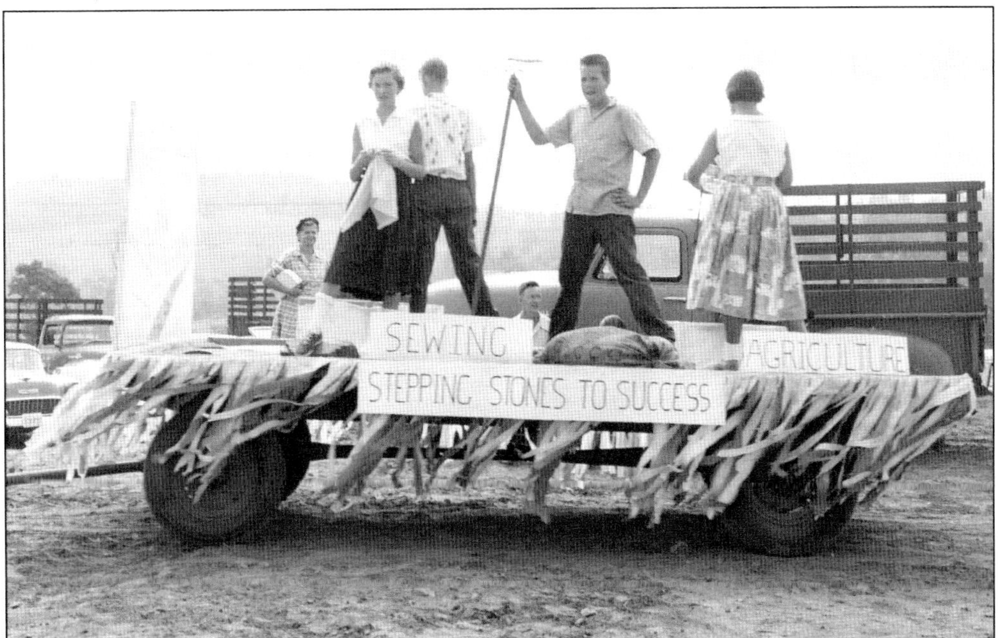

This float from an unidentified club is in a parade that was held on the fairgrounds outside of Leesburg in the late 1950s. The 4-H'ers on the float titled "Stepping Stones to Success" demonstrated various 4-H activities in which they took part within their club. (Courtesy of the William H. Cockerill family.)

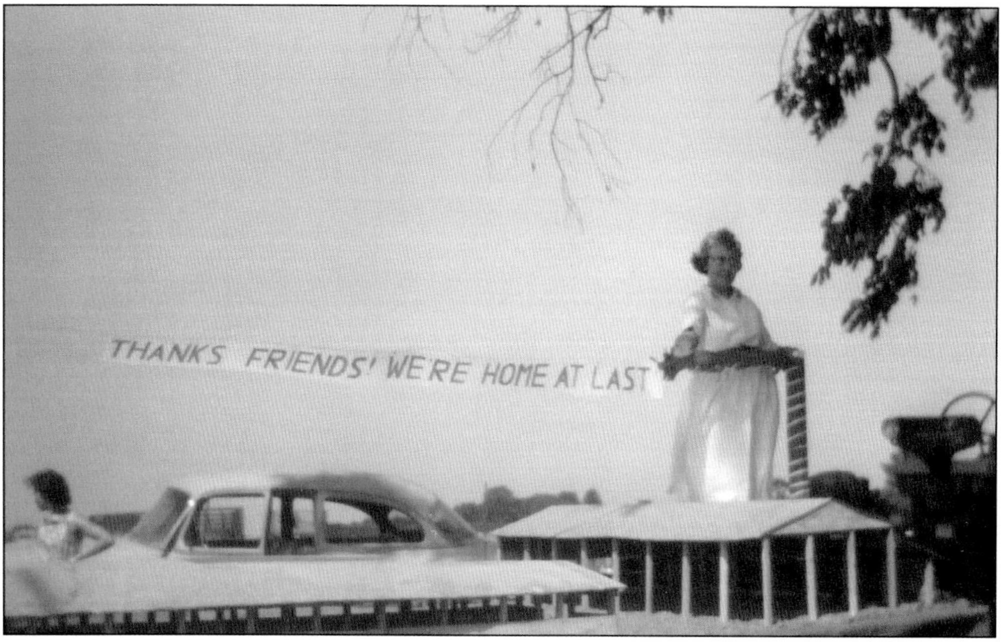

The photographs on this page are of the 1958 Lovettsville float. Since this was the year following the first fair held on the new grounds, the club wanted to celebrate the fact that they had a permanent place, a home for the 4-H'ers and the fair. The buildings on the float are replicas of the buildings on the grounds to date. In the above photograph is a clear view of the show pavilion. The angle on the image below shows the two livestock barns. Every detail was taken into account when the Lovettsville Senior Club designed this float. (Both, courtesy of Mary Virginia Keesling.)

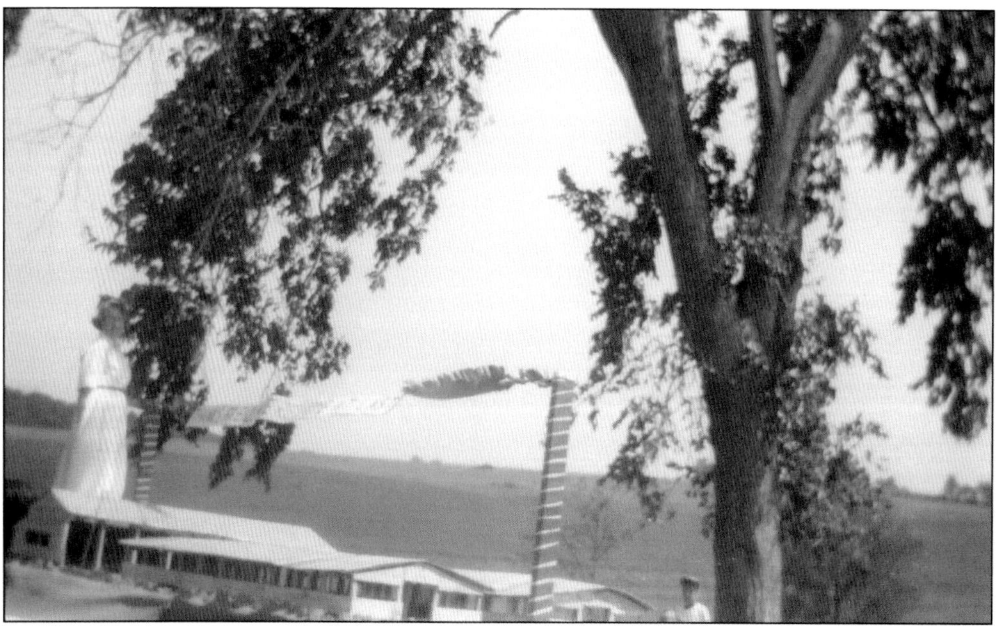

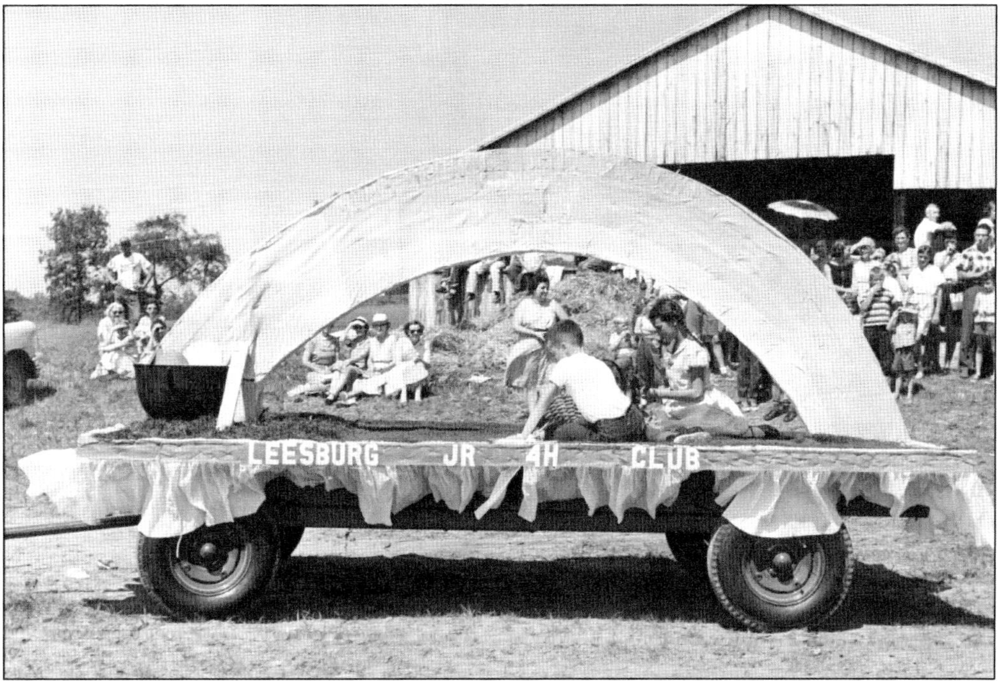

The Leesburg Junior 4-H Club float shows a pot of gold at the end of the rainbow, and in the background is one of the livestock barns. The junior 4-H clubs were as active in building and showing off their floats as the senior clubs. With each of the floats came a sense of teamwork and pride. (Courtesy of James Colbert.)

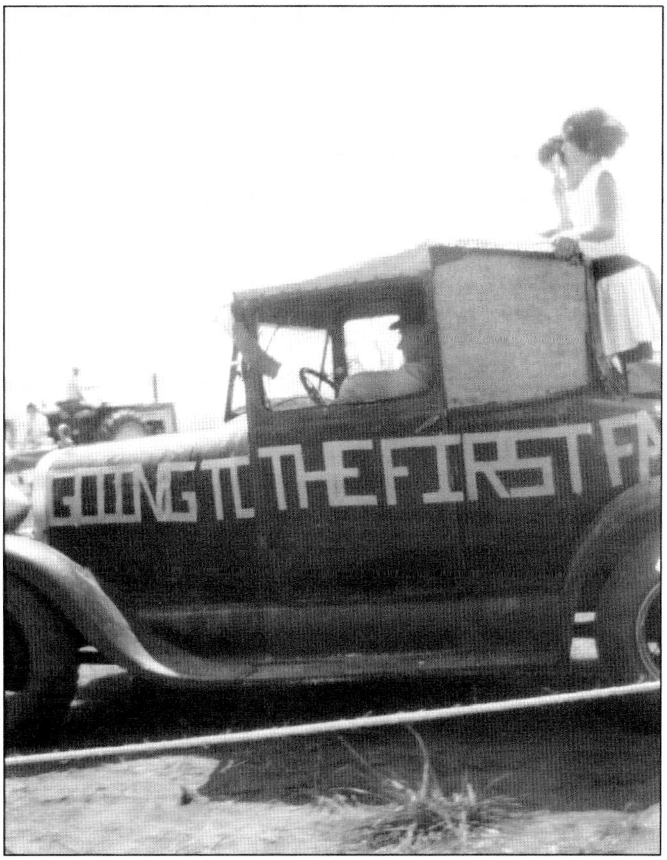

The truck in this parade from 1960 is the float. The theme of this float was "Going to the First Fair," looking back to the beginning from the 25th annual event. In the background, one can see a tractor pulling another float. (Courtesy of Mary Virginia Keesling.)

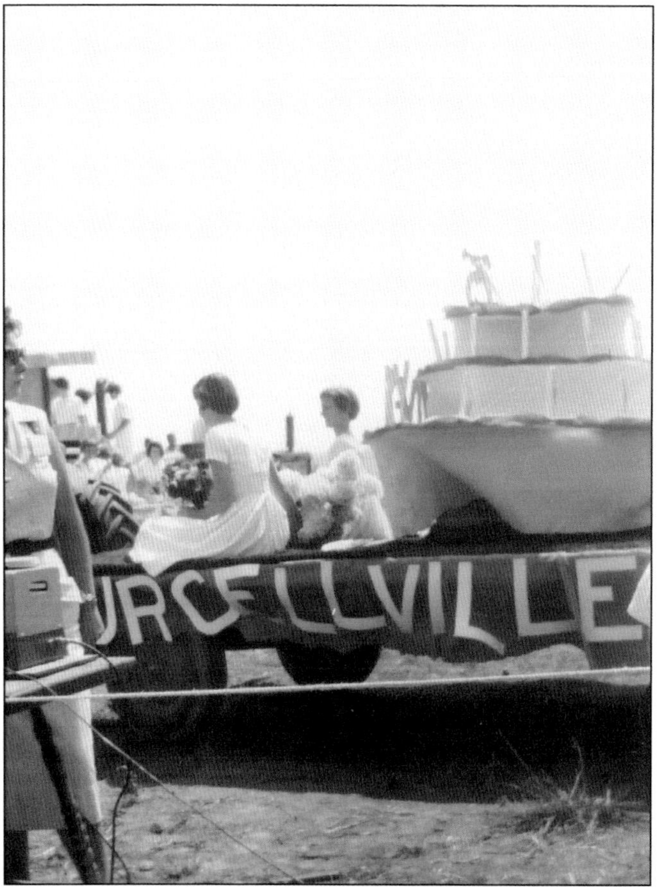

These images are from the 1960 parade. At left, the Purcellville float features a cake, celebrating 25 years of the Loudoun County 4-H Fair. Below is the Lovettsville Senior Club float, with members, from left to right, Jane Virts, Eleanor Smith (leader), Connie Smith, Frank Keesling, George Darr, and unidentified. The float, titled, "How Big is Your 4-H Clover?" was in a competition described by Frank Keesling as fierce. He also told the story of how this float was created. Chicken wire was wrapped around the form, and tissues were stuffed into the chicken wire. A.L. Hutton, an agriculture teacher at Loudoun County High School, just down the road from the grounds, let the club put the float together in the school shop so they did not have far to drive. (Both, courtesy of Mary Virginia Keesling.)

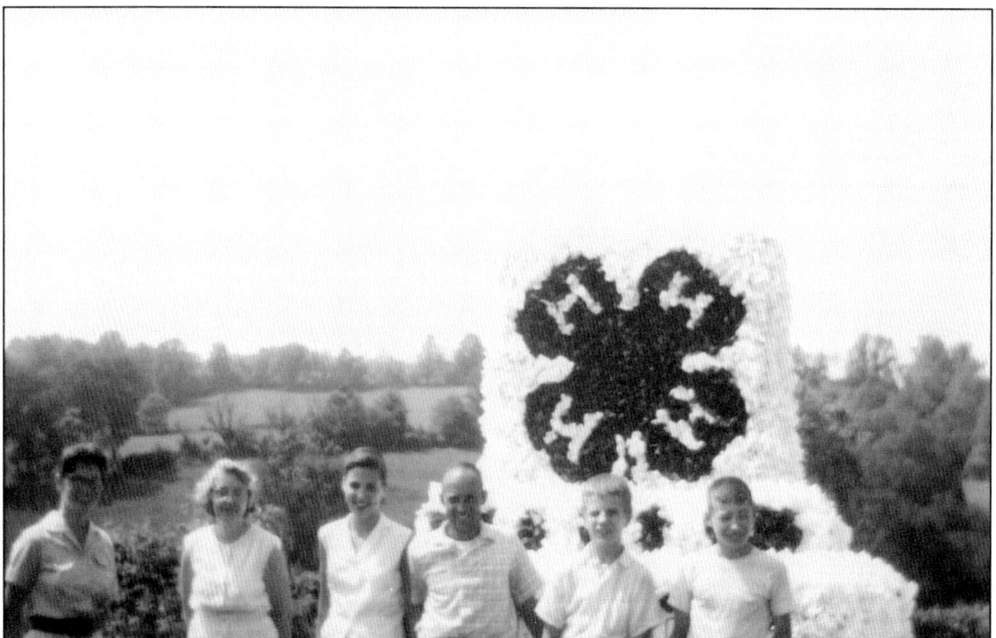

The floats in these photographs are passing by the show pavilion with onlookers observing from inside in 1962. In the image at right, the Lincoln Junior 4-H Club float sign salutes the Loudoun 4-H parents and agents. They are the "Cream of the Crop." Note that the children are saluting as they pass by the audience. The photograph below is of the Leesburg 4-H Club float. The theme of this float is "4-H Takes Time for Fun!" The signs the members are holding are examples of the things they do in 4-H that are fun—the fair, short course, and camp. (Both, courtesy of Mary Virginia Keesling.)

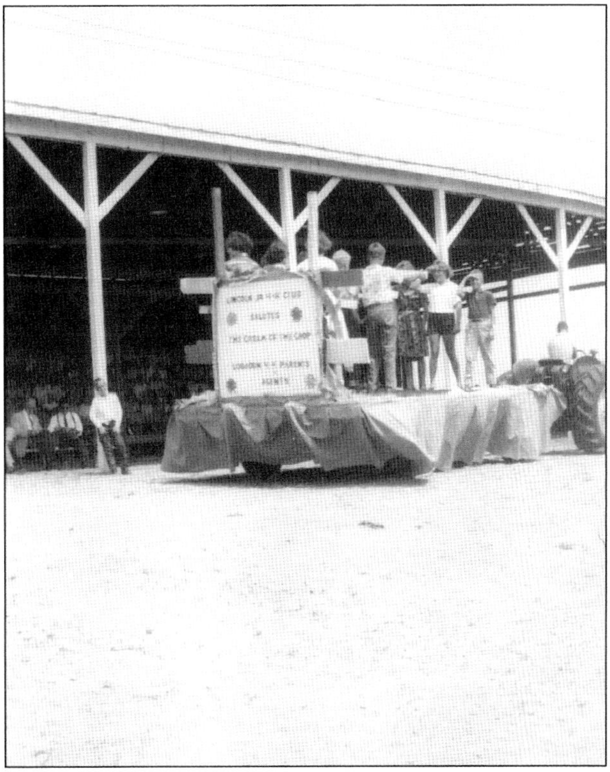

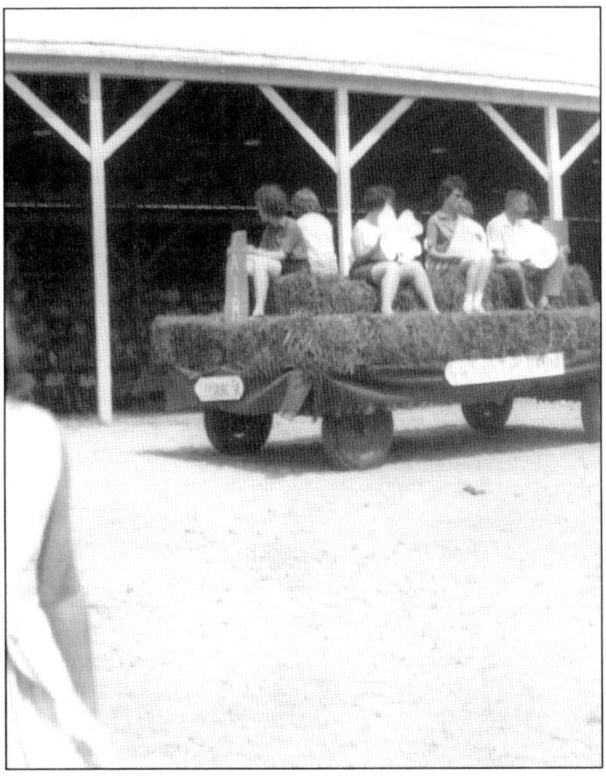

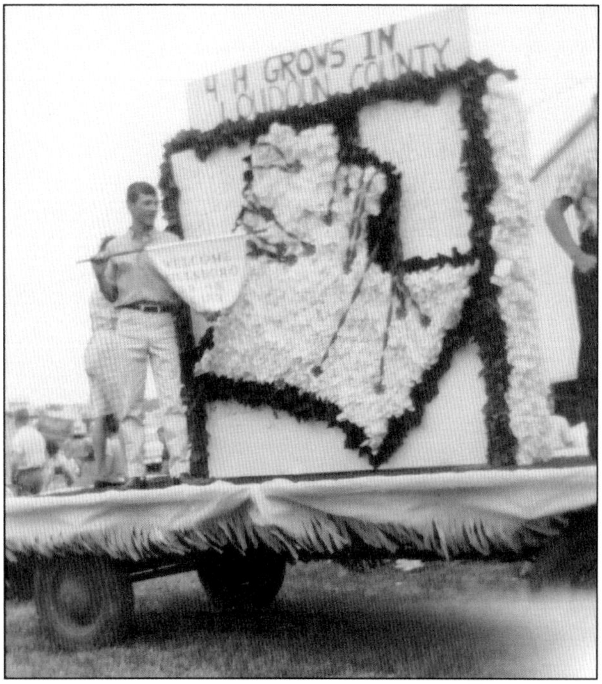

The parade floats on this page are also from 1962. At left is the Hillsboro Senior Club float with a theme of "4-H Grows in Loudoun County." The design in the center is of Loudoun County. Around the map are the names of the 4-H community clubs, and the dots point out the location of each of the clubs within the county. The float below is designed and shown by the Waterford Club. The signs on the float represent the 4-H pledge; "Clearer Thinking," "Greater Loyalty," "Larger Service," and "Better Living" are displayed. (Both, courtesy of Mary Virginia Keesling.)

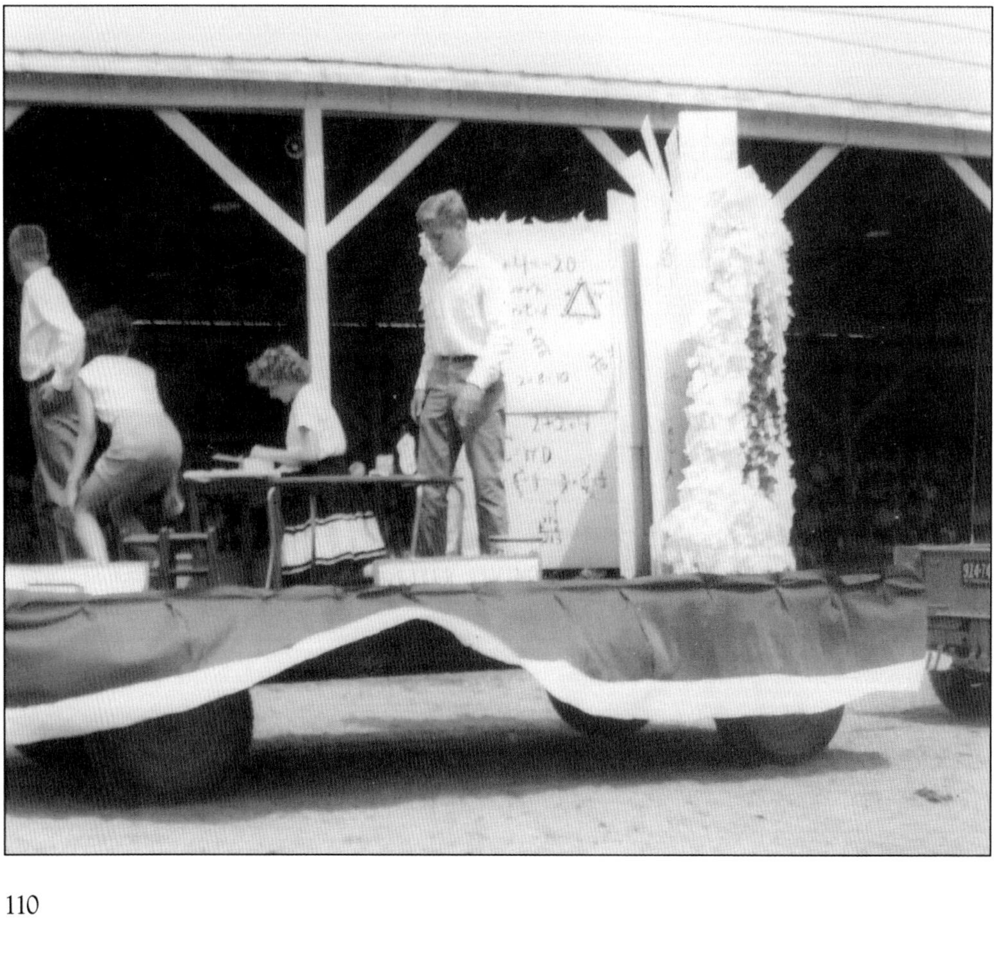

Seven

Scenes from Today

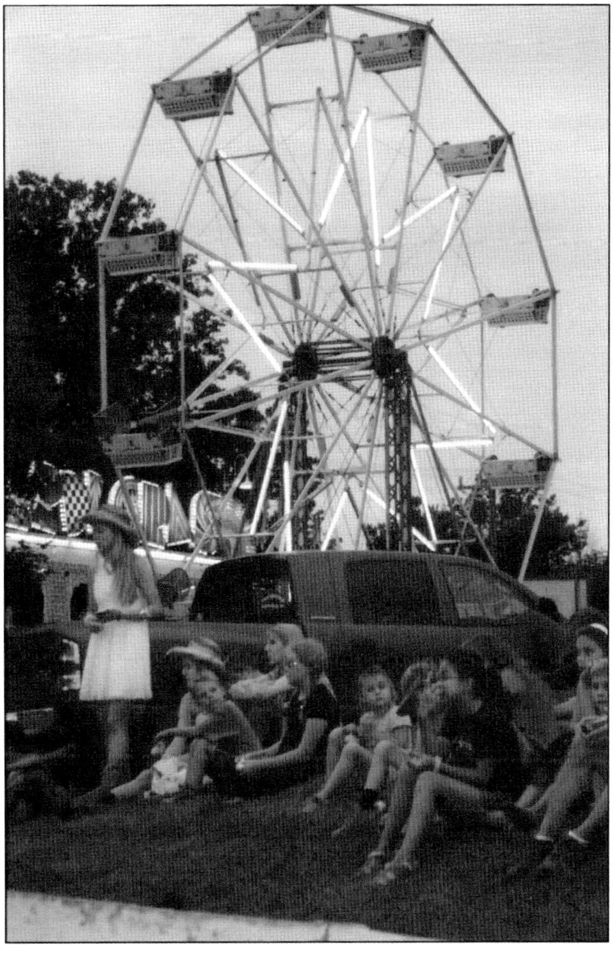

A carnival was added to the fair in the 1990s. In this photograph, the audience is watching a rubber-duck race sponsored by Ketterman's Jewelers in Leesburg on Sunday night, prior to opening day of the fair in 2014. The audience members are, from left to right, Cary Brown, Monica Stone, Sean Csizmadia, JoAnne Sulak, Catherine Klinkam, Brinn McClintic, unidentified, Caitlin Baltazar, and unidentified. (Courtesy of Mark Gaylord.)

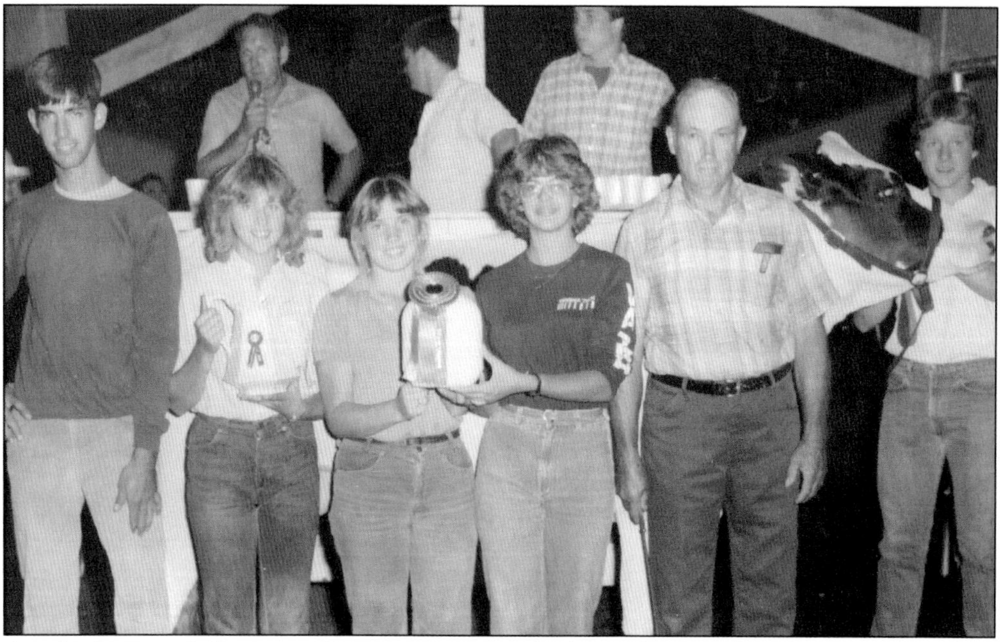

As a fundraiser to help support the maintenance and upkeep of the Loudoun fairgrounds, a gallon of milk from the Dairy Supreme Champion cow was entered in the livestock auction. From the beginning, this was a fruitful mission. In the nine years that a "Golden Gallon of Milk" was sold, it raised $54,000. In the above photograph, Greg Harrison (far right), owner of the Golden Gallon, is pictured in 1981 with his supreme champion Holstein. Also in the picture are, from left to right, Tim Potts, Bonnie Holiday, Karen McComb, Mary Schultz, and Nelson Ashby. In the photograph below, Kathy McComb stands with her supreme champion Holstein. The milk from Kathy's cow raised a record $20,000 for one gallon. Fellow 4-H member Chris Vest holds the gallon of milk. (Above, courtesy of William Harrison; below, courtesy of Carol Stowers McComb.)

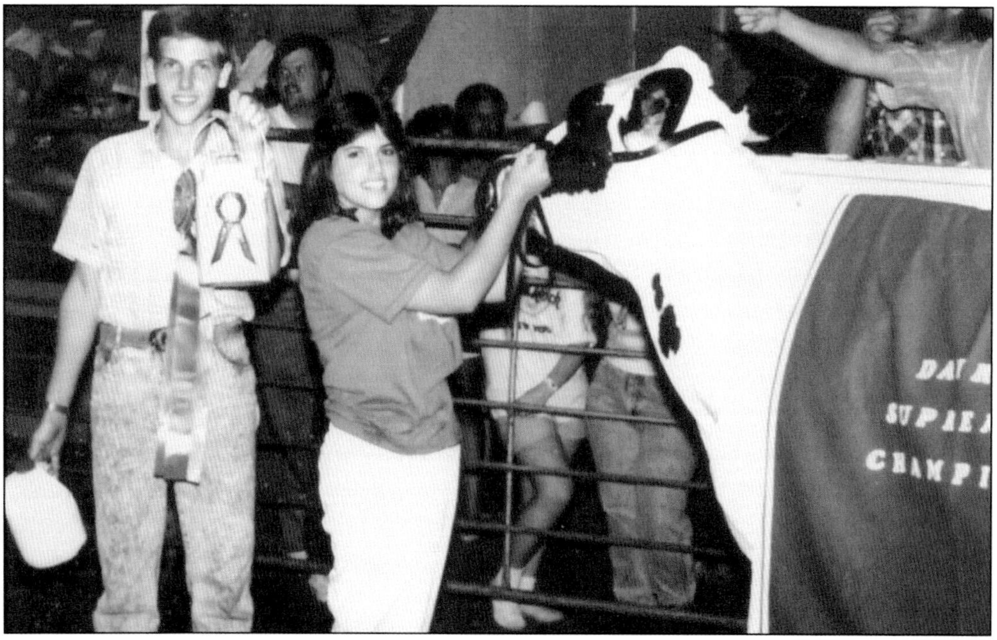

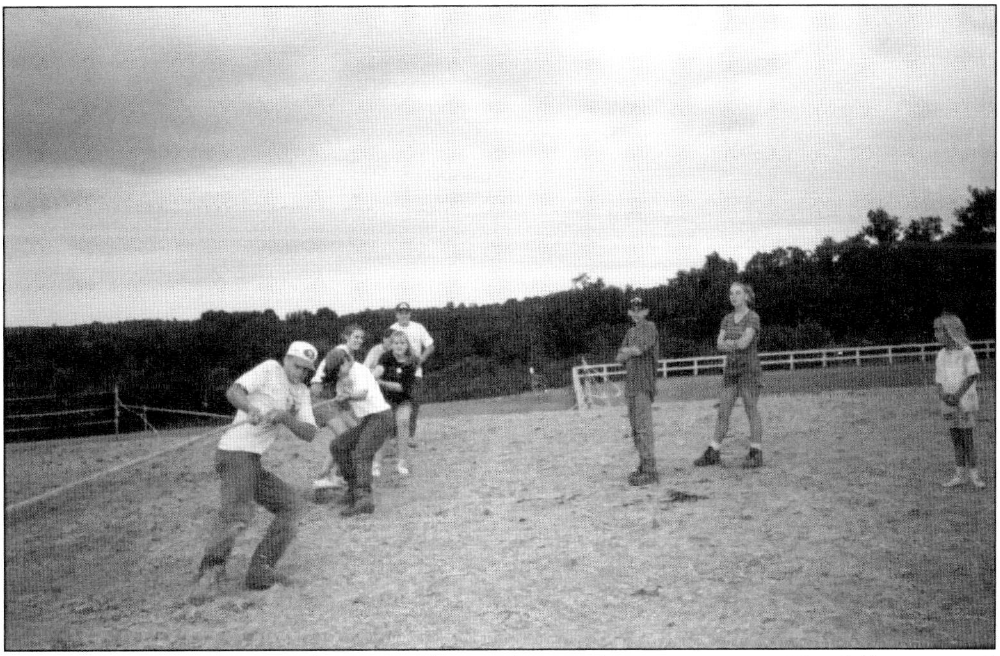

A fun time for participants and viewers alike was the tug-of-war competition. Two different tug-of-war competitions were held on a given year. A 4-H member and parent class consisted of 10 member teams, half of which had to be girls. A Jackpot class was open to the public. These teams had to pay $100 to enter. (Courtesy of Virginia Cooperative Extension: Loudoun County Office.)

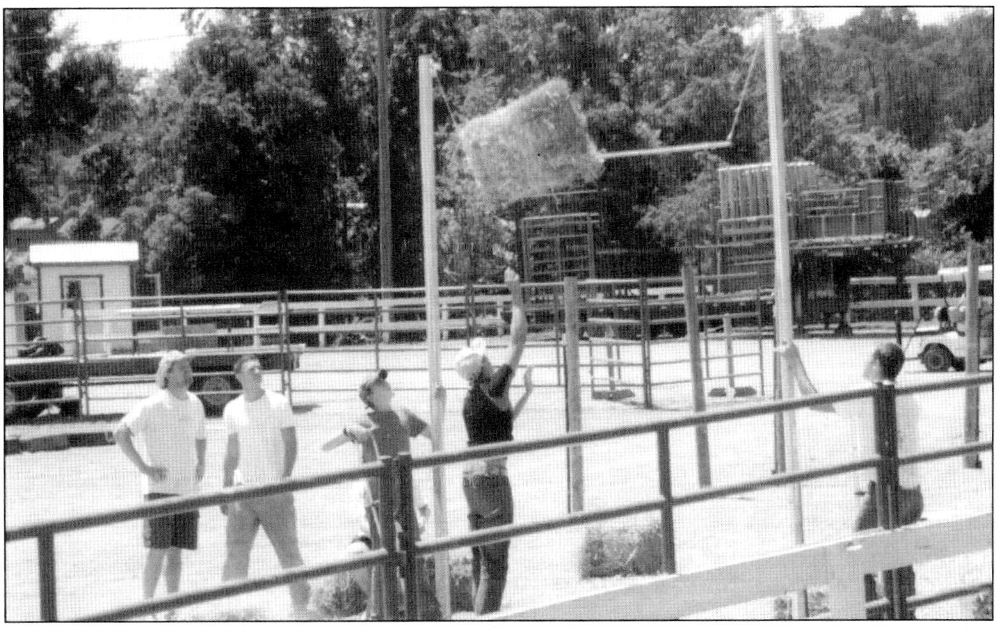

The Super Farmer competition was originally called the he-man competition in earlier fairs. In this event, couples worked together to complete challenges that may occur on the farm. These tasks could include a hay-bale toss, hay-bale stacking, a tractor pull, corn shucking, and a round-bale roll. In the photograph are, from left to right, Joseph Schwartz, Alex Skinner, Andrew Cockerill, Trevor Anderson, and Josh Cockerill. (Author's collection.)

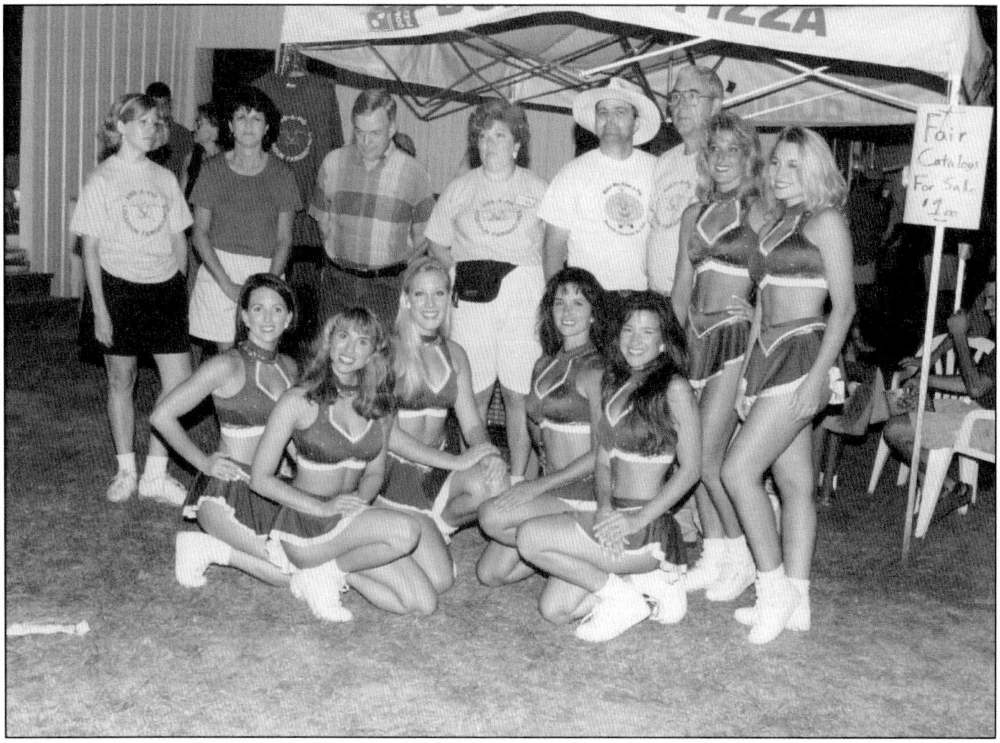

A fundraising event benefiting a children's shelter in Colorado gave Martha Potts the idea to ask community members to raise money for the fair. The person who raised the most money would kiss a pig; thus, the Kiss-a-Pig contest was formed. In the photograph, along with the Washington Redskins football cheerleaders are, from left to right, one unidentified individual, Milly Galahan, Joe May, Linda Tribby, Nolan Barzee, and unidentified. (Courtesy of VCE: Loudoun County Office.)

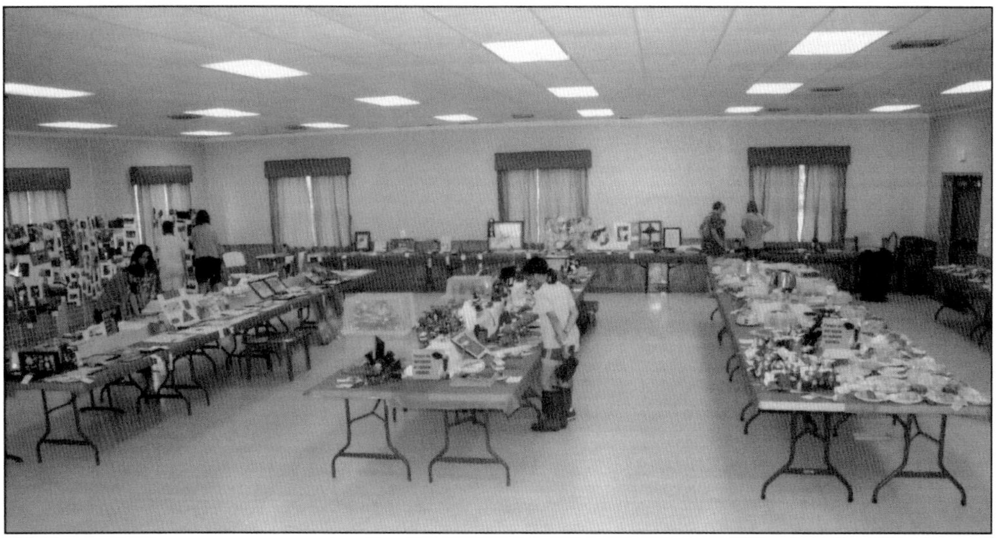

As in the early days of the fair, Sykes Hall still displays the home economics, garden, and general interest exhibits. Walking through the second floor, one will find canned goods, flower arrangements, photographs, project books, vegetables, baked goods, and clothing all made by 4-H'ers and members of the community. (Courtesy of Mark Gaylord.)

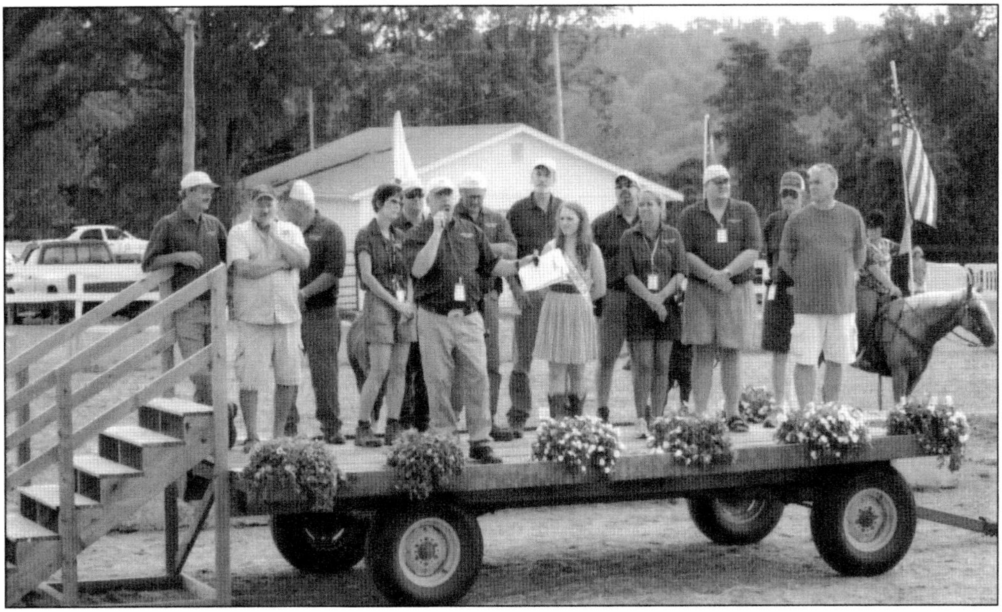

The opening ceremonies of 2012 had a skit featuring the 4-H youth, a presentation of fair dedication, and the national anthem with 4-H'ers from the Canterlopes Horse Club. From left to right are Mickey Lawson, Marty Beamer, John Smith, Claire Griffith, Doug Fidler, Terry Corle (fair superintendent 2003–2012), Luke Falconer, Kevin Murray, Franchesca Reilly (Miss Loudoun County Fair), Dave Brown, Tricia Wilkerson, Mark Gaylord, Mitch Miller, unidentified (minister of the ceremony), and Cassidy Carlton (on horseback holding the American flag). Below, the 4-H youth perform a skit based off the television show *Hee Haw* as part of the 2012 opening ceremony. From left to right are Jordan Ryan, Danielle McAllister, Marguerite Keane, Catherine Cockrill, Mary Elaine Boland, and Abigail Shires (partly shown). In the background is Mark Gaylord. (Both, author's collection.)

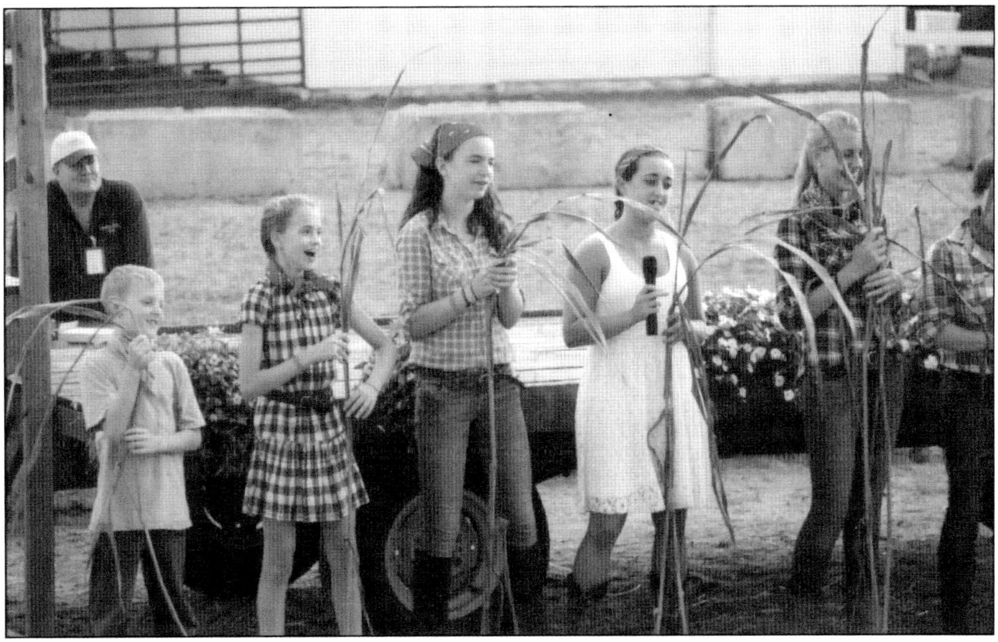

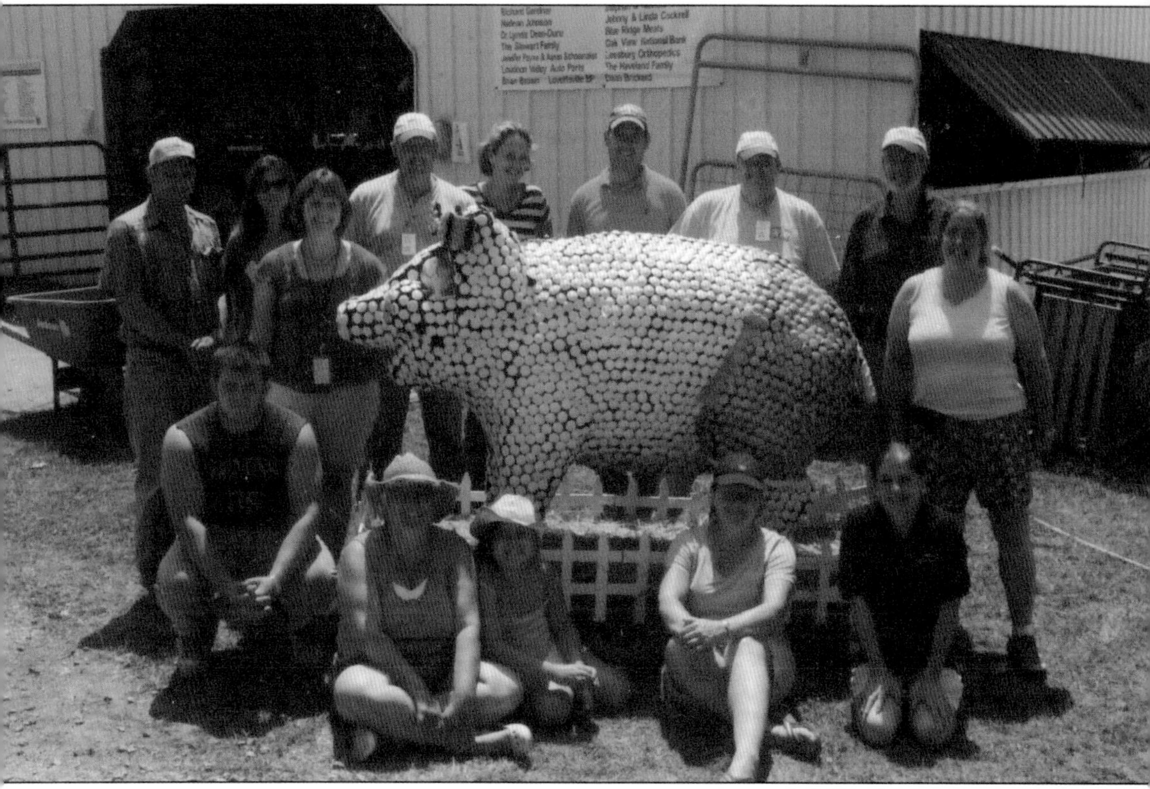

In 2012, the television show *DC Cupcakes* came to the Loudoun County Fair. As part of one of their episodes, the two sisters and business partners Katherine Kallinis Berman and Sophie Kallinis LaMontagne fashioned a pig out of miniature cupcakes. The pig, pictured here, was a hit with fairgoers. It was put to bid in the Friday night livestock auction. A group of fair parents and volunteers combined their resources and purchased the pig. Pictured here are, from left to right, (first row) Jarrett Bramhall, Pamela J. Bramhall, Mandy Bramhall, Elizabeth Shockley, and Sian Pugh; (second row) Mike Bramhall, Amy Lawson, Lynne Lott, Luke Falconer, Reece Murray, Rucker Slater, Mark Gaylord, Kevin Murray, and Karen Gaylord. The pig is still used today on display during the fair and in local town parades. In place of the cupcakes, pink tissue is used to give the pig color and texture. (Courtesy of Mark Gaylord.)

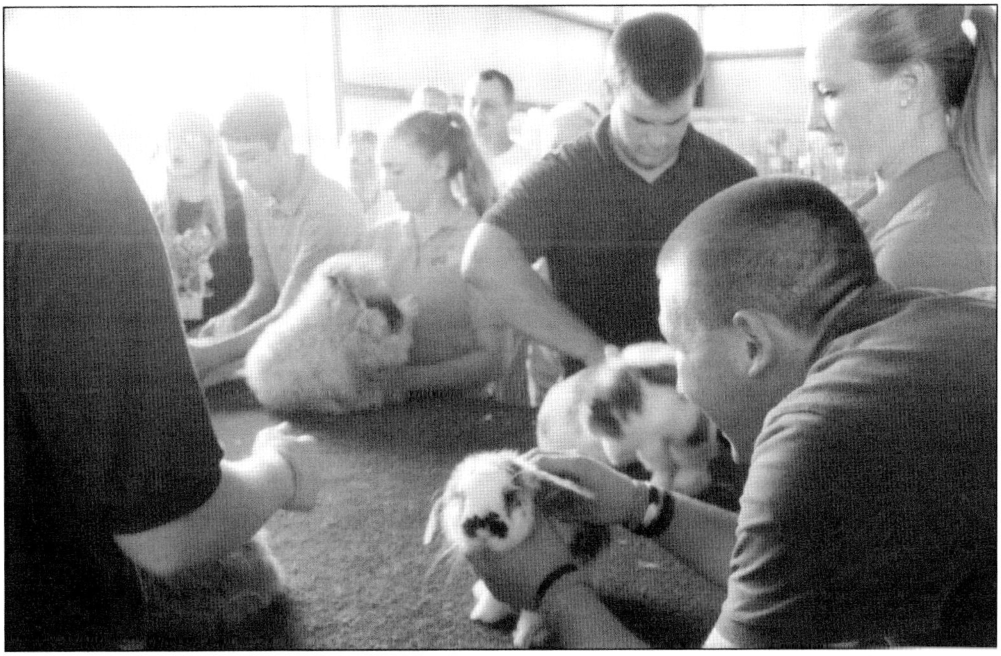

The Round Robin Showmanship is a chance for the winning youth of each discipline to learn how to show animals throughout all of the other disciplines shown at the fair. From left to right are Cary Brown, Tyler Rauch, Jessica McMann, Jarrett Bramhall, Annabelle Winants, and Matt Simpson (foreground). In the background are Jessica's parents, Christy and Corey McMann. (Courtesy of Mark Gaylord.)

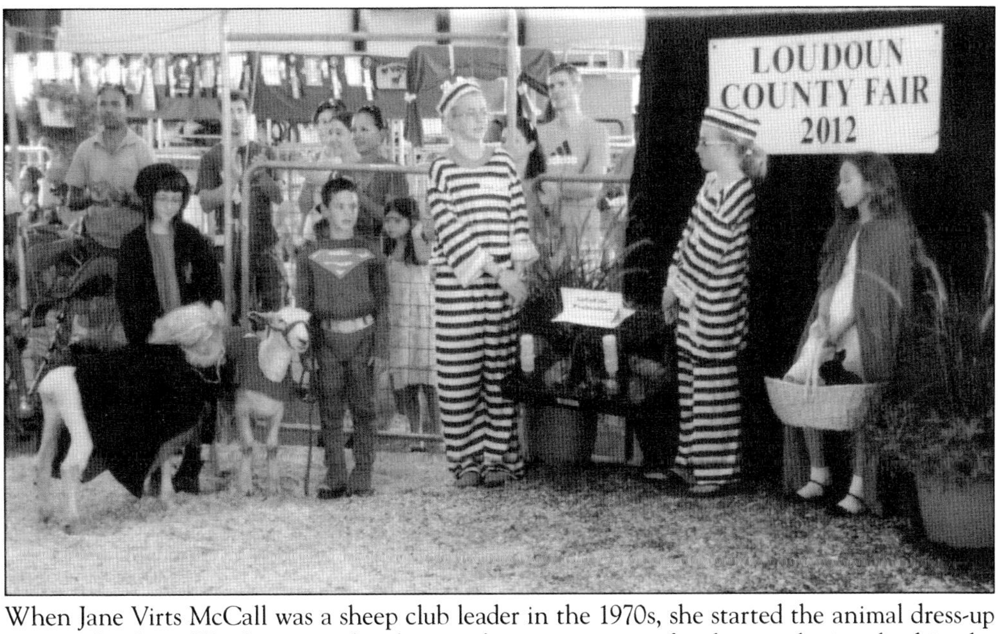

When Jane Virts McCall was a sheep club leader in the 1970s, she started the animal dress-up contest for the 4-H'ers' younger brothers and sisters as a way for them to be involved in the fair. 4-H'ers were included in this contest years later. In this 2012 photograph are, from left to right, two unidentified children, Cary Brown, Amy Brown, and Roxanne Howard. (Courtesy of Mark Gaylord.)

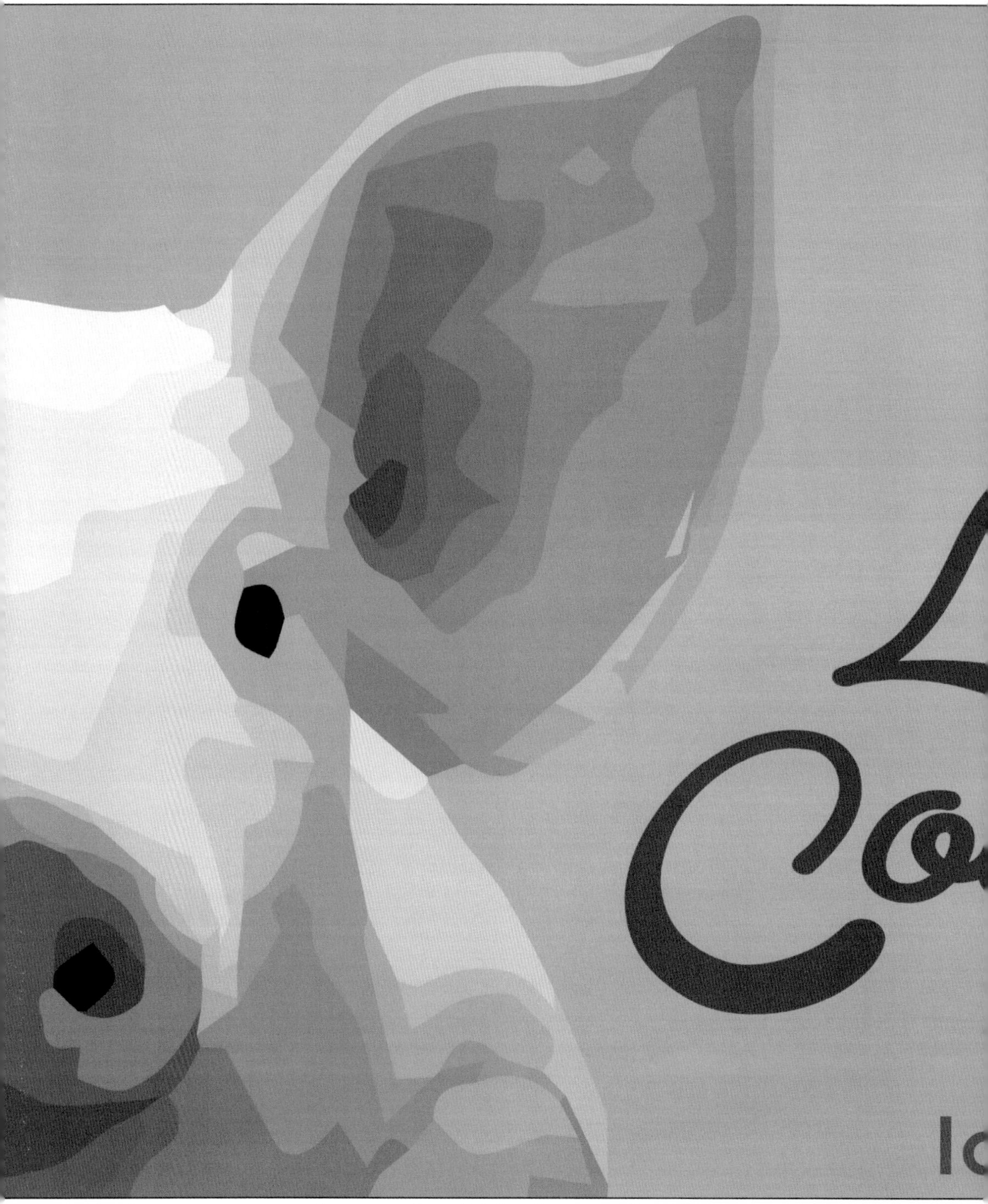

On this page is a poster advertising the 2014 fair. Former 4-H'er Allyson Conway designed the artwork with more than 11 images. Conway has started a new way of 4-H alumni giving back to the fair, having designed these posters for multiple years. The posters she designed were distributed to businesses and residents throughout the county and beyond to encourage people to attend the Loudoun County Fair. Advertising for the fair is conducted in many ways, one of

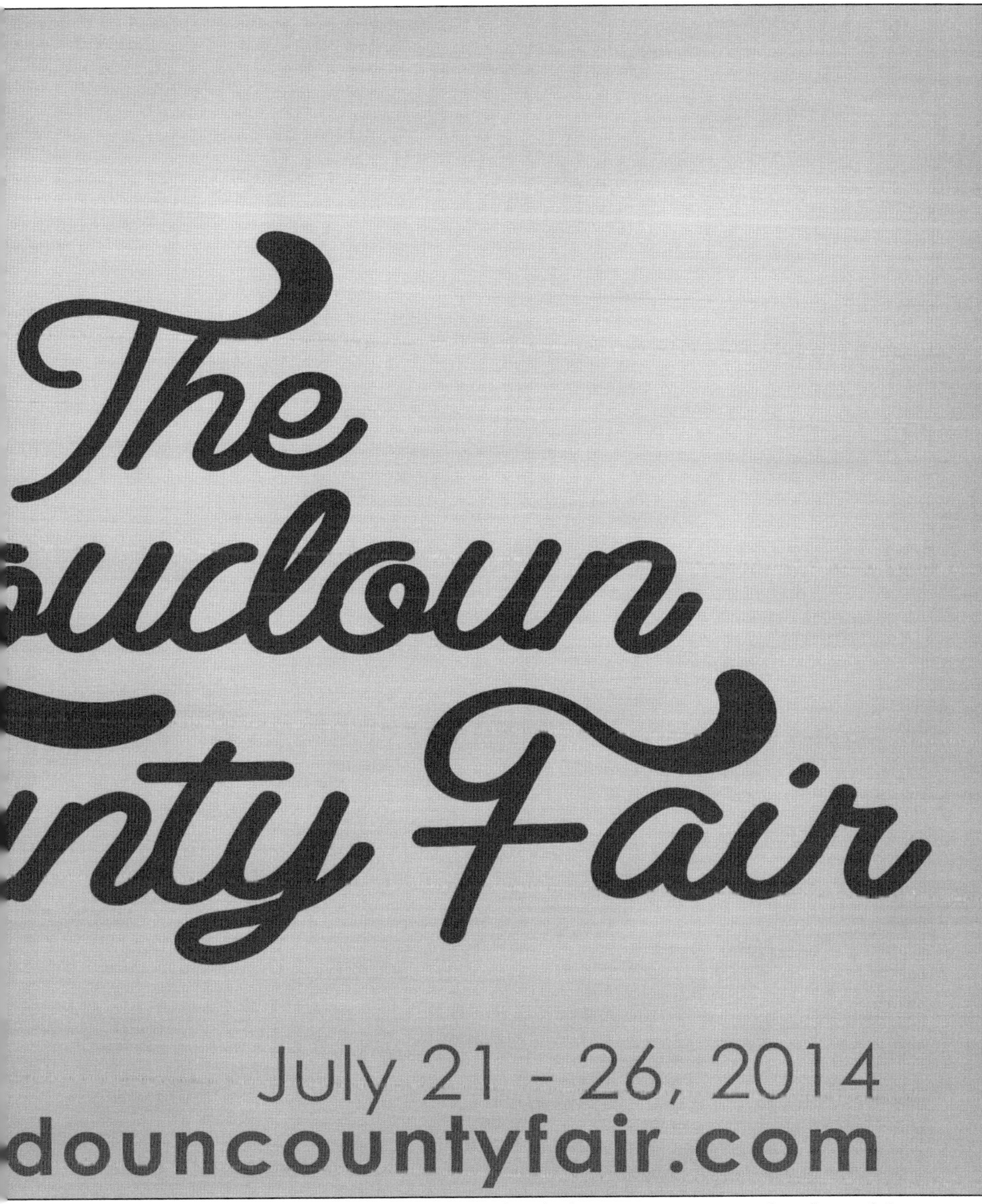

the best being word of mouth. Radio, newspapers, local television stations, social media, mobile applications, and the fair website are all mediums to get the word to the public. Fairgoers come from all over the county, the states of Virginia and Maryland, Washington, DC, and beyond. Many 4-H alumni come back to the area each year to reminisce about their days spent at the fair. (Courtesy of Doug Fidler.)

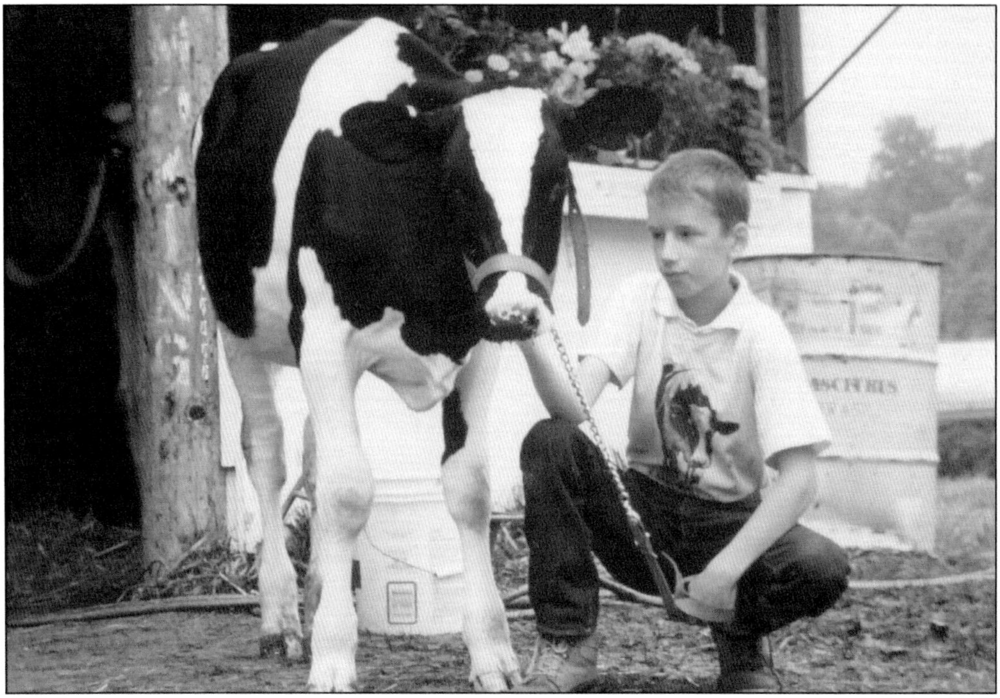

While the dairy industry in Loudoun is essentially a thing of the past with over 400 dairy farms in the 1950s to only one, Dogwood Farm in Lincoln, in the county today, there are still dairy cattle that participate in the fair. Justin Potts, shown here in the 1990s, is one of the youth that had cows as a 4-H project. (Courtesy of Martha Potts.)

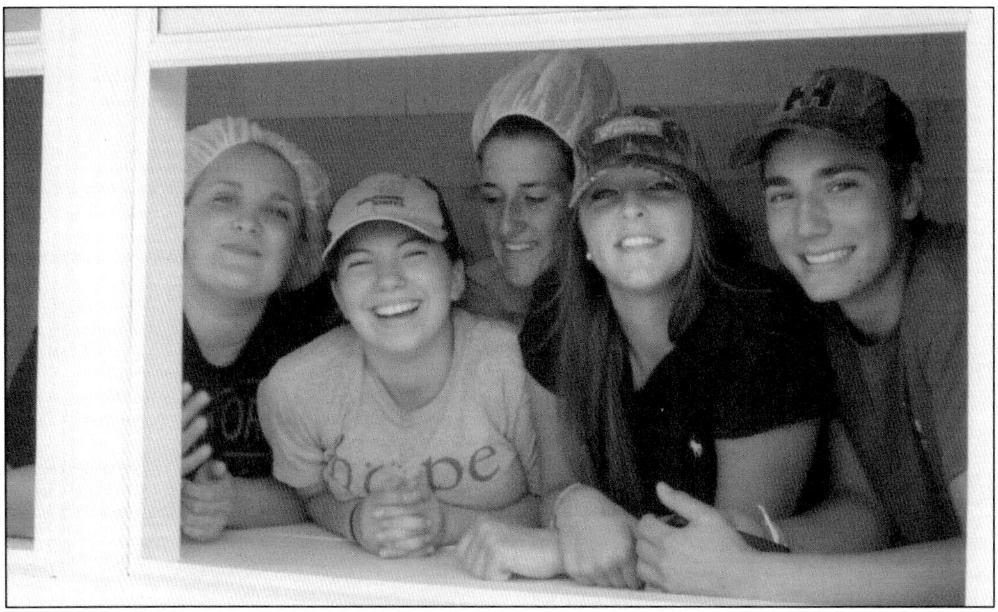

The Ice Cream Shack is managed by 4-H'ers and their parents throughout the week, and the money earned from the sale of the ice cream is used to benefit the fair. The 4-H volunteers helping on this shift in 2014 are, from left to right, Alexie Badura, Hailee Shockley, Cati Adele Slater, Hannah Small, and Matt Ferrari. (Courtesy of Kim Ferrari.)

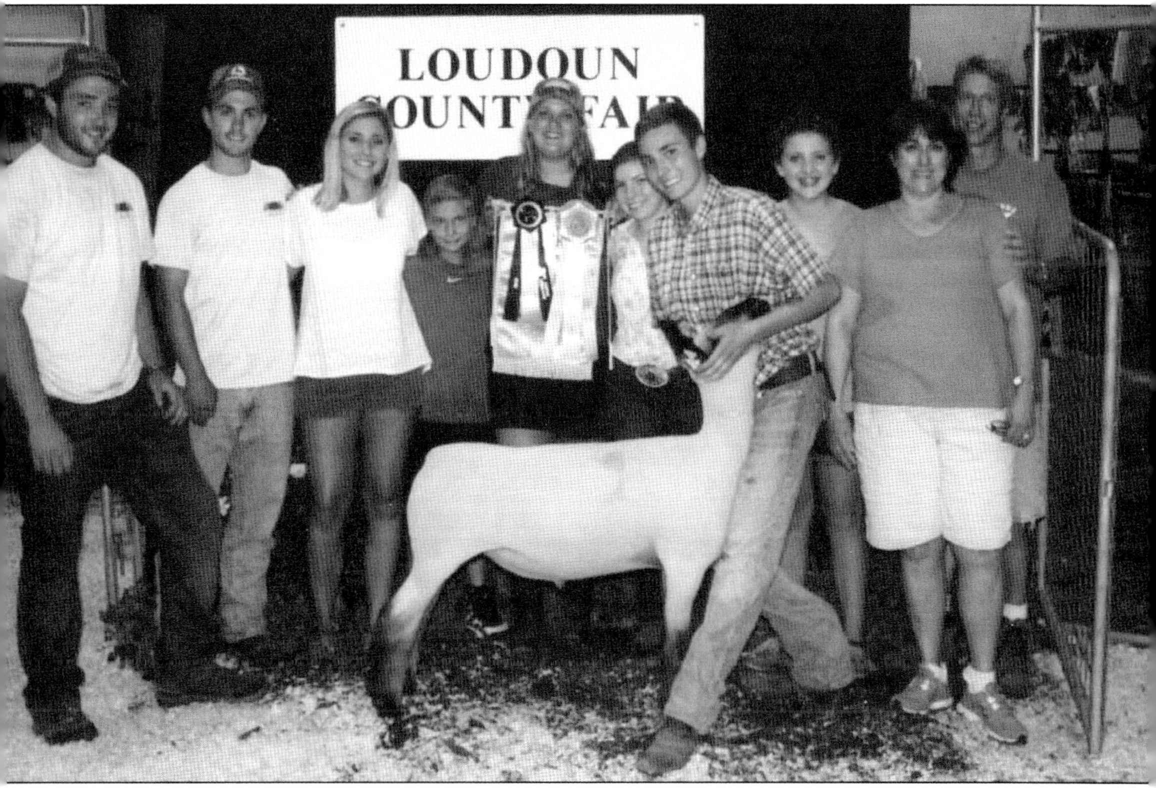

A proud moment in a 4-H'ers' career is receiving the honor of champion and grand champion. Matt Ferrari, senior 4-H'er, stands with his reserve champion market lamb. In this photograph are, from left to right, Matt Simpson, Scott Mumpower, Allie Galati, Ben Ferrari, Alexi Badura, Hailee Shockley, Matt Ferrari, Mikayla St. Clair, Kim Ferrari, and Paul Ferrari. The support of family, friends, mentors, and fellow 4-H'ers is important in the showing success. Raising an animal and learning how to show takes a great deal of time and effort, not only for the 4-H'er, but also for his or her supporters. Ferrari stands here with those who were a support to him throughout the 2014 fair. One of a 4-H'ers' biggest supporters are the parents. They drive the youth to meetings, attend competitions (some throughout the state), and provide financial backing, in addition to other tasks. (Courtesy of Kim Ferrari.)

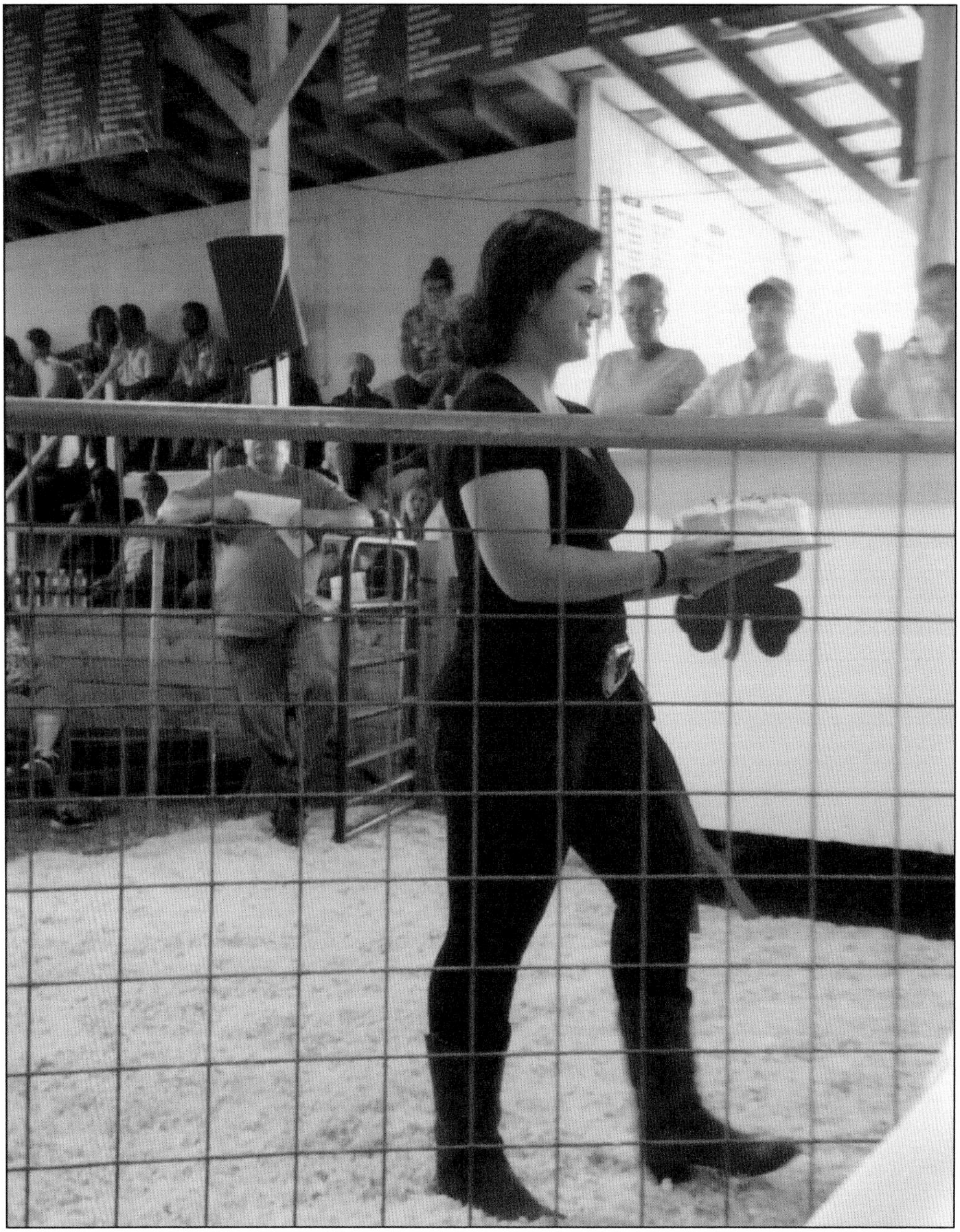

Cassidy Carlton was the grand champion senior cake winner in the 2014 livestock auction. The livestock sale was added to the fair in 1962 as a way for the 4-H'ers to market their prize-winning animals through auction. The first auction included animals such as steers, pigs, and sheep. Through the years, other animals have been added, including poultry, milk from dairy cows, rabbits, and cakes. The public has a chance to support the 4-H'ers by bidding on top-quality exhibits. Some auctioneers over the years have been Leonard Bowman, Bill Tillett, and Craig Damewood. Prior to the auction on Friday night, a bidder's dinner is held. For numerous years, the dinner was hosted by J.R.'s Festival Lakes. Currently Dry Mill Winery is the host location. (Author's collection.)

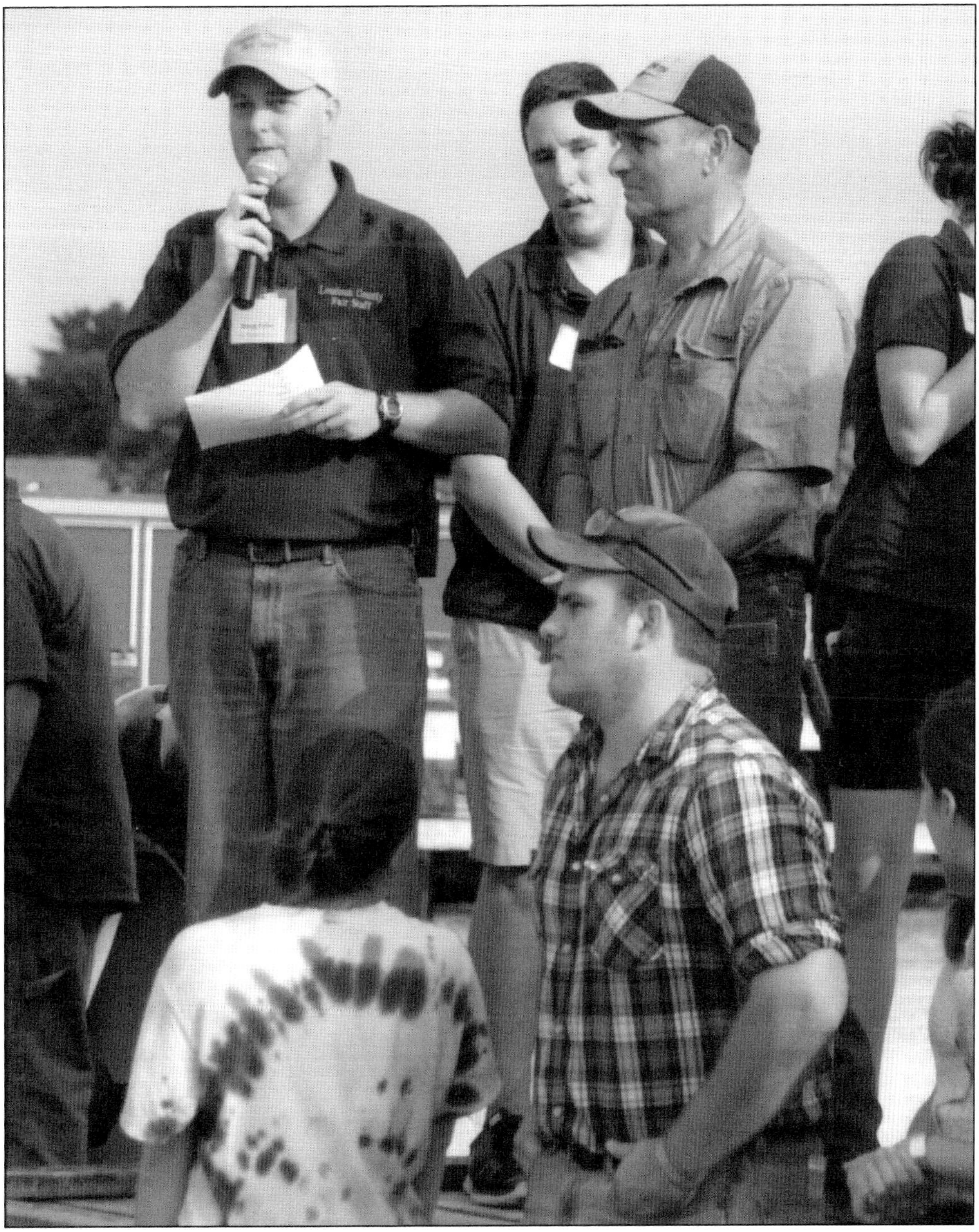

A tradition that was started back in 1963 is still an important aspect of the Loudoun County Fair. As a part of the opening ceremony, an outstanding volunteer is recognized for his or her service to the fair. In 2014, the fair was dedicated to Mike Bramhall, owner of Bramhall Trucking. Bramhall gives his time and resources in preparation for and throughout the fair week. In the photograph are, from left to right, (in front of stage) Jarrett Bramhall; (on the stage) Doug Fidler (fair superintendent), Tyler Rauch, and Mike Bramhall. Recent fairs have been dedicated to Charles and Gertrude Fletcher, the William Moreland family, Dan Clemons, Mabel Rollinson, Tommy and Tamma Payne, George Washington, Bob and Ann Hereford, Bill Tillett and Craig Damewood, John Smith, Robert and Katherine Kimble, and James "Jim" Colbert, in addition to many other dedicated individuals. (Courtesy of Mark Gaylord.)

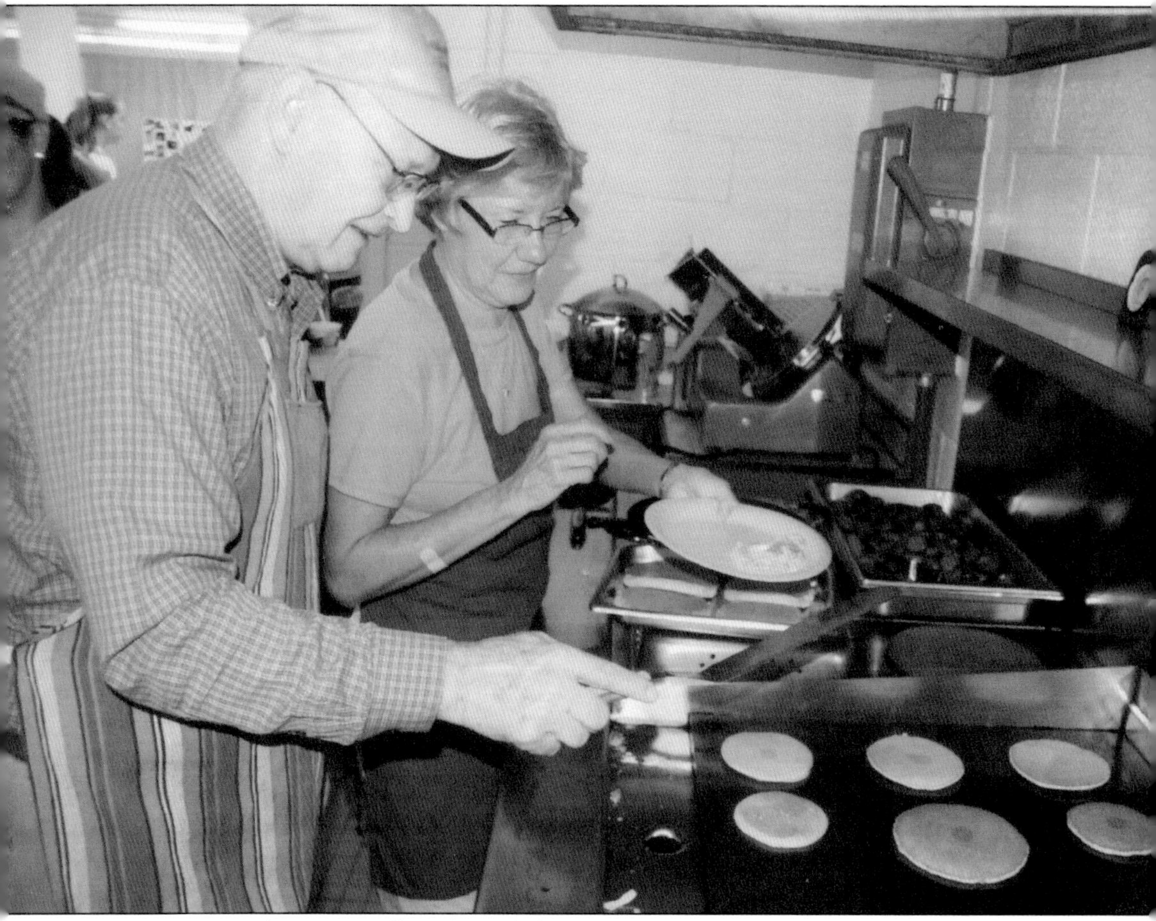

James "Jim" and Nancy Colbert have dedicated numerous hours to the 4-H and the fair. Jim showed at the fair during his youth, passing that tradition down to his and Nancy's own children. In addition to serving on the Loudoun Fair and Associates board, Jim comes to the fair before anyone else in the morning throughout the week to cook breakfast for the 4-H'ers and volunteers. Nancy is, of course, right at his side. The favorite day for the crowd is Friday morning's breakfast of biscuits and gravy. Fair staff and other willing adults assist Jim and Nancy in their task. The morning breakfasts give the youth and adults a time to reflect on the day before and plan the day ahead as well as getting to know others better. In the photograph are, from left to right, Jim Colbert and Nancy Colbert. Richlyn Norman is in the background. (Courtesy of Mark Gaylord.)

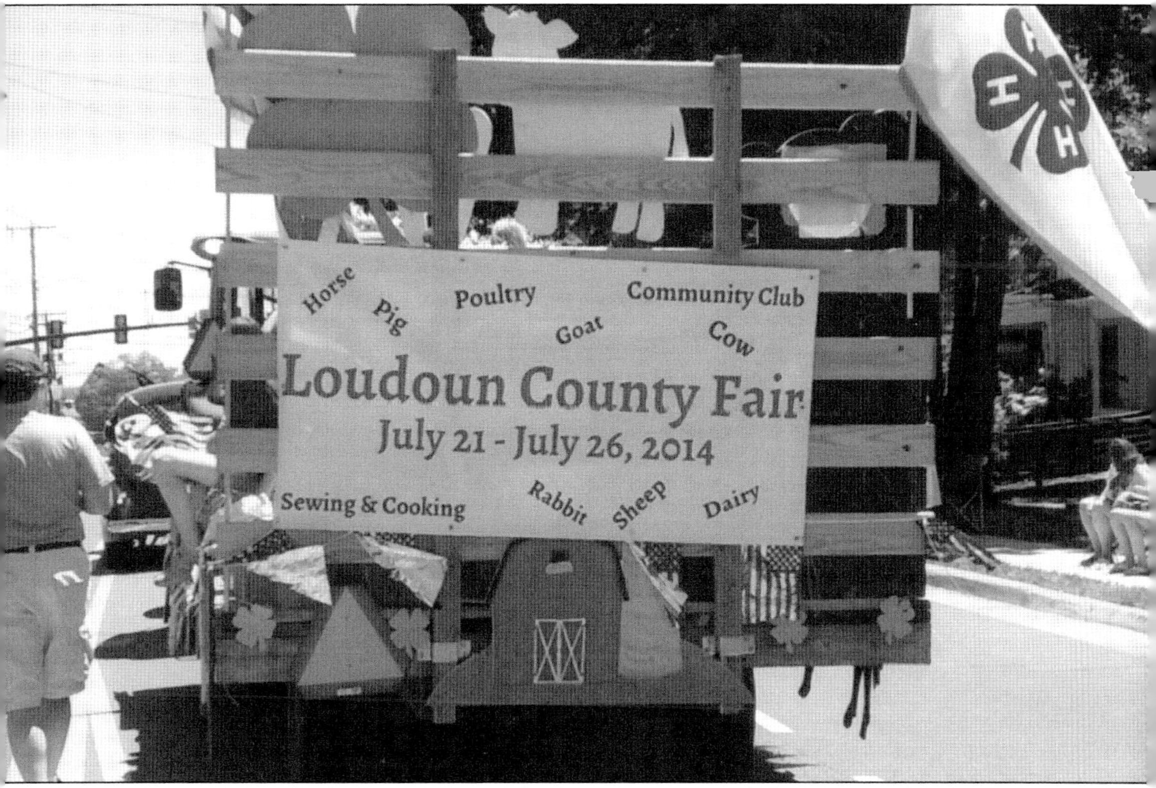

As in year's past, parade floats are a part of the fair experience. While a fair parade is no longer held as part of the event, 4-H'ers and leaders still get together to create a float for the local Fourth of July parades in Purcellville and Leesburg. Many hours from dedicated individuals are spent putting together a float to share the fair and 4-H with the community. The 4-H pledge embodies the 4-H'ers and volunteers of the Loudoun County Fair: "I pledge my Head to clear thinking, my Heart to greater loyalty, my Hands to larger service, my Health to better living; for my club, my community, my country, and my world." For 80 years, the Loudoun County Fair has been a part of tradition in Virginia. The volunteers, 4-H'ers, and community alike hope this is a tradition that continues for many more years to come. See you at the fair! (Author's collection.)

Index

Ashby, Nelson, 98, 112
Benedum, Mary Jane, 13, 19, 35
Benedum, Peggy Anne, 13, 63, 77, 100
Biggers, Carol, 12, 18, 20
Brown, Catherine, 6, 12, 14, 43
Brown, Jack, 19, 60, 74. 75, 88, 89
Bush Tabernacle, 21, 32, 51
Carlton, Cassidy, 4, 6, 115, 122
Clarke's Gap, 7, 35, 77
Cockerill, Anne, 40, 41, 93
Cockerill, Billy, 6, 39, 40, 41
Cockerill, Nancy, 39, 72, 75, 94
Cockerill, William H., 7, 11, 35, 39, 55, 65, 67, 72, 94
Colbert, James, 6, 17, 98, 123, 124
Cole, Bill, 37, 42, 77
Divine, Lynn, 6, 18, 20, 28
Fidler, Doug, 4, 6, 115, 123
Fletcher, Barbara, 12, 42, 47, 93
Fletcher, Tommy, 12, 13, 47, 93
Harrison, William, 18, 20, 47, 48, 49, 76
Herndon, John, 11, 12, 95
Herndon, Tommy, 11, 12, 93, 95
Hillsboro Club, 7, 65, 110
Keesling, Frank, 6, 16, 19, 65, 79, 102, 108
Leesburg, 7, 37, 57, 64, 76, 77, 83, 105, 125
Lincoln, 22, 23, 34, 75
Lincoln Club, 7, 21, 105, 109
Lintner, J.R., 2, 7, 67, 71
Livestock Sale/Auction, 56–58, 97, 112, 116, 122
Lovettsville Club, 7, 15, 16, 65, 102
McComb, Carol Stowers, 6, 47, 93, 100
Middleburg, 33, 35, 74, 75, 102
Norman, Rachel, 17, 36, 37
Payne, Tommy, 6, 57, 66, 97
Piggott, Mary Florence, 17, 36, 38
Potts, Edwin, 6, 12, 43, 47, 49, 91
Purcellville Club, 7, 108
Purcellville Fairgrounds, 24, 32, 33, 51–53, 68–69, 74, 101
Stowers Ellen, 16, 46, 94, 98, 99
Stowers, Joe, 18, 20, 46, 47
Sykes Hall, 7, 20, 26, 29, 80, 82, 84, 89, 91, 93, 114
Sykes, Eugene, 38, 45, 76, 83

About the Organization

The Loudoun Fair and Associates, Inc., is the governing body of the grounds on which the Loudoun County Fair is located. This nonprofit corporation has been in existence since 1956, when the grounds were donated, as a full-time location to hold the fair and other 4-H events. The objectives of the corporation are to:

Foster and encourage development of youth with encouragement and assistance from the Virginia Cooperative Extension Service and its 4-H programs; other county, state, and federal agencies, the business community; and groups and individuals that possess mutual interest through educational, recreational, social, and community programs of that general character;

Engage in various activities in connection with or incidental to such educational, recreational, social, and community programs and services having for their objective the development of a higher degree of efficiency in the training of youth in the development and use of improved practices and techniques of agriculture, to include agricultural products; livestock breeding, rearing, showing, and judging; home economics; artwork; hobbies; and skills;

Engage in such other activities as may be approved from time to time, that are designed for and carried on to promote the achievement of these objectives;

Maintain the corporation's physical properties in a good state of repair and to oversee and govern the use of those properties in a beneficial manner;

Manage the affairs of the corporation in a professional manner beneficial to the corporation, its membership, and the community; and

Assure that events related to and associated with the Loudoun Fair and Associates, Inc., are open to all people regardless of race, color, religion, sex, national origin, disability, or political affiliation.

Within Loudoun Fair and Associates, Inc., are several committees, one of which is the Loudoun County Fair Committee. The members of this group are volunteers who donate their time by organizing, planning, and facilitating the seven-day fair. This planning begins in August after the fair ends in July. The commitment and dedication of these individuals, additional volunteers, and the 4-H members are what makes the Loudoun County Fair possible each year.